A CURIOUS PLACE

The Industrial History of
Amlwch (1550-1950)

A Curious Place

The Industrial History of Amlwch (1550-1950)

Bryan D Hope

Illustrations by
Keith Shone

watch
house
books

Moelfre, Isle of Anglesey

A Curious Place
The Industrial History of Amlwch (1550 - 1950)
©1994 Bryan Hope

ISBN 0 9535268 1 X

Published in Great Britain by:

Watch House Books
Oriel
Moelfre
Isle of Anglesey
Wales
LL72 8HN

First published by Bridge Books, Wrexham 1994

CIP data for this book is available
from the British Library

Printed in Manchester by
MFP Design & Print

This book is dedicated to the people of Amlwch,
past and present, and to the memory of
Miss Gertrude Thomas
of Bryn Eilian,
who will always be remembered for her gentleness,
humour, freshly made *crempogau* and
delicious chocolate cakes.

*"The port of Amlwch also I have visited,
it is without exception the most curious."*

Thomas Beer, accountant to the 2nd Marquess of Anglesey.

Contents

Foreword   8

Acknowledgements   9

Prologue   10

Chapter 1   Introduction   11

Chapter 2   Changes & Early Industries   22

Chapter 3   Bayly & Hughes   28

Chapter 4   Sulphur   34

Chapter 5   Early Smelting   44

Chapter 6   The Francis Map   65

Chapter 7   Vitriol & Precipitation Works   75

Chapter 8   Later Smelting   82

Chapter 9   Chemicals   88

Chapter 10   Tobacco   92

Chapter 11   The Port   98

Chapter 12   Captain William Thomas   114

Chapter 13   Iard Newydd – The New Yard   121

Chapter 14   The Thomas Brothers   141

Chapter 15   Epilogue   150

Appendix 1   Amlwch Built Vessels   153

Appendix 2   Vessels in the Amlwch Copper Trade   155

Appendix 3   Amlwch Inns, Taverns and Public Houses   160

Appendix 4   Brand Names of Amlwch made Tobaccos   161

Appendix 5   William Williams, VC, DSM, Medaille Militaire   162

Notes   164

Bibliography   169

Index   171

Foreword

In 1973 when *Ships and Seamen of Anglesey* was first published, I indicated in the preface that what I was attempting was "not a narrative history but a series of studies to illustrate some of the ways in which the sea has affected the lives of the people of Anglesey", adding that "I recognized, however, that another twenty years and more research by many students, and many monographs on specialised subjects, were necessary before a comprehensive maritime history of Anglesey could be written." And here, twenty years later, Bryan Hope has written just the type of study I had hoped for, a thorough and detailed examination of the industrial development of Amlwch Port.

An engineer by profession, he brings a fresh approach to the fascinating story of this once busy copper-exporting port, and makes full use of the rich sources of documentary material relating to both the mines and the port itself. He has had access to much new material in the papers of the shipbuilders, William Thomas and Sons, and this, together with his own extensive knowledge, and the excellent, carefully researched illustrations by Keith Shone not only explain much that has hitherto been ignored or forgotten, but also bring to life in a telling fashion a little of what it must have been like to be a resident of Amlwch Port and the environs in its busiest days.

This book is surely essential reading for anyone interested in the history of Anglesey, providing ample material for further study by those with a specialist interest in industrial archaeology, but at the same time enabling the general reader to revisit Amlwch and look with new eyes at the town and the little harbour from which so many fine sailing ships once sailed.

Aled Eames

Bangor
June, 1993.

Acknowledgements

It is palpably true to say that a work of this nature can only be produced with the help of others, and I gratefully acknowledge the assistance given to me by many people during its preparation.

I am particularly indebted to Aled Eames however, not only for agreeing to write the foreword , but also for the kindly advice and direction he gave during the course of its preparation. Diolch yn fawr Aled.

The following have, however, given generously of their time in order to read and discuss the text, and their advice and suggestions have proved to be invaluable:

Dr Kath Davies	Researcher, Ynys Môn Borough Council
Gwilym T Jones	UCNW, Bangor
Elspeth Mitcheson	Director of Culture & Leisure, Gwynedd County Council
John Rowlands	Historian and author of *Copper Mountain*.
Dr R M Young	Associated Octel Co Ltd, Amlwch.

Contributors to the research who have made private documents, photographs, etc available to me, as well as others who have contributed by way of professional service and advice. It would nevertheless be remiss of me to omit the following, in whose debt I remain:

Messrs Greenall Whitley Ltd (Warrington), particularly Neil Chantrell and Mrs Margaret Lowe; Vera Bradford (Gwynedd County Archives); Jack Chapman (Menai Bridge); Cllr Eilian Hughes (Amlwch Port); Jean Hughes (Gwynedd Library Service); Margaret Hughes (Amlwch); Dr Bill Jones (National Museum of Wales, Cardiff); Eifion Jones (Amlwch); Elfed Jones (Cemaes); W A Rowntree (Llanfairpwll); John E Jones (Amlwch); John S Jones (National Museum of Wales, Llandysul); Trevor Morgan (Cumbria); Denny Rainford (Amlwch); Tomos Roberts (Archivist, UCNW, Bangor); Daphne Webster (Hereford); Elwyn Williams (Holyhead); Cllr Gareth E Williams (Llangefni); John E Williams (Amlwch); Robyn Williams (Holyhead); the Librarian, Camborne School of Mines.

I wish to express my indebtedness to Geoffrey Cliff, Managing Director, Jif Consultancy Ltd of Chester and Brisbane, Australia, whose most generous and practical assistance with computerised systems, and encouragement in their use, made my work infinitely easier.

Finally, I must record my grateful and sincere thanks to my wife Anne for her wholehearted support over the many years it has taken to research and write this book, without which it could not have been completed.

Bryan Hope
Moelfre
October, 1993

Prologue

The Isle of Anglesey, known in Welsh as Ynys Môn, is located off the north western coast of Wales. Measuring approximately 25 miles east to west and 20 miles north to south, it is separated from the mainland by the narrow and often turbulent Menai Strait. Facing Anglesey across the strait is a range of mountains known as Snowdonia, compared to which the island is best described as flat. It has nevertheless, several rocky ridges which rise to about 600 feet above sea level; some of which, as if by way of redress, are referred to by the islanders as mountains.

The name Anglesey is derived from the Norse for 'Ongull's Isle', and is an echo of the time when it was a Viking settlement in the 9th century. It's Welsh name is much older and is believed to have originated with early colonisers known as the Manapii, whom it is thought also gave their name to the Isle of Man, some 45 miles to the north of Anglesey.

There is evidence to show however that the island was inhabited some 2,000 years before the coming of Christ. Whilst it may be true to say that the early settlers were first attracted by its fertility and relatively mild climate, it is now evident that there was another, perhaps more compelling reason for their wishing to settle there.

The period in history dating from the beginning of the second millennium BC to 500 BC has since become known as the Bronze Age, because of the emergence and wide use then being made of the material. Bronze is an alloy from which were fashioned vitally important survival tools such as knives, arrow heads and axes. Its warm colour resembling that of gold, led to its further use in the manufacture of items of personal adornment; and such was its importance as a raw material that it became a prized and much sought after commodity, not only in the British Isles but also in the whole of continental Europe.

It was during this period that the industrial history of that north eastern area of Anglesey, later to become known as Amlwch, began.

Chapter 1
Introduction

Bronze is not a naturally occurring metal, but is a man-made alloy composed mainly of copper, to which a small amount of tin and zinc, and sometimes lead or arsenic is added. In its pure form, copper is quite soft, making it of limited use in the manufacture of weapons and tools. Bronze on the other hand is much harder by comparison, and cutting tools made of it retain their sharpness longer.

Until recently, there was little evidence to support the theory that copper mining had in fact been carried out in Britain before the Roman occupation in the 1st century AD, and it was believed that the raw materials from which the Bronze Age artefacts found in the British Isles, had been imported from the continent of Europe. Some archaeologists thought otherwise however, but lacked the means to prove their theories. The development of carbon dating techniques has now made it possible to prove conclusively that copper mining was extensively carried out at several sites in Wales, and elsewhere in the British Isles during the Bronze Age. Foremost amongst the prehistoric mining sites are those at Nantyreira and Cwmystwyth in mid Wales, Great Orme's Head on the North Wales coast, and Parys Mountain on Anglesey.[1] The latter, known in Welsh as Mynydd Parys, is little more than a low lying ridge, two miles inland from the town of Amlwch, on the island's northern coastline. Some early workings had been discovered there during the 19th century, as the following extract from a treatise on Parys Mountain published in 1848 records:

> The subterranean architecture in the workings of these mines is sublime and extensive, and, of late, several Druidical works have been discovered, which have added an additional interest in the antiquities of them. In these workings large stones were discovered, evidently used as hammers, with several pieces of timber and charcoal ready to be ignited, which were in ancient times, successfully used in mining operations before the invention of gunpowder.[2]

An investigation carried out in 1935 by Oliver Davies of Queen's University, Belfast, into the remains of early mining at Parys Mountain[3] confirms the earlier account by referring to the discovery of stone hammers underground at the mine. Many were also found scattered around the northern slope of the ridge, and he was inclined to the belief that these dated to the Roman occupation of Britain; although he stated quite categorically that their use was in no way representative of Roman mining techniques. The majority of the hammerstones were of quartzite, which could only be found locally on nearby Porthwen beach, or in glacial debris deposited further inland. Expert opinion at the time was in no doubt however, that there was no way the stones could have found their way onto the Parys hillside by anything other than human agency.[4]

Much of present day knowledge relating to early mining in the British Isles results from practical investigations carried out by the Early Mines Research Group, members of which have made notable discoveries at the sites of several ancient copper mines in north and mid Wales. Under the sponsorship of the British Museum and the National Museum of Wales, the group undertook systematic searches of the underground workings of several of the old mines, and their discoveries have led to a significant redrafting of British prehistory.

As might be readily imagined, equipped as early miners were with only the most primitive of tools, they faced a daunting task when it came to extracting ore from rock. Davies's research at Parys Mountain and elsewhere demonstrated however, that there was clear evidence of a relationship between the use of stone tools, and a method of mining known as fire-setting.[5] This technique involved the building of a substantial log fire against the rock face, as a result of which, the rock either cracked or softened, depending on its nature. If the rock was particularly hard, the effect was augmented by throwing cold water on to the heated rock, after which it was comparatively easy to remove the fragmented ore using antler picks and hand-held stone tools. Shattering the rock face was sometimes achieved with far less effort by simply crashing large stones suspended from wooden frames against it.[6]

Experiments have since shown that in general, the burning of a given weight of wood results in the release of twice that weight of ore[7] and such is the extent of some of the underground galleries ascribed to the Bronze Age miners, that had this method been widely used, the number of trees required to fuel the operation would have been vast. How far the Bronze Age workings extended at Parys Mountain, and how much had been excavated by fire setting will never be known, for the scale of subsequent mining operations destroyed much of any remaining evidence. The little which has survived has been invaluable however, for the charcoal remains of fire setting discovered there, have been subjected to radiocarbon dating at the British Museum. The results confirm that copper mining had indeed been carried out at Parys Mountain during the Bronze Age, for the charcoal was shown to be the remains of mature oak dating back to the period between 2040 and 1690 BC.[8] Comparable results were obtained from other mines in Wales, and the dates were further confirmed by a similar test on a piece of bone tool discovered in the Great Orme copper mine.

Ore removed from the mine had first to be broken up in order to separate the rich from the poor, the latter being discarded. Because the useful ore often contained sulphur compounds which inhibited its smelting, it was discovered quite early on that its quality could be substantially improved by roasting.

One of the curious results of research into copper smelting methods, is that little evidence has been found of Bronze Age smelting sites and methods: the absence of slag, which is a product of later smelting techniques, further adds to the mystery. Three possibilities present themselves: either slag did once exist, and has since decayed, or slag still exists, perhaps at some distance from the mine, but remains undiscovered, or the Bronze Age smelting process did not produce slag.

One characteristic of slag is its great durability, and had any existed, it would undoubtedly have survived but, despite intensive searches in the vicinity of known Bronze Age settlements in Britain, no evidence whatsoever has been found of slag deposits. The only remaining possibility therefore, is that the early smelting process did not produce slag, and recent experimental work indicates that this is indeed possible under certain conditions.[9] It has been recorded that small amounts of metallic copper have been formed by simply roasting chalcopyrite, which is by far the most abundant of the several copper

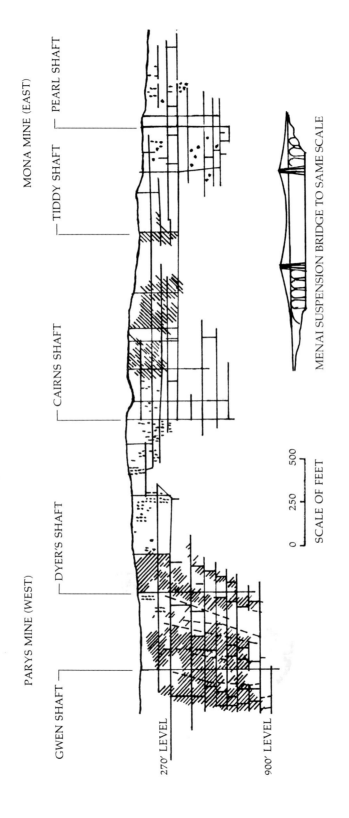

SECTION THROUGH PARYS MOUNTAIN SHOWING MAIN LEVELS AND LODES
BASED ON A DRAWING BY EDWIN COCKSHUTT

ores found at Parys Mountain, in open heaps without the need of a formal furnace. This would not have resulted in sufficient amounts of metal to have made it worthwhile, and it is now believed that the most likely method involved the intense heating of crushed, roasted ore, using charcoal as a fuel.

This would not appear to have been the view held by the late Edwin Cockshutt, a recognised authority on the history of Parys Mountain, who in a conversation with the author claimed to have discovered an ancient smelter on the Parys hillside. It would seem that on one of his frequent walks around the mountain he had stumbled across a dried up gulley, the existence of which he had previously been unaware, for the whole area had, until a recent fire, been thickly covered with gorse and heather. What made the gulley unusual was that for a considerable part of its length it had been packed with ore which had then been covered with large stones sealed with earth and clay. Both ends of what he described as a long sloping chimney, had been left open. The lower end had however, been packed with kindling, and this would have been sufficient, Cockshutt believed, to have induced a sufficiently hot draught of air up the chimney, to smelt the ore.[10] Uncharacteristically, Cockshutt declined to reveal the whereabouts of the gulley, partly because he wished to carry out further investigations of the site himself, and partly to protect it from unwarranted exploration. What he may have discovered during a subsequent investigation of the site has never been published, and numerous attempts by the author to discover the gulley's whereabouts have proved fruitless.

It is unlikely that the furnace so described was a smelter; for the temperatures such an arrangement could have attained, even with an ample supply of fuel, would in all probability, have been insufficient to smelt the ore. What is more likely however, is that the assemblage was a primitive kiln, used to improve the quality of the ore.

The main impurities found in the Parys ores were compounds of sulphur, which if heated to a sufficiently high temperature, ignited and continued burning of their own accord. Setting fire to the kindling at the lower end of Cockshutt's kiln could quite easily have generated sufficient heat to ignite the sulphur contained in the ore in contact with it, and which in turn would have extended the chain reaction upwards. Depending on the quantity and the quality of the ore in the kiln the process could have taken several months to complete, leaving the ore somewhat similar in appearance to cinder from a domestic fireplace, but much heavier. This would, with little difficulty, have then been crushed into a coarse granular form suitable for smelting.

Owen Griffith, a miner who had been employed at the Parys Mountain mine during its latter years, described an incident which occurred sometime around 1870, which may well have a bearing on this particular subject. At the time, the miners were working on a vertical vein of ore which had been extended so far upwards that it was possible for them to hear the rumble of carts passing overhead.[11] One day the roof collapsed with little or no warning, and amongst the rubble which fell to the lower level were some 20 stones, described by Griffith as resembling cobblers' lapstones, such as might be found on a sea shore. These, he described as being *glân*, which can be translated as either clean, or polished. Under the circumstances, it is reasonable to discount the first interpretation.

What made the stones extraordinary was the fact that each bore the impression of four fingers and a thumb. Their discovery promoted a great deal of interest and speculation amongst the miners, despite the fact that it was not unusual for them to come across stone tools and other evidence of ancient workings during the course of their work underground. No rational explanation was put forward at the time regarding the use to which the stones had been put, but of one thing the miners were certain,the stones would not have survived sufficiently long to have had indentations worn into them had they been used to break hard, ore bearing rock.

Little credence would appear to have been given to the legend of the indented stones recalled by Griffith, but there may well be a logical explanation to the riddle, if it is assumed that the stones were used to crush burnt ore, by way of preparation for the smelting process. The fact that the ore in that condition was brittle meant that it could readily be crushed by light hammer blows, and if this was followed by a grinding action using the stones as pestles, the ore could have been readily reduced to a coarse powder suitable for smelting.[12] This technique would have had little or no ill effect on the stones themselves, and for that reason it could be argued that they would have had a long life. The burnt ore would have been highly abrasive, and any particles sticking to the miners' fingers, would with constant use, have worn away the stones at the points where they were being held, at the same time imparting to them a polished finish.

Whether the exploitation of the mines continued without interruption into the first century AD when the Romans are known to have worked them, may never be known; but with their advanced mining and smelting technology, they were probably the first to exploit the mountain to any significant degree.

All ore mined within the Roman Empire belonged to the state, and it is as likely as not, that the majority of the miners who worked at Parys Mountain mine during that period, were slaves.[13] It is also equally likely that the mine managers were themselves slaves, whose skills had been learnt in the Roman mining school at Rio Tinto in Spain.

The evidence for Roman working of the mine lies in the fact that copper bun ingots, now in the British Museum, which were discovered on the western flank of the mountain, bear what are taken to be Roman inscriptions. With the collapse of the Roman Empire however, the demand for bronze diminished, and it is generally true to say that as a result, many of the mines under its control fell into disuse. It is possible however that after the Roman withdrawal, mining for both copper and lead would have continued at Mynydd Parys on a much diminished scale.

In 1557, an effort was made by Mary Tudor to revitalise the defunct British copper mining industry, when she granted limited mining rights to the Earl of Northumberland. This licence was later rescinded by her sister Elizabeth, who justified her action by claiming that as gold and silver ores, which were then the sole property of the Crown, were frequently found alongside copper ores, it must therefore follow that copper mining infringed royal rights.

In order to fully exploit copper mines to the Crown's advantage, Elizabeth established the Company of the Mines Royal in 1564, which relied heavily on German finance and expertise; a fact which reflected the shortcomings in native mining technology. The new venture had exclusive rights to copper mining in Wales, and it turned its early attention to Anglesey where, according to Sir John Wynn of Gwydir, there was in 1570, 'a great mineral work'.

In 1579, Lord Burghley, President of the Mineral and Battery Works, a sister company to the Mines Royal, commissioned a mineralogist named Medley to investigate the properties of the mine water which issued out of the Parys hillside, with a view to its commercial exploitation. The following description of Medley's experiment is an extract from a letter sent by Sir John Wynn to the President of the Marches, Lord Eure:

Plan of the Haven at Amlwch. [Crown Copyright: reproduced by permission of the Controller of HM Stationery Office] This document is endorsed: 'A Plotte of the woorkes and havens n[ow] fitt for that purpose'. Another endorsement, much faded and in a different hand, reads: '. . . only mention is made of . . . Haven at Amlewyhe . . . et S. Hillaries church et Bpi House standing neer ym.' The map has been considerably damaged where it was once folded. It shows in elevation the bishop's house, a chapel, a windmill, St Hilary's church, houses, hills, trees, ships and human figures. Distances from the mines are given. The map is drawn in ink on paper and measures 2 feet 11 inches x 1 foot 1¹/₂ins. It is undated but, from the style of the script, is undoubtedly Elizabethan.

First: a quantitie of iron was beaten small into powder, which was put into the water in a great boiler of lead, whereof there were either half a dozen or more. Manie of these boilers, having flat bottoms, and not verie deep, not unlike the form of a cooler, did contain manie barrels of licker, beinge that water; which beinge boiled with an exceeding hot fire of turf to a great height, and afterwards suffered to coolle, there was congealed in that water a threefolde substance; the one copperas, beinge green, highest; the second alome, beinge white, in the middle; and the thirde, called the earth of iron, beinge yellow, in the bottome. The alome and copperas seemed both to be perfectlie good. The earth of iron, after it was fullie dried, grewe to a substance like the ruste of iron which had beene canckered, yet yellowe. Of this earth of iron I have a great quantitie laid upon charcoale in a bricke furnace, and blowne down and smelted like lead; and downe came a great quantitie of iron synders, intermingled here and there with copper. A $^{1}/_{10}$th parte of that which came downe proved to be copper; whereof parte was sent to the Lo(rds) of the Counsell that were partners in the worke, part to others of the nobilite; and everie gentleman of qualitie the represente had parte to carrie in his pockette, who were of opinion that the worke would not quitte coste; and so it proved, for that in a while it was given over.[14]

Medley's experiment proved that whilst it was possible to recover copper from the mine water, the cost of doing so then, was prohibitive; but an adaptation of his method was nevertheless successfully exploited during the later life of the mine.

A time ravaged map discovered amongst the State Papers Supplementary [15], depicts in a very crude fashion, the coastline of north east Anglesey. Several annotations written on it in small, neat script, dates it to the time of Queen Elizabeth I. Unfortunately no additional papers relating to the map have been identified, but its purpose can nevertheless be readily deduced for it identifies the havens of Amlwch and Dulas, and a third inlet lying between the two, described as "a cricke by St Hillarie's C(hurch)". St Hillary and St Eilian are synonymous, and a sketch of the church alongside the inlet bears a remarkable similarity to the present day church of St Eilian, which it is clearly meant to represent. A small church shown to the west of the Amlwch haven, is without doubt, meant to be that associated with the Celtic St Elaeth; the size and character of which compare unfavourably with the larger and more ornate church of St Hillary.

A surprising feature of the map is an illustration of a large, very opulent Elizabethan style house referred to as the Bishop's House, standing on the western side of the Amlwch haven. The proportions of the building, which has the appearance of being divided into four sections, far surpass others shown on the map, including one described as a parsonage, situated close to St Hillary's church.[16]

More importantly, the map entitled "A plotte of the woorkes and havens n(ow) fitt for that purpose", reveals that the haven of Dulas, and the church of St Hillary, were both 2 miles from "the mines", whilst the haven at Amlwch was shown as being 1 mile distant from them. On the assumption that the recorded distances are tolerably accurate, it is evident that the mines referred to were located on the eastern flank of Parys Mountain, near the place now known as Hen Waith (Old Workings).

The title of the map is a clear indication that work had by then been undertaken to prepare the havens for what must have been their role in the exportation of ore, for the Mines Royal Company had by then established a copper smelter in the Vale of Neath in South Wales.[17] The fact that it was considered necessary to prepare two havens to serve the mines is interesting, for it is highly unlikely that the quantity of ore raised from them was sufficient to require this. There are however, two theories which may account for this.

The first is that the haven at Amlwch was unsafe when the wind was from a northerly direction, and that Dulas, although a little further from the mines, was safe at such times. The second takes into account the fact that there is known to have been a copper mine close to the estuary at Dulas, which may have been worked at one and the same time as those at Parys Mountain. Despite the inherent danger at Amlwch, it is probably true to say that its nearness to the mines, and the topography of the land in between, made it the preferred haven.

The absence of information relating to the tonnages of ore passing through the port at Amlwch during that time makes it difficult to assess the extent to which facilities had been necessary in order that it should be considered "fitt for that purpose", but the essential features can perhaps be deduced.

The absence of built-up roads meant that heavy goods would have either had to be transported by pack horse or in horse drawn sleds, the use of the latter having continued well into the 20th century in some parts of Wales. In either case, individual loads would have been in the region of 2cwt (224lbs), and because of this, numerous journeys to and from the mines would have been necessary to load even a small vessel. It would have made sense therefore, to provide storage facilities on the quayside for a minimum of one full cargo of ore, amounting to about 20 tons.

The natural formation of the land alongside the creek would have had a profound effect on the way in which the port was used. Access to the eastern side would then have been very limited because of the steepness of the rocks, and the early use of the port would in all probability, have been restricted to its landward end and western side. Any storage facilities would of necessity have been built alongside the quay in such a way as to facilitate the loading of the vessels directly from it, and provision would have had to be made to deliver the ore into the storage areas from whatever means were used to deliver it from the mountain. One method, used later at the port, was to tip the ore down chutes into bins from the roadway above, from where it could be loaded directly into a vessel lying alongside. There is reason to believe that this was the method also adopted in Elizabethan times. It is impossible to be precise with the limited amount of information available, but there is one site in the port as it now is, which satisfies these criteria. The creek (for it would have been little else then), lies on a line which runs roughly north to south, and on its western side there is a 60 feet length of wharf which has on it the remains of buildings which have never been identified. The wharf itself is unusual inasmuch that at each end there were stone steps leading down to it, implying that access to that level was denied to wheeled vehicles. If this is proved to be the case, then the wharf was built some time before the formation of roads in Anglesey in the middle of the 18th century.

The steps at the southern end lead to the remains of a stone building, which must at one time have been a storehouse. The wharf's back wall supports a road which is on average, 10 feet higher than its floor, from which it would have been possible to tip ore on to the quayside. Close inspection of the wall reveals that there were once two openings in it, both of which have since been filled in; the curious thing about which is that they had rounded sills, and around which the stones have been worn away in a manner which suggests that they were at one time used as chutes.

There can be little doubt that the wharf did in fact form part of the early development of the port; but there is little likelihood of it being dated accurately without an archaeological dig under the tons of slag which now cover part of the site.

The sea has been described as the highway along which the commerce of western Europe developed, and the numerous beaches and havens along the coastline of Wales, many of which are now renowned tourist attractions, were in the 18th and 19th centuries used by a myriad of small trading vessels. The Irish Sea was criss-crossed by well established shipping routes, and any creek which provided a safe anchorage became a haven. The heavy dependency which the inhabitants of any small island have on the sea is self evident, but the inhabitants of Anglesey had the added disadvantage of being further separated from the remainder of the country by the Snowdonian range of mountains which face it across the Menai Strait. This had the effect of making the island's lines of commerce and communications by sea not only faster and cheaper, but infinitely better than tedious and frequently hazardous journeys overland.

The port of Beaumaris, located at the northern entrance to the Menai Strait was the principal port of North Wales in the 18th century, and one which controlled the length of coastline between the Conwy and Mawddach estuaries. The port's account book which records those cargoes passing through the port in 1729, names three vessels as being of "Amblwch". These were the *Hopewell*, the *Speedwell* and the *Swallow*, not one of which was recorded as carrying goods to or from its home port. In October and December 1730 however, two Conwy vessels, the *Cotton* and the *Pembroke*, are recorded as carrying Oak and Owler (Alder) timber from Amlwch.

The variety in the cargoes carried by the vessels is surprising, for quite apart from cereals and dairy products, exports from Beaumaris included timber, slates, bacon and red herring.[18] The inclusion of kelp in the list suggests that a local industry existed to harvest this particular type of seaweed, the ash of which was a source of iodine and potash, used amongst other things in the manufacture of alum and glass.[19] As might be expected, imports were those necessities not produced locally, which included: bars of Swedish iron, noted for its consistent high quality, and `britt' iron from Aberdyfi, which in all probability was cast iron, which is brittle. 'Grindle stones' (grindstones), wire and iron loops were also imported in considerable quantities. Coal was another import, which although mined in Anglesey at that time, was of very poor quality, unlike that mined in Flintshire, Lancashire and South Wales. Domestic utensils such as iron and earthenware pots, brass pans, brown paper, tallow and candles were also included.

From Dublin came numerous horses, linen and corkwood as well as chopped oak bark for leather tanning and textile dyeing. Two chests of oranges, 500 lemons, and 10 barrels of raisins imported from Malaga, suggest that at least part of the population enjoyed a varied diet. Further imports included building materials such as bricks, planks, window glass, nails and pipes. At a time when it was usual for cottages to have nothing better than hard, well trodden earth floors, the importation of stone flags amongst the other building materials is an indication that living standards were improving.

The significant increase in sea-borne trade meant that the number of vessels using the Irish Sea in the first half of the 18th century was such as to prompt the Lords of the Admiralty to commission a survey of the Welsh coastline from Anglesey to Pembrokeshire. This was done primarily to provide mariners with reliable information relating to safe anchorages and harbours along what had been proved to be a treacherous coastline. The man chosen to undertake the survey was Lewis Morris, a Customs Officer at the port of Holyhead; who was one of four illustrious brothers brought up at Pentre Eirianell, a farm overlooking the estuary at Dulas. In his report published in 1748, [20] Morris was somewhat unimpressed with the haven at Amlwch, for he wrote:

I did not think it worthwhile to publish a plan of this (place) as it is now, because it is no more than a cove between two steep rocks where a vessel hath not room to wind, even at high water. But a large vessel might be saved here in case of necessity, provided the mouth of the harbour can be discovered which is now difficult for a stranger.

By way of overcoming the last objection, he proposed the building of

Two white houses, for land-marks, one on each side (of) the harbour's mouth, would make the entrance conspicuous to any stranger; the eastern-most Mouse, a small island near the place, being a good direction till you come close to the shore.

Although the cove had its limitations, Morris nevertheless described it as a place where: "vessels load corn, butter and cheese etc and here the Liverpoole [sic] Pilot Boats lie afloat, to be ready to meet any vessels in the offing."

In his *History of the Island of Anglesey* published in 1775, John Thomas described the harbour at Amlwch:

Amlwch harbour in the North West part of Anglesey, is a small cove, formed as it were by an excavation of a large rock, the extension of which, as far as navigable, we compute, without measurement, to be 40 perches, and from side to side, which are uncommonly steep, no more than 5 perches. When the tide is in, 'tis here nothing strange to see men fishing while they stand only on the brim of the cavation: in this agreeable pastime they avoid those commotions often concomitants of sea fishing. The harbour is much frequented by small sloops: here the Liverpool pilot-boats usually moor, to be ready to give assistance to such vessels as are unacquainted with the coast.[21]

In 1780, a survey of land belonging to the Bod Ednyfed and Glanllyn estates was carried out by Richard Owen,[22] who has undoubtedly proved himself to be Anglesey's foremost surveyor in the 18th century, but about whom unfortunately, little else is known.

Although the haven formed no part of either property, Owen included it on the map, probably as a reference in locating land belonging to adjacent landowners. Because of this, he does not appear to have lavished the same degree of care in plotting the creek as he did on the remainder of the map, and its accuracy in this respect cannot be relied upon. Nonetheless a few buildings which are shown lying close to the harbour correspond remarkably well to those shown on a later, more accurate map of the area, and for that reason, the map can be taken as a reliable indication of the development that had taken place by 1780.

A dozen or so buildings shown clustered around the very end of the creek, were clearly the beginnings of the port, and their location corresponds to that of a group of private and commercial premises later known as Lower Quay Street. Although not immediately apparent from Owen's map, later evidence indicates that some of the buildings he recorded lay alongside an inlet which could accommodate small vessels. The remains of these early warehouses, the windows and doors of which have since been filled in, can still be seen flanking the eastern side of the concrete slipway which now leads down to the harbour floor.

As the buildings were built right up to the very edge of the inlet in order to allow goods to be loaded directly into the vessels lying alongside, access to them had to be from the back. The narrow track hewn out of the bedrock, which was used to deliver goods to and from the warehouses, is now used as a pedestrian access to the present quayside.

Some short distance inland from the end of the harbour, Owen's map shows several buildings grouped around a large, almost square compound, bounded on its western side by a stream shown running into the creek, and on its southern side by what is now known as Chapel Street. The site is interesting inasmuch that a half century later it was occupied by a brewery, and the fact that there had been little change either in the compound itself, or in the orientation of the buildings associated with it, suggests that it may well have had a similar use in 1780.

Chapter 2
Changes & Early Industries

In order to have a better understanding of the rapid and far reaching changes which transformed the industrial way of life in Amlwch from the middle of the 18th century onwards, it is important to briefly recall the social, economic and industrial conditions which prevailed generally before that time.

In the first half of the century, large numbers of the nation's population were destitute; as a result, begging, vagrancy, thieving and prostitution were ways of life that were very much the norm. Rural life had seen little change from that known in the Middle Ages, and although depicted by many artists as being almost idyllic, it was in truth a way of life that was enjoyed by very few, and endured by most. Despite that, most of the Anglesey parishes reported in 1790 that they had no poor people in their midst.

Land was mainly unenclosed by walls and fences, which meant that the traditional practice of open field cultivation required the close co-operation of neighbours in order to succeed. This resulted in a working system which did not readily lend itself to improvements or change of any kind, and consequently, land yields generally were no greater than they had been in the time of the first Queen Elizabeth, a century earlier.

Anglesey was once described by a traveller as a naked and unpleasant country, which was mainly uncultivated, and which did not produce one tenth of the yield of which it was capable. In fact, agriculture was then able only to provide employment during the middle months of the year, whilst at other times the population found other work: fishing, quarrying, cutting turf and coal mining.

Housing conditions for the majority were poor, for the traditional and often windowless, stone cottages were far too small to accommodate the average family in anything approaching hygienic conditions, and it was not unknown for domestic animals to share the meagre living space. Thatched roofs were invariably infested with disease-carrying rats, and wells and streams from which drinking water was drawn, were more often than not polluted. Little attention was paid to personal hygiene, and as a result, diseases such as typhus and tuberculosis were rife. Although coal had been discovered on the island as early as 1450, peat and wood continued to be the staple domestic fuels. The island's scattered communities were generally self sufficient regarding food, and surplus produce was taken to any one of the island's markets either on foot or by packhorse.

Evolutionary changes had been taking place in Wales, albeit slowly, but these were accelerated by a phenomenon which became known later as the Industrial Revolution. The factors which brought it about were numerous, and their interdependence makes it almost impossible to determine which made the greatest contribution to the course of events. It is probably easier therefore to highlight a few of the factors which came together in the right place and at the right time, to change in a most profound way, the course of British history. The use of the word industrial to describe the changes which took place, tells only part of the story for the changes were equally of social and intellectual importance. In his history of the Industrial Revolution,[23] T S Ashton describes the changes as resulting more from a revolution in ideas, than from the technology which followed in their wake.

The extent to which land enclosure contributed to the process is still the subject of debate, but it cannot be denied that it was of great significance. The improvements in land drainage and reclamation which followed in its wake meant that many more acres could be brought under the plough. Landowners benefited greatly from new ideas regarding crop rotation and soil betterment, and experimentation with new varieties of crops and livestock strains paid great dividends. The introduction of root crops for winter animal feed meant for example, that fresh meat became more readily available throughout the year: one such case being the introduction in 1765 of the Swedish turnip into Anglesey by Thomas Williams, who was later to distinguish himself as the driving force behind the British copper industry. The rural infrastructure also benefited greatly from the construction of new roads, which permitted the accelerated and wider distribution of goods and produce.

The sustained growth of the home market, which since the union with Scotland in 1707, represented the largest free trade area in Europe, was crucial to the development of the industrial revolution. The growing demand for consumer goods became the impetus behind the now familiar factory system of mass production. At first however, the various industries had successfully met the increased demand by intensifying their existing production methods, as well as by sending more work out to the small outlying cottage industries. This expedient was short lived however, as the benefits of factory operation and economies of scale became more fully realised. In such factories, newly invented machinery, more often than not powered by wind or water, replaced the drudge of human power and workers were drawn to them in their thousands. Many of the new factory workers were those made landless by the process of enclosure, and jobless by the more efficient farming methods which were becoming widely used.

New towns were thus established and, although the demands made on the workers by the oppressive nature of much of the work were often extreme, the factories did at least offer an improvement in the quality of life to those who had known nothing better than abject poverty throughout their existence. Many, by frugal living, were able to start businesses of their own and many artisans turned their knowledge and skills towards the design and manufacture of improved versions of the machines they once laboured over.

The expansion of home trade was matched by that overseas, and the importation of raw materials from countries such as Canada, India and America was balanced by the exportation to them of finished goods. This two way trade encouraged the establishment of banking and insurance houses, which in turn provided capital for further investment thereby adding further momentum to the whole process.

A growing awareness of the need for personal hygiene, coupled with the availability of a plentiful supply of cheap soap, fresh food and easily laundered cotton garments, added greatly to people's health and well being. As a result, there was a significant decrease in the infant mortality rate, which in turn added to the number of people available to meet the employment requirements of the emerging industries and these, because of their increasing wealth, represented a rapidly growing consumer market for all manner of products.

Requirements for both machinery and power, stimulated by the factory system, led to a phenomenal growth in engineering and technology and in consequence of which, the market for iron and coal became almost insatiable. The demand for non ferrous metals came second only to iron in the general clamour for raw materials created by the emerging engineering industries and this again stimulated a previously unparalleled search for new sources of the basic raw material, copper.

The most common of the early rural industries were, as might be expected, those associated with agriculture, and itinerant tradesmen such as carpenters, saddlers, shoemakers and weavers, travelled the countryside in pursuit of business. Others, such as millers and fullers established mills where they could rely on near constant natural sources of power.

The depiction of a post mill on the Elizabethan map relating to the Parys mines, would seem to confirm the belief that flour milling was then being carried out in Amlwch. Although such mills were in regular use well into the 20th century elsewhere in the country, their design was unsuitable for the island. Post mills differ from the later Anglesey windmills insofar as the whole of their upper structure rotates about a central wooden post, in order to bring the sails to the wind. It was this feature that made them unstable, and many were consequently toppled over by strong winds such as are regularly experienced in Anglesey. In order to overcome this problem, it became the custom in Anglesey to build mills, in which only the cap rotated, out of stone, and it is the empty shells of these that are now familiar sights all over the island.[24]

The use of wool to ward off the cold, began when early man took to wearing fleeces and stuffed wool gathered from brambles and the like, into his shoes, where it matted to form a warm and comfortable inner lining. The insulating properties of wool thus became known, and the evolution of the woollen industry, which is known to have existed on the island in the 15th century, was marked by the introduction of three quite distinct technical innovations: the spinning wheel, the horizontal loom and the fulling mill.

The first stage in the development saw the wool being used simply for knitting purposes in preparation for which it had first to be washed, for wool is naturally very greasy. It had then to be lightly oiled so that it could be disentangled and separated into individual strands, a job normally undertaken by women and children, using nothing more sophisticated than thistles and teasles by way of tools. The strands were then gathered together into skeins ready for spinning, a process which twisted the individual fibres into one long continuous thread. This was made possible by the scaly nature of the individual strands which interlocked to such a degree when twisted together, that they became more or less permanently entwined. This fundamental process required the use of nothing more than very simple hand spindle made of wood, which when rotated as it hung suspended by the thread, imparted a twist to the wool as it was drawn out of the skein held in the spinner's hand. The degree of evenness to which the yarn could be spun, depended to a great degree on the skill of the spinner.

This once laborious process was speeded up considerably with the introduction of the hand operated spinning wheel, which was later superseded by a foot operated wheel with which most people are familiar. By thus freeing one hand, this new development enabled the spinning of finer and more even yarns suitable for weaving. This improvement, coupled to the development of the horizontal loom, made possible the weaving of long lengths of cloth from which garments could be tailored. Early wooden looms were extremely basic in their design and were more often than not built by the weaver himself. The need to house the loom in what was already cramped living accommodation, limited

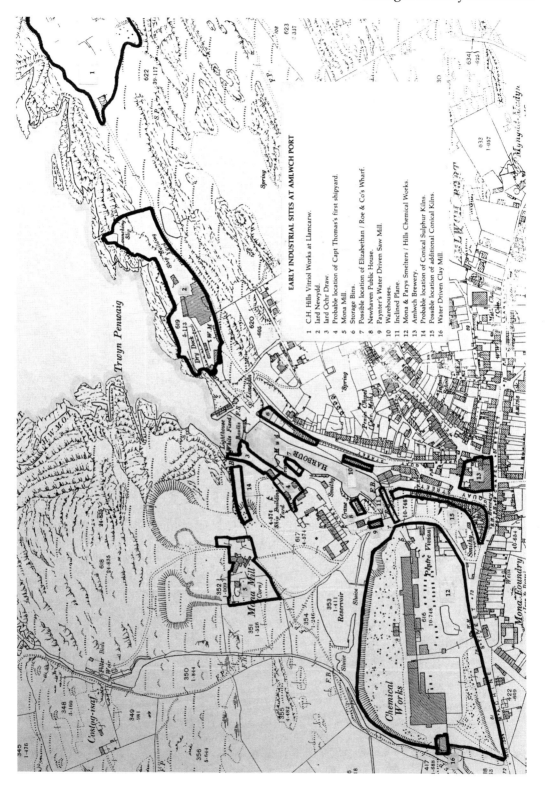

EARLY INDUSTRIAL SITES AT AMLWCH PORT

1 C.H. Hills Vitriol Works at Llamcarw.
2 Iard Newydd.
3 Iard Ochr Draw.
4 Probable location of Capt Thomas's first shipyard.
5 Mona Mill.
6 Storage Bins.
7 Possible location of Elizabethan / Roe & Co's Wharf.
8 Newhaven Public House.
9 Paynter's Water Driven Saw Mill.
10 Warehouses.
11 Inclined Plane.
12 Mona & Parys Smelters / Hills Chemical Works.
13 Amlwch Brewery.
14 Probable location of Conical Sulphur Kilns.
15 Possible location of additional Conical Kilns.
16 Water Driven Clay Mill.

its size, and this in turn governed the width of the cloth that could be woven on it. Not all weaving took place in the weavers' homes however, for many of the wealthier landowners had their own weaving sheds set apart from the main house. Because of their size, the sheds accommodated considerably larger looms which permitted the manufacture of broadloom cloths.

Early domestic looms, at which the weaver sat, required the constant use of hands and feet, which made the work physically demanding and for that reason, weaving was considered to be man's work. This meant that the task of dyeing and spinning the wool was left to the remainder of the weaver's family.

Dyeing was carried out using colourants extracted from a variety of plants which included foxglove and rock moss, which were gathered locally and one yellow dye frequently used in Anglesey came from seaspurge, which grew along the sea shore at Malltraeth. Dyes do not always take readily to wool however, and it was discovered that a better and more permanent result could be obtained by first soaking the yarn in a mordant known as lye, which was obtained by steeping wood ash in water. The grey *brethyn cartref* however, perhaps the best known of the Welsh cloths, was left undyed, and its colour resulted from the use of a mixture of wool taken from mountain and valley sheep, each of which had its own peculiar characteristics.

The cloth, as it came off the loom, was not as might be expected, the final stage in the process for it was both uneven and of open texture and of little use to the tailor. In order to overcome this problem the cloth had to undergo a finishing process known as fulling, which matted the weave, making it both warmer and of more even texture.

During the lengthy and tedious fulling process, the cloth was soaked in a succession of very basic chemicals, one such being stale human urine which was collected daily from families living nearby, and which provided the fuller with a very cheap and readily obtainable supply of ammonia. Other chemicals used in the process were lye, and an absorbent form of clay known as Fullers' Earth. The demand for chemicals created by the expanding textile industry soon outstripped that which could be supplied by traditional sources, and this resulted in the creation of the chemical manufacturing industry.

Initially the cloth was matted by trampling it underfoot as it lay spread out on the ground, and there can be little doubt that this was the most irksome part of the fuller's trade. The nature of the process as well as the chemicals used in the various stages meant that it was vitally important to ensure that the cloth was frequently and thoroughly washed. For that reason fulling mills were invariably sited alongside streams which could provide adequate amounts of clean, fresh water.

As more and more trades were becoming mechanised it was only natural that the fuller should also have looked to the same source to supply his power, and the first operation to be mechanised relieved the fuller of the need to trample the cloth underfoot. The power to do this was obtained by extending the axle of a water wheel into the mill where it was a relatively easy task to use its rotation to operate large wooden trip mallets to beat the cloth. This first stage in the mechanisation process was later followed by a mechanical means of raising the nap of the cloth, a process that had until that time, been done by hand using teasels.

Of the early Anglesey *pandai*, as fulling mills are known in Welsh, at least one is known to have existed in the parish of Amlwch. Its exact location is unrecorded, but an undated land schedule bearing the signature of the then Bishop of Bangor, refers to a parcel of land known as Cae'r Pandy [25] close to Plas Farm. Through this land passes a stream referred to in early documents as Afon Amlwch, but which in later years became so heavily polluted with effluent discharged by industries associated with the mines, that it became known as Afon Goch, the Red River. As nothing short of clean, fresh water would have served the fuller's purpose, it must follow therefore that the discharge of effluent into the river occurred at a later date.

The precise location of the mill has not been discovered, but it is thought likely that a water driven clay mill associated with a later industry may have been a development of the original fulling mill. This would have made sound economic sense in that the new clay mill could have made use of the original mill pool, leats and sluices.

There was evidently another fulling mill in Amlwch, near Pentrefelin Adda (now known simply as Pentrefelin) for the 1841 census lists one fuller and two weavers as being resident in what was referred to as the "Factory", somewhere in that neighbourhood. The exact location can not be proven, but local legend suggests that the mill later known as Rholdy, which is close to Pentrefelin, was originally a *pandy*.

Chapter 3
Bayly & Hughes

In the mid 18th century, Parys Mountain was in the joint ownership of two Anglesey families. The eastern half of the hill, known as Cerrig y Bleiddiau,[26] was in the sole ownership of Sir Nicholas Bayly of Plas Newydd, whilst the western half, known as Parys Farm, was a moiety shared by Sir Nicholas and William Lewis of Llys Dulas. In 1753, Bayly negotiated a 15 year lease with William Lewis for sole rights to work Parys Farm. The lease, for which Bayly paid an annual rent of £25, effectively gave him the sole mining rights to the whole of the mountain: the surface rights having already been let to Thomas Price, a local farmer.

It has been hitherto believed that apart from undertaking exploratory works, Bayly was in no way involved in the commercial exploitation of Parys Mountain before the summer of 1761. This would not appear to have been the case, for a cash book entry, dated September 1762, records disbursements incurred by Mr Cartwright, a former bricklayer who was then Bayly's mineral agent, in reopening the old works at Parys Mountain.[27] The sum included Cartwright's salary for 2 years and 11 months, which probably meant that Bayly had been working the Parys mine since October 1759, at the very latest. This would accord with the fact that Bayly had clearly intended to mine the property when he negotiated the mineral rights with Lewis in 1753.

In view of his eagerness to mine the Parys ground it is reasonable to suppose that before entering into an agreement with Lewis, Sir Nicholas had explored the possibility of mining his own half of the mountain; but that the results fell short of expectations. Despite that, it is known that in 1762 a Scot named Alexander Frazier, who with his partner Hugh Owen, had been working the nearby Rhos Mynach mine, persuaded Bayly to allow him to explore the Cerrig y Bleiddiau land where he believed there to be a great body of ore.[28]

Trial shafts were sunk and, true to his word, Frazier discovered ore; but before any significant amounts could be raised however, the workings were overcome with flood water. Whether the flooding was beyond their capacity to overcome, or whether the quality of the ore raised was poor, it is clearly evident that neither party was prepared to invest further in the venture, for the work was then abandoned.

In 1764, Bayly agreed a 24 year lease on the Cerrig y Bleiddiau ground to Roe & Co, of Macclesfield, which was already leasing his Penrhyn Du lead mine in Caernarfonshire. It would seem that Bayly, no doubt basing his judgement on Frazier's abortive attempt to work the ground, was far from convinced that it held any worthwhile mining potential, and he agreed to terms which were later to prove less than favourable to him.

Initial exploratory work proved to be unfruitful, and the company was on the point of abandoning the lease when the decision was taken to make one final attempt at finding ore. The company sent for its agent at Penrhyn Du, a most capable and experienced Derbyshire miner called Jonathan Roose, to direct the search. According to Pennant, Roose

... divided his men into ten several companies, of three or four in a partnership, and let them sink shafts in several places, about eight hundred yards eastward of a place called the Golden Venture, on a presumption that a spring which issued from near the spot, must come from a body of mineral. His conjecture was right; for in less than two days they met with, at the depth of seven feet from the surface, the solid mineral, which proved to be that vast body which has since been worked to such advantage. The day that this discovery was made was March 2nd, 1768; which has ever since been observed as a festival by the miners. [29]

Under the terms of the agreement, Bayly was allowed to claim duty ore amounting to one eighth of all that brought up from the mine, but for some unexplained reason he had tried to buy his way into the Macclesfield company on the 15th of February, 1768, two weeks prior to the discovery. It has since been suggested that Bayly had somehow come into possession of confidential information relating to the discovery before the company itself was made aware of it, and was as a result, trying to gain from his new found knowledge.

If Pennant's reportage of the facts is correct, the ore was discovered within two days of beginning the final search, which meant that the search began no sooner than the 28th February which would exonerate Bayly of any charge of impropriety. It is clear that Charles Roe did not welcome Bayly's attempt to buy himself into the company however, and although at least one attempt to expedite matters had been made, it was not until December 1768 that he offered Bayly, through his agent John Cartwright, an eighth share in the concern. A day after accepting the terms Bayly changed his mind and demanded a quarter share. Despite a personal meeting with Roe, Bayly refused to accept the earlier offer, and the matter was left in abeyance. Not surprisingly perhaps, the relationship between the two men deteriorated rapidly and many disputes subsequently arose between them, regarding mining operations at both Penrhyn Du and Amlwch.

In an attempt to ease the worsening situation, Roe again offered Bayly the original one eighth share, conditional upon him extending the terms of the original lease by three years, and agreeing not to further harass the company. A time limit was imposed for the acceptance of the offer, but for some unexplained reason Bayly failed to respond, and he was ultimately to be much the poorer for not accepting what was, with hindsight, an extremely generous offer.

When William Lewis died in 1761, his share of the Parys moiety passed to his niece Mary and her husband, the Reverend Edward Hughes, to whom Bayly made all payments relating to his lease of the moiety. In 1769, a year after his original lease with the Llys Dulas estate had ended, Bayly discovered a very promising lode of copper ore, and he tried in vain to interest his fellow landowners in exploiting the find. They refused however: "on account of the great risk and expense that attended it", and at some considerable personal expense Sir Nicholas carried on unilaterally and "did raise a large quantity of ore thereout."[30]

Documents relating to the workings of the early Parys mine give an insight into the way it was managed on Bayly's behalf. One such is an account of expenditure over a four month period in 1770, "for work and labour done for and on behalf of Nicholas Bayly Bart in carring [sic] on the copper and lead mines in the Undivided Estate called Baris [sic]."[31]

Lead mining at Mynydd Parys was nothing new, and Pennant describes how "this place been worked for lead ore in very distant times. In the bottom of the pool was found an ancient smelting hearth of grit stone, and several bits of smelted lead, of about four inches in length, two inches in breadth, and half an inch thick."[32] It is evident however that the amount of lead ore raised by Bayly during that quarter was small, for only two cargoes, each of 16 tons, left Amlwch for the Flint smelters during that time.

Imports for the use of the mine included timber and bricks, thousands of which were delivered by ship from Pwll Fanogl, close to Bayly's home on the Anglesey shore of the Menai Straits.[33] No indication was given regarding the use to which the bricks were put, but one possibility is that they were intended to floor precipitation ponds, in which copper was recovered from the mine water.

Mining has always proved to be a dangerous occupation, and perhaps never more so than in the latter half of the 18th century, when the demand for minerals of all kinds became so great that the welfare of the miners would seem to have been of little consequence. It may be surprising to find therefore, that despite his reputed antipathy towards the working miner, Bayly agreed to pay a local apothecary to provide medical attention to those he employed at Parys Mountain. His concern extended towards their spiritual well-being in a similar way, for the same records show that he paid the sum of £10 to the Reverend Richard Owen for reading English Services. As this item was entered under the mine's operating costs, it is probably correct to assume that the services took place there, and not at the local church.

By 1770, Bayly was exporting sufficient ore, made up of that from his own workings together with the duty ore received from Roe & Co, to warrant the construction at the port of a storehouse and new bins in which to store the ore awaiting shipment. It is known that Bayly later owned storehouses in Lower Quay Street, which were originally recorded on Owen's map of 1780.

The total amount of copper ore sent by him to Dumbell's Warrington smelter in the year ending March 1772, came to 972 tons, which was made up of almost equal amounts of burnt and raw ore. In the succeeding 6 months however, the total increased to 1,284 tons, which was made up almost entirely of raw copper.[34] As only the poorer quality ore needed to be burnt by way of improvement, it must follow that Bayly was raising only that of good quality. Mine lessees have often been known to maximise their short term profits by concentrating only on those areas yielding the best ore, leaving the poorer sources untouched. The fact that the Hughes family accused Nicholas Bayly of doing just that at Parys Farm, could therefore have been well justified.

By way of preventing what he considered to be the wasteful manner in which the mine was being worked, Edward Hughes sought an injunction denying Bayly the right to continue his operations, until such time as the matter could be resolved in court. The injunction was granted but, whilst it was in force, men employed by Hughes broke into Bayly's storehouses and removed tools and working instruments which they then used to work the mine themselves. Considerable quantities of ore were reputed to have been raised in this way, but precise details of the amounts were kept secret from Bayly.

Whilst the injunction remained in force, Bayly's activities were more or less confined to the burning, washing and exportation of the duty ore paid him by Roe & Co, but the importation by him of old iron from Chester and elsewhere is the clearest indication that he was also exploiting a process known as precipitation, in which copper was recovered from the sulphate rich waters emanating from the mine.

It took two frustrating years, during which he could only stand and watch Hughes mining the moiety, before Bayly succeeded in having the injunction lifted, by convincing the court that his mining methods were not altogether wasteful. A period of uneasy peace between the litigants then followed, during which both parties mined the property together, but it appeared to Hughes that Bayly was seeking to gain an unfair advantage by employing more men on his side of the workings. So angered was he by this, that in 1775, he took Sir Nicholas to court yet again. Seeking the court's direction to have the number of people Bayly could employ at the mine limited to 50 miners, 2 agents, and an Assay Master; and also trying to prevent him from opening new pits and carrying away more than half the ore. The Court resolved that by common agreement, three agents should be appointed to run the affairs of the mine, and that a man called Hugh Price be appointed receiver and distributor of all profits on behalf of the respective owners who were themselves restrained from working the property. The third agent was not appointed however, probably because each side having appointed its own man, they could not agree on the appointment of the third, who was supposed to be neutral. Over and above this, Hugh Price was evidently having problems in getting the parties to disclose their accounts in working the mine prior to his stewardship, and this led to yet another court appearance. As a result, the Master of the Rolls decreed that both parties should disclose their accounts to Price, under oath.

The relationship between the two sides worsened even further, for Hughes appealed to the court in December 1775, to have Sir Nicholas committed to the Fleet prison in London, better known as a debtor's prison, for failing to agree to the appointment of the third agent. The court did not accede to that plea however, but did order that the two agents previously appointed, be allowed to divide the ores equally whilst both parties in the dispute were invited to nominate a third agent of their choosing, for consideration by the court. The court chose Henry Staples, who was Edward Hughes' nominee, who, together with the other two agents, became responsible for dividing the ores equally between the owners.

Throughout the course of the litigation, Edward Hughes and his family were represented by an Anglesey born lawyer called Thomas Williams, whose career up to that time, although successful, had given little indication of the depth of his innate capabilities. His involvement in the lawsuit proved to be the key that opened the door for him to enter a new career in which he rose to become a figure of international importance. Such was his success that Professor J R Harris, in his biography of this outstanding man,[35] claims that he became one of the greatest figures among the businessmen of the 18th century. Indeed, so considerable did his power and influence become, that industrial giants such as Mathew Boulton, and his partner James Watt, the pioneer of steam power, the steelmaking Wilkinson brothers, and the pottery magnate Josiah Wedgewood, all nationally revered figures, regarded him with awe. Moreover it was Mathew Boulton who first referred to Thomas Williams as the 'Copper King', and described him as one who "has really created new consumption of copper that did not before exist . . . He constantly receives accounts of the price of copper at every market and the produce of every mine in Europe, and hath certainly done more in the copper trade than all the other drones in it."[36]

Unlike other, far lesser men born on Anglesey however, Thomas Williams' achievements have gone unrecognised by his own people, and such is his obscurity that the most that is now likely to be known about him on the island is that he was in some way associated with the Parys mines, where he was known as *Twm Chwareu Teg* [Tom Fair Play].

Thomas Williams, son of landowner Owen Williams of Treffos, received his legal training at Caerwys before returning to Anglesey, where he built up a successful practice acting as land agent and advisor to many of the island's landowners. Amongst his clientele was Nicholas Bayly, who, because of their previous business association, took great exception to the fact that Williams now represented his adversaries in matters relating to the mine, particularly as this was done to such devastating effect.

Williams' ability to see problems for what they were, was but one facet of his genius and, as a means of simplifying the complexities surrounding the rights of the several heirs to the Lewis family's share of the Parys moiety, he arranged to lease the land himself, in trust for Edward Hughes. The move not only solved the problem, but also cleared the way for Williams to take an active part in the running of the mine, as opposed to being simply an advisor.

The effect which many years of litigation had had on Bayly must have been profound, for there can be little doubt that he lost the will to continue his battle against Hughes. His utter disillusionment extended even to his activities at Parys Mountain, for he gave up mining and offered to lease his share of the moiety to Roe & Co, whose lease of the Cerrig y Bleiddiau land was about to expire. They declined the offer however, and the fact that the relationship between them was hardly ever good may well have coloured their decision.

In 1778 however, Bayly agreed to lease his share of the mine for a period of 21 years, to a London banker named John Dawes, who immediately, and probably much to Bayly's surprise, joined forces with the Hughes-Williams partnership. The possibility that the merger was premeditated cannot he ruled out, for in view of all that had transpired between them, it is unlikely that Bayly would have offered the lease to his former adversaries. Dawes was involved purely on the financial side of the newly formed Parys venture, whilst the undoubted power behind the business lay with Thomas Williams.

Much of our knowledge of the working conditions which existed at Parys Mountain during the years in which it developed from a copper mine, similar to many others then to be found in North Wales, into one which allowed it to dominate the world markets, comes from several sources. Mine records and correspondence relating to the Plas Newydd family, successors to Sir Nicholas Bayly, provide a wealth of information regarding legal matters, quantities of ore raised, and materials purchased. Very little can he gleaned from them however to show how the agents, miners and others went about their business, and the technology they used. Fortunately for us however, several scientists, artists and writers were attracted to the mine by its reputation, and their impressions provide us with graphic illustrations of the place as they experienced it.

One of the earliest of these accounts was that by Thomas Pennant, whose *Tours in Wales* was first published in 1784, some 16 years after Roose's great discovery. This was at the time when Roe's lease of Cerrig y Bleiddiau was coming to an end, and Thomas Williams was both a major shareholder and the main driving force of the Parys Mine Company.

In his narrative, Pennant relates how:

Nature has been profuse in bestowing her mineral favors on this spot; for above the copper ore, and not more than three quarters of a yard beneath the common soil, is a bed of yellowish greasy clay, from one to four yards thick, containing lead ore, and yielding from six hundred to a thousand pounds weight of lead from one ton; and one ton of the metal yields not less than fifty seven ounces of silver. Mixed with the earth, are frequently certain parts of the color of cinnabar: whether these are symptomatic of the sulphurous arsenical silver ores, or of quicksilver, I will not pretend to decide. Something interferes with the successful smelting of this earth in the great(*sic*): insomuch that it has not yet been of that profit to the adventurers, which might reasonably be expected from the crucible assays of it; and they have at this time about eight thousand tons on bank undisposed of.

There was little doubt in Pennant's mind that the hill had also been worked for copper by the Romans using fire setting techniques, for "vestiges of the antient operations appear in several parts, carried on by trenching, and by heating the rock intensely, then suddenly pouring on water, so as to cause them to crack, or scale." By that time, the mines were, according to him, supporting no fewer than 8,000 people, of whom 1,500 were employed directly by the two companies. The full extent of the ore body had not been determined, although its depth had, by driving a level under it, been found to be no less than twenty four yards. The ore varied greatly in quality, some being quite rich, but the majority was poor in that it contained a high percentage of sulphur.

A vein discovered at the western end of the mountain had however proved to contain between 16% and 40% copper, although the ore was "not got out in the common manner of mining, but is cut out of the bed in the same manner as stone is out of a quarry. A hollow is now formed in the solid ore, open to the day, and extends about an hundred yards in length, about forty yards in breadth, and twenty four yards in depth."

It is evident that mining was carried out simultaneously above and below ground, for the account goes on to state that the ends of the excavation "are at present undermined, but supported by vast pillars and magnificent arches, all metallic; and these caverns meander far underground." It has been suggested that the systematic removal of ore from these supporting pillars over a period of time, caused an unexpected and catastrophic roof fall.[38] That was evidently not the case, for he went on to say that the caverns "would soon disappear, and thousands of tons of ore be gotten from both the columns and roofs."

The Reverend Edward Bingley's [39] account of his visit to Parys Mountain during the summer of 1798, gives a vivid description of the frightening conditions under which the men worked:

> Having ascended to the top, I stood upon the verge of a vast and tremendous chasm. I stepped upon one of the stages suspended over the edge of the steep, and the prospect was dreadful. The number of caverns, at different heights along the sides; the broken and irregular masses of rock, which everywhere presented themselves; the multitudes of men at work in different parts, and apparently in the most perilous situations; the motions of the windlasses, and the raising and lowering of the buckets, to draw out the ore and the rubbish; the noise of picking the ore from the rock, and of hammering the wadding, when it was about to be blasted; with at intervals, the roar of the blasts in different parts of the mine, altogether excited the most sublime ideas, intermixed with sensations of terror. Leaving this situation, and following the road, which leads into the mine, my astonishment as again excited, the moment I entered. The shagged arches and overhanging rocks, which seemed to threaten annihilation to any one daring enough to approach them, when superadded to the sulphureous smell arising from the kilns in which the ore is roasted, made it seem to me like the vestibule to Tartarus, described by Virgil. To look up from this situation and observe the people upon the stages, 150 feet above one's head to see the immense number of ropes and buckets, most of them in motion; and to reflect, that a single stone casually thrown from above, or falling from a bucket, might in a moment destroy a fellow creature, a man must have a strong mind not to feel impressed with many unpleasant sensations. The sides of this dreadful hollow are mostly perpendicular. Along the edges are the stages with the whimsies by which the buckets are lowered; and from which the men descend to their stations upon the sides. Here suspended, the workman picks with an iron instrument, a place for a footing, whence he cuts out the ore, and tumbles it to the bottom, where it rests with a thundering crash. After working the place into a cavern he removes to a new station.

Chapter 4
Sulphur

The size of the ore bearing rock delivered up from the mine was totally unsuitable for smelting for it was far too large, and it was necessary to reduce it to a suitable size, described by one observer as approaching that of a domestic hen's egg. The work was carried out by women, who were known locally as 'Copper Ladies'. In his book, Owen Griffith, a miner and later official at the mines, paints graphic word pictures of the many colourful characters who worked there, amongst which were the 'Copper Ladies', for whom he had nothing but praise.

The women were easily identified by their unusual clothes, for each wore a black hat referred to locally as a Jim Crow under which was worn a yellow spotted scarf, tied in such a way that it covered the hair and most of the face and neck. The clothes were clearly as practical as they were colourful and were chosen to protect the wearer both from the cold and from the dust laden atmosphere of the dressing sheds, as their workplaces were known. Although not referred to by Griffith, the women were also known to wear stout leather aprons at their work.

The sheds in which the women worked were long, large wooden buildings, built on levelled areas of hillside, as near as possible to the shafts from which the most ore was being raised. The women, of whom there could have been as many as 80 in any one shed, sat one in front of the other in long rows. As the ore was barrowed in from the mine, it was tipped into a heap alongside each of the 'ladies', and then replenished as was necessary. In front of her, each woman had a square block of iron known as a knockstone, on to which she placed the ore to be shattered. A 4lb hammer with a long, narrow head, was used to shatter the ore, and in order to reduce the number of accidents to the ladies' hands, the fingers of each glove were protected by stout iron rings. The women's working day was of 12 hours duration, which was half as long again as that of a miner working underground.

Despite the demanding nature of their work, the 'ladies' were renowned for their chatter, and Griffith relates an amusing tale of how a New Year visitor to the dressing floor was driven to declare that unless he could escape from the endless prattle he would be driven mad. In reply, the supervisor very wittily suggested that there would be considerably less of it in the course of the following month.[40] Griffith recounts how the subject matter of the women's discussions was both wide and varied, and often of little consequence, but there were times when the mood was more serious and they recited and sang at their work.

Reducing the ore by hand provided the women with the opportunity to discard those pieces which contained little or no ore, a task at which they were most adept. This most important form of quality control was probably achieved by assessing the weight of each lump against its size and appearance, a skill no doubt acquired only by long experience. Several groups of lads attended the 'ladies' as they worked, and part of their duties was to scrutinise the discarded ore to ensure that none that was good had slipped the net, and their lynx-eyed quickness in selecting the copper from the waste,[41] was described as nothing less than astonishing.

An Amlwch 'Copper Lady'.

When the ore prepared in this way was of good quality it was first washed before being sent directly to the smelter; but the discovery that the washing water contained recoverable copper as a result meant that it was far too valuable to be wasted, and was therefore channelled away to be processed. The material rejected by the Copper Ladies however, although it almost always contained a very small quantity of ore, was thrown on to vast waste heaps on the mountainside where it still remains.

As previously mentioned, most of the ore raised at Parys Mountain contained sulphur compounds which made it difficult, and therefore more expensive to smelt. In order to make it more commercially acceptable however, the sulphur was removed by a process known as calcination which was little more than a roasting operation. The remarkable thing about this process was that it used the sulphur contained in the ore as fuel, which made the whole operation highly cost effective. The basic principle behind the process nevertheless remained the same as that employed in the kiln discovered by Edwin Cockshutt, but the quantities of ore burnt at any one time were vastly greater.

There were several stages in the evolution of the ore roasting process, the earliest involving little more than small heaps of ore piled on to wooden fires out in the open. In this way the ore became sufficiently hot to ignite the sulphur contained within it – a

Sulphur Extraction Kiln, c1765.

process which having begun then became self sustaining. The process continued until such time as the sulphur had been completely burnt off, or as no doubt frequently happened, when it was extinguished either by heavy rain or through lack of oxygen. Both problems were easily overcome however by sealing the heap with stones and clay, and by ensuring that there was an adequate number of air vents leading into it.

As the quantity of ore to be processed increased, the mounds became larger and more regular in shape, and instead of building them directly on the ground, false floors made up of numerous cast iron plates supported on pierced brick walls ensured an adequate supply of air to the kiln. Containment walls were then built around the rectangular floor, and the open, box-like structure filled with ore. When this had been done the kiln was then roofed over with rubble, and sealed with clay, leaving a few vents through which smoke could escape. Using whatever fuel was available, small fires were then lit under the ore to begin the calcining process, which continued until all the sulphur compounds were spent. In this way, large kilns were left to burn themselves out over a period which could last for many months. When the dense and acrid sulphur dioxide fumes given off by the burning ore abated, it signalled the end of the process, and the kilns were allowed to cool. The stone shell of the structure was then dismantled, and the burnt ore removed to the smelter, leaving the flooring plates to be recovered for further use.

The cast iron plates used for the kiln floors were manufactured by the well known ironmaster John Wilkinson at his Bersham works, and imported through Amlwch Port in large numbers. These had a limited life however, for the simple reason that the sulphur dioxide generated during the process combined with the water that was always present within the kiln, to form sulphuric acid, which corroded them very quickly. Although this added appreciably to the cost of improving the ore, the end product was, according to Pennant, an ore reduced to a fourth part in quantity, but considerably improved in quality.[42] What exactly he meant when he stated that the ore was reduced to a quarter of its previous quantity is uncertain, for it is thought unlikely that neither its volume nor its weight would have been diminished to that extent by the process. Some loss in weight could be expected however, partly from the burning of the sulphur bearing compounds in the ore, and partly because the ore was acted upon by the hot sulphuric acid that had been formed.

The calcining process was carried out, as indeed were most other tasks at the mine, on a contract basis, with payments varying from 3s 6d to 5s 0d for every 100 tons of ore burnt. Why the rates should have varied so much is not clear, but they may have reflected the quality of the ore being processed, some of which was possibly easier to burn than others. The best of the calcined ore contained about 10% copper, and the poorest about 4%.

The temperature generated within the kilns had to be in excess of 248°F (120° C) for the sulphur to burn, and the corresponding expansion of the tightly packed ore must have presented problems regarding its containment. Drawings of later kilns show them filled to capacity with ore, which would when heated, have created sufficiently high lateral pressure on the dry stone walls to break them apart – unless of course they were adequately reinforced. Not one of the many descriptions of the kilns refers to the need for reinforcement however, which is surprising, but which suggests that another method was used to solve the problem. One possible way would have been to include with the ore a combustible material which would have wasted away during the process, thereby allowing the expanding ore to occupy its former space. Wood for example, would have been an obvious choice, but its cost would undoubtedly have been prohibitive and it is possible therefore that the peat and gorse known to have been cut for the burning of copper ore, was used for this purpose, and not just as a fuel by which the ore was initially ignited. Peat, which has traditionally been cut from its bed in rectangular blocks about the size of two or three present day house bricks, could have been used to build partition walls within the kilns. These walls, against which the ore would have been piled, would have been reduced to a fine ash during the burning process, thereby allowing the ore to expand inwardly with little or no danger to the containment walls.

Valuable as the use of peat may have been in protecting the walls it is likely that a further, perhaps somewhat unexpected benefit may have resulted from its use in this way. The peat known to have been used at the mine was obtained either directly off the mountainside or from one of several large turbaries skirting Parys Mountain. Unlike normal peat, that which came from sites close to bodies of copper ore frequently contained pure metallic copper. This had been formed in the plant's structure as a result of a chemical reaction between the plant cell material and the copper rich salts with which the peat was saturated. This phenomenon frequently results in the copper assuming the shape of part of the host plant such as: a stem, a leaf or even a nut. Cupreous Peat as it was known, could be very rich indeed in copper, and according to Pennant, "It is quarried out of the bed in vast masses; is broken into small pieces; and the most pure part is sold raw, at the rate of about £3 to £6 per ton, or sent to the smelting houses of the respective companies to be melted into metal." The highest price obtained for cupreous peat was twice that which could be had for the best of the burnt ores.

The effect the fumes from the kilns had on the environment was catastrophic, and Pennant's description of the scene on Parys Mountain is most graphic:

> Suffocating fumes of the burning heaps of copper arise in all parts, and extend their baleful influence for miles around. In the adjacent parts vegetation is nearly destroyed; even the mosses and lichens of the rocks have perished: and nothing seems capable of resisting the fumes but the purple Melic grass, which flourishes in abundance. [43]

The effect the fumes had on the wider locality however, was considerably less than it might have been, for the prevailing wind which blows almost constantly over Mynydd Parys blew them away seawards. By way of comparison, the same process carried out in Roman times at the Tharsis copper mine in Spain, has left the surrounding area still barren almost 2,000 years later.[44]

It is a recognised fact that the establishment of one industry frequently generates a need for another, either to provide specialist products or services to support its own operations or, as sometimes happens, to make use of its byproducts which would otherwise have been wasted. The latter was true of Amlwch, where a brand new industry was created which, apart from the wealth it generated in its own right, significantly improved the environment.

Gunpowder for artillery and other uses had been known in Europe since the 13th century, and the European wars of the late 18th and early 19th centuries meant that there was an almost constant demand for sulphur, one of its three constituents. This demand however was nowhere near as great as that created by the newly emerging chemical industry for the production of sulphuric acid. It had long been known that sulphur dioxide fumes would on release into a cool, dry atmosphere, condense into an amorphous state known as Flowers of Sulphur and it was the application of this knowledge that formed the basis of a new industry at Amlwch.

During the ore burning process, great volumes of sulphur dioxide fumes were released into the atmosphere, and there was little or no incentive to prevent the pollution until it was realised that sulphur could be recovered directly from them. As with many other branches of science and technology, the means by which the sulphur was commercially recovered began in what an only be described as a very basic and crude way, but which ,with time, evolved into a most efficient process.

It will be recalled that initially, Nicholas Bayly paid to have his ores calcined, but made no attempt to increase his profit margin by extracting sulphur from the process, and it was Roe & Co (who then had the lease of the Mona Mine), who were first to benefit by the process at Amlwch.[45] In 1778 however, John Champion Jnr, a member of the well known Quaker smelting family, joined forces with Charles Roe's son William, to calcine ore at Amlwch, the partners agreeing to calcine the mining company's ores free of charge, in return for the sulphur they could produce.

One very important source of information regarding the operation of the Parys mines at the turn of the century, is a series of ten letters published as a book in Leipzig, in 1800. The letters, written by Doktor Augustin Lentin, of Leipzig University, describe in a most thorough, and scientific manner, the way in which the various processes associated with the mines at Amlwch were carried out.

It is evident that two methods were developed to produce sulphur. The first, favoured by Champion,[46] being a batch process using large horizontal ovens developed from the original ore improvement kilns. The second method was a continuous process in which the raw ore was introduced into the system at one end, at the same time as calcined ore was taken out at the other.

The first reference to continuous sulphur extraction kilns would appear to be that in a letter written in 1787 by Matthew Boulton, one of the nation's leading industrialists, to his son:

> About a fortnight ago I was obliged to go to Brosely, Shrewsbury, Bersham, Chester, Hollywell (sic), Conway, Bangor, and to the Isle of Anglesey where I spent 3 or 4 days in inspecting the

Anglesey Copper Mine which is a tremendous mine for a Cornish miner to behold. It is not like a deep Cornish mine but is an open work like a quarry or a gravel pit, and worked by open daylight. The ore is not very rich as it yields about 7 or $7^1/_2$ percent of fine copper, but they can get almost any quantity, and have now from 80 to 100 thousand Ton of Ore upon the bank which they calcine in kilns built of brick in a conical form A and as it burns the sulphur arises to ye top and is condensed in the form of flowers of Brimstone in the Condenser B which is a big empty space built with brick in the ground.

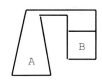

The second reference to sulphur production at Amlwch was made by Augustin Lentin in the sixth of ten letters he sent to Germany at the close of the 18th century, and which were later published as a book in 1800.[47] It is evident from Lentin's detailed account that both the batch and continuous methods were then being used simultaneously at Amlwch. The drawings which accompanied his narrative show that the roasting oven or kiln used in the batch process was very similar indeed to that introduced by Champion[49]; and was a rectangular, stone built building some 70 feet long by 27 feet wide, the sloping walls of which rose to a height of 8 feet. The roof of the kiln sloped upwards to a height of about 12 feet, in a manner similar to that of a slate roofed house, but which was built of stone. A second, smaller building, measuring some 60 feet by 8 feet, was built immediately alongside the kiln, into which the sulphur dioxide fumes from the latter were directed by means of what would appear to be wooden ducts connecting the two buildings. The roof of the condenser chamber, as the smaller of the two was known, was built of brick and arched to a height of 6 feet. The fact that the walls of both of the buildings were built on underground foundations indicates quite clearly that they were permanent structures, quite unlike the original calcining kilns which were dismantled after each firing. Unlike the condenser building which had a large door at one end, the kiln had 4 openings along its side and one at each end, which although restricted in size, appear to have been the means by which it was loaded and discharged.

As a result of the preliminary washing process, the ore was almost always damp when it was put into the kiln, and this resulted in the formation of steam which effectively prevented the sulphur from condensing satisfactorily. By way of overcoming the problem, it was the practice to vent the fumes given off in the early stages of the process, out to the atmosphere. Only when all the water had all been driven off were the fumes allowed to pass into the second chamber where the sulphur condensed in the form of a bright yellow powder, referred to by Boulton as Flowers of Brimstone. In this form, the sulphur did not lend itself easily to handling and transportation, and it was necessary to convert it into another form known either as cake or stone sulphur, a process further described in Boulton's letter:

> . . . it (the powder) was put into a Cast Iron Cylindrical Vessel and melted by a gentle heat into a solid form & laded out and poured into moulds. This Brimstone is sold for the purpose of making Oyl(sic) of Vitriol and they make at Anglesey about 3,000 Ton (worth £10 per Ton = £30,000 per year).

The cylinders thus produced were exported through Amlwch Port in their thousands. In order to reconvert the cake sulphur back into its original form, all that was necessary was to reheat the cake, and then allow the resulting fumes to condense as before.

A Curious Place

The importance of the process, whether as a means of recovering valuable sulphur, or as a method by which the ore was improved, was such that large areas of the Parys hill side had to be levelled in order to accommodate the many kilns that were required to process the amount of ore then being raised. One such area on the northern flank of the hill was known as the Brimstone Yard, but little more than a few tumbledown walls now remain there to remind us of that once important industry.

In the 1810 and later editions of Thomas Pennant's book, the description of the sulphur kilns suggests that the basic technology had changed little if any, during the ten years since Lentin's account was published. The kilns themselves had evolved however, for the single condenser building had been replaced by two, running parallel to the main kiln, with a third built at a higher level and at right angles to the others. The roofs of the later chambers were arched and the structures had the appearance of having been built throughout in dressed stone or brick.

Lentin's letter goes on to describe in detail a second method by which sulphur was recovered at Amlwch. Although the new technique, touched upon by Boulton, was a significant departure from the old, it nevertheless relied on the same basic principle as that used previously. The appearance of the kilns differed greatly however. Unlike the original horizontal kilns, those described by Lentin were vertical, and were loaded with ore from a charging platform located above the roasting chamber, in a manner similar to that used to roast limestone. There are however, significant differences between those written about by Boulton in 1787 and those described by Lentin some 13 years later.

According to Boulton, the kilns he saw were built of brick, and had their condensing chambers built into the ground, whilst the later ones were described by Lentin as having been built mainly of stone, with their condensing chambers built above ground.

Although they lacked the capacity of the horizontal kilns, the vertical kind were very impressive structures nonetheless, rising as they did to a height of some 35 feet above ground level, in the shape of huge, inverted cones. The base of each kiln was a square of 25 feet and 7 feet high, on top of which was built the inverted cone of the calcining kiln. At its base the cone was 20 feet in diameter, and at the charge face, some 28 feet above that, it was reduced to 6 feet in diameter. The 2 feet thick walls were inadequate to resist the stresses induced in them by the expanding ore and they were heavily reinforced by longitudinal iron bars and hoops 4 inches wide, $1^1/_2$ inches thick. At the base of the cones there were four vents lined with firebrick, each leading from the outside to the centre of the kiln where they formed an open square. The opening and closing of the vents closely controlled the rate at which the combustion took place. In order to facilitate the loading of the cone from the top, each kiln was built against steeply rising ground, the top of which was accessible to carts bringing the ore from the mine.

Connecting the top of the kiln to the adjacent high ground was a bridge which contained a duct through which the fumes from the burning ore could be led to a small condensing chamber measuring no more than 4 feet by 10 feet, built on the high ground against which the kiln was built.

In order to begin the process, the fuel, which could have been either wood or coal, was placed at the bottom of the chamber, which was then half filled with ore. A fire lit on the windward side of the kiln, was left until the burning ore could be heard crackling. At that stage, when the process had become self sustaining, more ore was added until the chamber was two thirds full. The kiln was then left for a period of 14 days, during which time the

Artist's impression of the Conical sulphur
kilns, Amlwch Port, c1798

duct to the condensing chamber was kept firmly shut, and the fumes vented to the atmosphere. Six weeks were normally allowed to elapse to allow the lower part of the charge to roast, at the end of which it was discharged manually into the cellar within the base structure. There the treated ore was left to cool before being examined to ensure that it was adequately processed for smelting. Any ore found to be unburnt at that stage was added to later charges, which were introduced into the kiln at twice weekly intervals. Sulphur was first removed from the condensing chamber some 8 weeks after the beginning of the roasting process, and every two weeks thereafter. One kiln processed some 10 tons of ore each week, during which time as much as $1^1/2$ tons of brimstone could be recovered.

According to Lentin there were as many as 45 conical kilns at Amlwch when he left Anglesey some time before 1800, some of which were built on Mynydd Parys but the majority he reported as being located close to the port. Exactly where these structures were located in the vicinity of the harbour has never been discovered, for their exact whereabouts do not appear to have been recorded by any of the contemporary writers. This is somewhat perplexing, for the sight of so many large structures clustered together must surely have been such that most chroniclers would have been anxious to describe them. Bearing in mind the extraordinary lengths to which the builders went to reinforce the kilns with iron bars and hoops, one might be forgiven for asking why none has survived – particularly as less robust buildings from the same period have, even if only in part.

The answer may well lie in the question itself. It will be recalled how vast quantities of scrap iron were then being imported into Amlwch, for use in the precipitation ponds and, in an age when resources were hardly, if ever wasted, the considerable quantity of iron used to reinforce the structures would undoubtedly have been recovered for that purpose when the kilns ceased to be used. In a similar fashion, the stone from which the kilns were built would also have been recovered for use in other structures, obviating the need for costly quarrying and cartage.

By referring to Lentin's detailed description of the kilns however, it may well be possible to determine their location by looking more closely at the facts he recorded:

(a) The kilns were built up against steep ground, to a height of about 35 feet.

(b) The base of each kiln was about 25 feet wide, which meant that even if they had been built with their base structures touching each other, they could not have been accommodated in a length of less than 698 feet. It should be realised however that there is no requirement for the kilns to have been located all together, and they may well have been distributed over several sites.

(c) The ore was fed into the kilns from the top, and as it was at that time brought down from the mountain by horse and cart, it follows that the land above and behind the kilns must have been accessible to that form of transport.

One site which satisfies the criteria is located on the western side of the port, alongside the Treweek shipyard on Ochr Draw, where the land is now somewhat higher than the quay and supported by a retaining wall. There is evidence to show however, that the present level of the land behind the retaining wall is artificially high due to the slag that was dumped there by the smelters.

A recent investigation has revealed that the curved rock face which bounds the area to the north and west has been worked in several places. In one such place the remains of a rusted iron bar set vertically into a narrow ledge can still be seen, and in another, a wide channel has been cut into the solid rock immediately above the rock face. What is perhaps more telling, is the discovery of a cluster of crystals under a ledge on the rock face, which had been formed by the combination of sulphur dioxide and lime. The rock face at this site however is not long enough to accommodate as many as 28 kilns, and it is thought possible that the remainder were located under the rock face which now lies behind the western side of Quay Street, where the rock has also been worked.

The possibility of finding evidence of the kilns is slender, but there is a chance that the remains of the square bases on which the cones were built, continue to lie beneath the made up ground at the side of Treweek's yard – a possibility that warrants further investigation.

Chapter 5
Early Smelting

It was clear to Thomas Williams that the ore producers were, to a large extent, held to ransom by the large smelting cartels, and he was quite determined to maximise the mine's profits by establishing a smelter in which the company's own ores could be refined at cost.

Anglesey's inability to produce supplies of cheap, good quality coal, coupled to the fact that the government had imposed a crippling tax on all coal that was carried by sea, meant that there was little, if any incentive at all, to undertake smelting operations locally. However, despite the difficulties, it is evident that this was precisely what Thomas Williams had in mind from the very beginning for Edward Hughes, no doubt at his prompting, declared as early as 1775, his intention to erect a smelting works in Anglesey. [50]

In order to make the proposition commercially viable however, Hughes had to overcome the problem of the duty payable on the coastal shipment of coal, and in 1776 he petitioned Parliament to that end. His plea was unsuccessful, and on the grounds that a concession was needed to permit the fuelling of steam pumping engines for the mine, he placed further petitions before Parliament in 1779, 1782 and again in 1783. These proved to be no more successful than the first, for the simple reason that they were strongly opposed by Cornish mining interests, who had found an ally in no less a person than Sir Nicholas Bayly.

Sir Nicholas was not entirely driven by animosity, but more by the economics of the proposals, which he saw affecting the value of the duty ores he received from the mining companies working Cerrig y Bleiddiau, or the Mona Mine as it was to became known. He reasoned that the Hughes, Dawes, Williams partnership would not be pressing for such a concession unless it profited them financially and in that case, they would then be better placed to undermine his own profits.

Frustrated by his failure to bring the coal to the ore, Thomas Williams decided instead to take the ore to the coal and in 1779 he leased land on which to build a smelter at Ravenhead in Lancashire. The site, adjacent to a coal mine belonging to John Mackay, whose own operations had been badly hit by the American War of Independence, was prepared to supply all the coal Williams required, at what was even then, a ridiculously low price. The site chosen by Williams had the added advantage of being located alongside a canal which was connected to the River Mersey, along which, vessels of up to 40 tons burden could navigate. This made it possible for the ore carrying ships to sail from Amlwch Port to the smelter directly, without having to transfer their cargoes to smaller canal boats for the last part of the journey.

The scope of Thomas Williams' forward strategy can be gauged by the fact that having only just embarked on the Ravenhead project, he then went on to purchase the Upper Bank Works, which was an established copper smelter in Swansea. This was not as might be supposed, intended to give him additional smelting capacity, but more especially to give him a vital foothold in the Cornish mining industry which had traditionally sent its ores to Swansea for smelting. He later exploited this masterly move to great effect.

Henry Paget, 1st Earl of Uxbridge.

Sir Nicholas Bayly died in 1782, and he was succeeded by his eldest son Henry, who was created Earl of Uxbridge in 1784 (he had assumed the surname Paget upon succeeding to the barony of Beaudesert in 1769), one year before the end of Roe's lease of Cerrig y Bleiddiau. However much Sir Nicholas may have disliked Williams, it is clear that his sentiments were not shared by his son for both men joined forces in 1786 to form what was later to be referred to as the 'old' Mona Mine Co, which carried on where Roe & Co had left off. The company, three quarters owned by the Earl, was under the direction of Thomas Williams, who owned the remaining one quarter share. The stewardship of the mine itself however was placed in the hands of John Price, who had by then become Lord Uxbridge's agent.

During the course of their lease of Cerrig y Bleiddiau, Roe & Co had effectively plundered the mine by working only the rich ores, and disregarding those which were least profitable. This made matters extremely difficult for their successors who had to spend over £60,000 putting matters to right. At that stage, both the Parys and the Mona mines were operated quite independently of each other insofar as each had its own officials. The fact that Thomas Williams was intimately involved with both companies however, meant that they had a common direction, and that there was close co-operation between them.

Further pressure put on the government by Thomas Williams, to have the duty on

Parys Mountain – the great open cast workings photographed in 1981. The shell of the pumping windmill can be seen on the skyline. [Don Williams]

seaborne coal rescinded, ultimately proved successful; for in 1786, there was a partial remission of duty amounting to £1,500 per annum, on coal imported through the port of Amlwch, irrespective of the use to which it was put. The existence of the duty had not prevented Thomas Williams from establishing a smelter in the town before that time however.[51] The economics of the situation must clearly have benefited him to import coal to smelt locally, rather than to have the ores exported in their raw or burnt state. The fact that no less than 40 tons of coal were then needed to produce 1 ton of fine copper meant that the greatest financial benefit was gained by partially smelting the poorest of the ores into what was known as a regule,which could then be fully refined elsewhere.

Smelting at Amlwch would appear to have been carried out in two distinct phases, the first begun under Thomas Williams' direction, is unfortunately, the one about which least is known. What is known however, is that the first smelter was located alongside Afon Amlwch, close to Plas Farm, on the site of the present Craig y Don estate. The original building was about 112 feet long by about 50 feet wide, alongside which there was a large water driven clay mill. A contemporary plan of the early smelter [52] shows also how Afon Amlwch was diverted to provide water, not only to the clay mill, but to the smelter and brewery as well. Arthur Aikin, a contemporary writer, wrote in 1797 of his visit to Amlwch, describing the operation of the clay mill:

> Adjoining to the smelting houses is a rolling mill, upon the same construction as malt-mills, for grinding the materials for fire bricks: these consist of fragments of old fire bricks, with clunch, (a kind of magnesian clay found in coal pits) procured from near Bangor ferry.

The description of what he describes as a rolling mill indicates quite clearly that it was not a copper rolling mill as had hitherto been supposed, but a conventional clay mill. For the purpose described by Aikin, it is almost certainly true to say that it would have employed one or more edge rollers, which are best described as heavy wheels driven in a circular path within an open pan, under which the material to be milled is thrown. Such wheels were often made of stone, but as scrap iron was then being imported for the precipitation ponds from Abraham Darby's ironworks at Coalbrookdale,[53] they may well have been made of cast iron.

On the early map of the smelter previously referred to, the road from Parys Mountain to the port is shown passing the smelter site, and when this is projected on to a later Ordnance Survey map of the area, it is quite evident that it led directly to that area of the western side of the port later known as Turkey Shore. This fact supports the theory that the early development of the port took place on that side, and the remains of buildings and yards thought to have been built to accommodate the later shipbuilding industry, were in all probability first associated with the mines.

By 1797 however, Amlwch had two smelting houses employing some 90 workers, and the following description by Aikin throws some light on their operation:

> The two smelting houses, of which one belongs to each company, contain thirty one reverberatory furnaces, the chimneys of which are 41 feet high; they are charged every five hours with 12 cwt. of ore, which yields $1/2$ cwt. of rough copper, containing 50 per cent of pure metal; the price of rough copper is about £2 10 0 per cwt. The coals are procured from Swansea and Liverpool, a great part of which is Wigan slack. From experiment it appears, that though a ton of coals will reduce more than the same quantity of slack, yet, owing to the difference of price, the latter is upon the whole preferable; the prices of the two at Liverpool being, coals 8s/6d per ton, slack 5s per ditto.[54]

Although Aikin's prime reason for visiting Amlwch was to learn about the copper industry, he was so impressed by the people he met there that he recorded how he and his companion

> . . . were much pleased with seeing the scars of rock between the town and the sea occupied by numerous groups of men, women and children, all neat in their best clothes, it being Sunday, who were enjoying the mild temperature of a summer evening, rendered refreshing by the neighbourhood of the sea. In one place we observed a circle of men gathered round a point of rock, on which was seated the orator of the party reading a newspaper aloud, and commenting upon it. On other little eminences were seen family parties, the elder ones conversing, and the younger children gamboling about them, or running races with each other; in a new mown meadow close to the town we passed by a large company of lads and lasses seated on a green bank, chatting, laughing, and full of mirth and frolick.
>
> To one who had been a spectator of the gross and riotous delight too frequent on holiday evenings in the outskirts of the metropolis, or any large town in England, the contrast could not fail of being very striking, and much to the advantage of the inhabitants of Amlwch: out of the whole number we did not see one drinking party; the pleasures of society and mutual converse needed not the aid of intoxication to heighten their relish.

Aikin returned to the district the following year and added to his previous impressions by recording:

> I am acquainted with no place the manners of whose inhabitants are so unexceptionable (as far at least as a stranger is enabled to judge of them) as Amlwch; and the favourable opinion which I was led to entertain of them on visiting the town last year is confirmed by what I have observed at present. Not a single instance have I known of drunkenness, not one quarrel have I witnessed during two very crowded market days, and one of them a day of unusual indulgence, that I passed at this place; and I believe no gaol, or bridewell, or house of confinement exists in the town or neighbourhood. Most of the miners are methodists, and to the prevalence of this religious sect is chiefly to be attributed the good order that is so conspicuous.

The 21 year lease held by the 'old' Parys Mine Company comprising of Hughes, Dawes and Williams, ended on 12 November 1799; by which time the ores were steadily becoming exhausted. A new company was then formed on 5 March 1801, which had Lord Uxbridge, Edward Hughes and Thomas Williams as its shareholders. Despite this commercial alliance, there was increasing personal animosity between Lord Uxbridge and Thomas Williams, resulting partly from Williams' autocratic style of management, and partly through his attempt to have his nephew appointed Receiver General for Anglesey [55] – a matter which found no favour with Lord Uxbridge.

The decline of the mines, on which Amlwch and much of the surrounding area had come to depend, coincided with a decline in Thomas Williams' health, and his grip on the copper empire he had so assiduously built, relaxed. During his lifetime he had gained control of both the Parys and Mona mines; three smelters in South Wales and two in Lancashire; the Garston Vitriol Works in Liverpool; two copper and brass factories in Flintshire, as well as two in the Thames Valley. In addition, he had offices or copper warehouses in London, Liverpool and Birmingham and he controlled banks in Chester, Bangor and Caernarfon. He had also been elected Member of Parliament for Great Marlow and his death in 1802, at the age of 65, brought to an end a brilliant career which saw his rise from being a modest country lawyer to becoming one who, by "matching greatness of achievement to grandeur of imagination, helped to open men's minds to what industrial and commercial revolution had made possible."[56]

In one of his letters, Lentin described how by 1800, there were by then only 20 furnaces operating in the Amlwch smelter [57], a fact which reflected the decline in the mines' fortunes.

In 1801, the same year as the 'new' Parys company was formed, Lord Uxbridge gave notice of his withdrawal from the Stanley Company, the smelting concern associated with the Mona Mines. This arrangement however does not appear to have included his interest in that part of the Amlwch smelter owned by the Mona Mine, in which Thomas Williams' sons were also shareholders.

It is not clear how long the Parys smelter continued its own operations after this, but the number of vessels entering Amlwch had by 1808, declined to such an extent, that the *North Wales Gazette*, which published details of local shipping movements, excluded the port from its returns. This must be taken as an indication that by then the work of the smelters had, to all intents and purposes, come to an end.

Owen and John Williams finally severed their family ties with the Anglesey mines in 1810, which then reverted to their original ownership, represented by Lord Uxbridge and the Reverend Edward Hughes.

Although the mines had by 1811, seen better days, James Watt, the pioneer of steam power, wrote to a friend who was proposing to visit Wales, that he should "call at the port of Amlwch on the north coast of Anglesey, and visit Parry's [sic] mountain, a very great copper mine within 2 miles of it."[58] As it is known that both he and his partner Mathew Boulton were regular visitors to the Cornish copper mines where many of their engines were installed, the remark could be taken to mean that he had himself been to Amlwch.

In the same year, Lord Uxbridge was offered a favourable contract by John Vivian and Sons, of the renowned Hafod smelting works in Swansea, for his share of the ore from the Anglesey mines. This was a means whereby the Vivians sought to ensure a regular supply of ore for their own smelter, by diversifying their business interests,[59] but they also had much to offer, for their expertise extended well beyond the copper smelting industry. The family owned shares in several copper mines in their native Cornwall, where John Vivian also played a prominent role in the management of the Cornish Metal Company. He was later to became Vice Warden of the Stannaries, a position of great power and influence in the West Country mining industry. Quite apart from the technical expertise they possessed, the Vivians were also able to provide much needed capital through the Miners Bank at Truro, of which John Vivian was joint owner.

Of the shares in the new company, Lord Uxbridge owned 40, the Vivian brothers, Richard Hussey and John Henry, each had 9 and a further 2 were held by another Cornishman, Captain William Davey. The overall direction of the new company was entrusted to John Henry Vivian, who in turn assigned the practical day to day running of the mine to Captains Davey and Treweek.[60] The latter arrived to take up his new duties in Amlwch in October, 1811.

Lord Uxbridge's business involvement with the Vivians proved to be short lived, for he died in 1812, and was succeeded by his 44 year old son Henry William. In the same year he gave notice of his withdrawal from the Greenfield concern as well as the Stanley and Ravenhead smelters – all of which had been established by Thomas Williams.

The drastic reduction in the output of the mines following the exhaustion of the easily mined open cast ore, was followed by the run down of the Lancashire smelters, both of which had closed down by 1814. Following their closure Edward Hughes concentrated the smelting of his own ores at Amlwch,[61] in that part of the smelter complex belonging to the Parys concern, and William Morgan who had been the Refiner at Ravenhead under Hughes' son Michael, came to Amlwch when that smelter closed. The Mona smelter, located alongside the Parys smelter, had in all probability closed down in 1812 when Lord Uxbridge disassociated himself from the other Mona concerns.

Part of the agreement between Uxbridge and the Vivians was that the latter would supply coal to the Amlwch smelter. As this contract was to last only until 1813, it could hardly be thought of as an inducement to invest either in the mine or in the smelter unless of course, they were persuaded that there was great potential for profit in the alliance. Bearing this in mind, it is also highly unlikely that Captains Davey and Treweek, with all the mining expertise their titles imply, would have invested either their money or their futures in a blind venture. It is reasonable to suppose therefore, that both men had surveyed the mine on behalf of the Vivians long before any agreement was reached, and that their assessment of its potential was favourable. The very fact that the open cast method of mining had come to an end meant that the only possibility for future development lay in conventional mining, and with their expertise in the deep mines of Cornwall there could perhaps have been no better assessors.

Under the Vivians' direction the smelter began work with 8 furnaces, indicating that early operations in that field were modest, by comparison with those in Thomas Williams' time. This may be somewhat misleading, for the Vivians' share in the Mona Mine Company entitled them to dispose of a third of the mine's output, including those ores belonging to Lord Uxbridge.[62] The possibility remains therefore that only the least productive ores were, under that arrangement, being smelted locally.

In 1815, Lord Uxbridge distinguished himself on the field of Waterloo where he was second-in-command to the Duke of Wellington and was created Marquess of Anglesey. By coincidence, Richard Hussey Vivian, the elder of John Vivian's two surviving sons also served in the campaign, as commander of a cavalry brigade.

Despite a sixfold increase in the output from the Mona Mine between 1811 (when Treweek arrived at Amlwch) and 1816,[63] the Vivians, for some unexplained reason, declined an offer to renew their lease. Notwithstanding the Cornish family's withdrawal, Treweek chose to remain in the Marquess' service, and it is thought very likely that it was he who persuaded his employer to go it alone.

Word of the new development soon got around and, in 1817, the Marquess received several unsolicited applications for the post of Smelter at the Amlwch works. These were accompanied by other applications for the post of Cashier and Clerk from one who had been informed "that it was His Lordship's intention to work the extensive and valuable copper mines on his own account in preference to letting them on lease."[64] A suggestion put forward by a member of the Williams family that William Morgan, former Smelter at Ravenhead, should take over the joint management of both the Mona Smelting Works and the Parys works, to which he had moved when the Ravenhead smelter closed, was agreed to by the Marquess.

Despite the apparent departure of Vivian & Sons, it would appear that the family still had a say in the smelting operations at Amlwch for Treweek, in a letter addressed to the Marquess' agent John Sanderson, stated that he had received a letter from J H Vivian stating that he was very willing for them to begin on the inferior ores and that he would take the best, which he would begin smelting directly.[65]

Restarting operations at Amlwch was not so easy however, for in another letter to Sanderson, dated a week later, Treweek had to admit that, "We cannot possibly begin to smelt at the Mona Works yet as there is Copper Bottoms in every furnace that must be taken out and rebuilt. If you could borrow two furnaces at the other works we might begin directly. I will write to Mr Vivian about the furnace bottoms."

The copper bottoms, referred to by Treweek, were the solidified remains of partially smelted ore which had been left in the furnaces when smelting work was abandoned and which had to be removed before smelting could be restarted. This required the dismantling and rebuilding of each furnace, and the proposal to borrow two furnaces belonging to the other works is a clear indication that the Parys smelter had capacity to spare.

Reopening the smelter was the least of Treweek's problems at that time however, for that year saw widespread poverty and hunger throughout the whole of Wales. At the heart of the problem were the recently enacted Corn Laws which prohibited the importation of cheap grain and which represented an attempt by government to perpetuate the high cereal prices which had prevailed during the Napoleonic Wars.

The problem at Amlwch, where many miners were unemployed because of the decline in the mines' fortunes, was particularly bad and made even worse by the number of soldiers and sailors who had by then returned from the wars. To further exacerbate the situation, the island's grain harvest was delayed and much reduced, following an exceedingly wet summer. The herring season, on which many families depended for both food and income, had also proved to be disastrous. The price of bread rose so much that it could barely be afforded, and the number of people reduced to begging was so high that one landowner claimed that Beaumaris gaol and castle together, would not have held the swarm of tramps and beggars to be found there, had the vagrancy laws been strictly applied.

There were several proposals to try to ameliorate the situation, one of which was to borrow money from the mine owners to purchase grain for selling on to the needy at a reduced price. There were, however, conflicting views as to the severity of the problem, but in the minds of many there was little doubt that a great famine was imminent. The absurdity of the situation lay in the fact that adequate supplies of corn were readily available – at a price – and locally produced grain continued to pass through Amlwch port, destined for the more affluent towns and cities.

The sight of waggonloads of oats and oatmeal being taken to the port for loading on the *Wellington* was, quite understandably, the catalyst which brought the people of the town on to the streets in protest. Faced with the need to prevent the ship from sailing, the mob removed her rudder, without causing hurt to either the crew or damage to the vessel. The incident must have taken place during the hours of darkness, for the rudder was immediately carted away to the churchyard at Llanwenllwyfo, some 3 miles south of the port, where it was carefully hidden from sight. Its weight was such that several men were needed to lift and carry it, but the secrecy surrounding the affair meant that few others could have known of its whereabouts.

In an effort to defuse the situation, another meeting was called at the Ty Mawr,[66] in order to discuss what practical action might be taken to either solve the problem or at least to ameliorate its effects. After much deliberation, a decision was made to try and raise £2,000 by public subscription, which could be used to purchase corn and potatoes for distribution to the needy. James Treweek was one of two mine officials present at the meeting and a request to borrow money from the mine owners through their good offices was met with a refusal to consider any sum in excess of £300. When the response became known, a great deal of anger was generated amongst a section of the townspeople and they gave vent to their feelings by taking to the streets, their anger, perhaps unjustifiably, being mainly directed towards the mine owners.

Before the obligatory establishment of county police forces in 1856, the maintenance of law and order and the protection of property depended on the deployment of Special Constables, who were enrolled unpaid, on an *ad hoc* basis. Their authority was given to them by local Justices of the Peace, who were in turn supported by Assize Courts. In extreme cases of public disorder however, when all else had failed, it was not unusual for the authorities to resort to the use of military force.

Six days after the removal of the *Wellington's* rudder, two of the island's magistrates were despatched to the town to restore peace and order and, following an assessment of the situation, their first act was to enrol thirty Special Constables to assist them. The enrolment was achieved more by coercion than by consent for, no sooner were they sworn in, than the constables "seemed to consider their duty at an end, and disappeared, except five or six who were totally inactive, with the exception of one",[67] which could be taken to mean that many of the townspeople were sympathetic towards the rioters.

Having only a token force available at their disposal, the magistrates could only detain those they considered to be the most active in promoting the disturbances, not one of whom offered the slightest resistance to his arrest. Although the situation was grave, it is evident that a great measure of self control was exercised by the protestors who were clearly anxious to prevent matters getting out of hand. This unusual fact was substantiated by one of the magistrates, who reported that, "no acts of violence were committed, and only a few scores of women and children made their appearance, who were rather unruly and abusive, but not to the magistrates". [68]

Having arrested the ringleaders, the magistrates were then faced with the problem of transferring them to the gaol at Beaumaris, where they could be tried by an assize judge. Having only one constable available for escort duty, there was no way this could be achieved and the magistrates were reluctantly forced to release two of the men on bail, holding only the prime suspect in custody. Their plan was to march the prisoner to Llanerchymedd, from where he could be taken the remainder of the way by carriage. When this became known, the inn where the man was being held was quickly besieged by sympathizers and the escort, comprising of one constable assisted by two men, had to resort to subterfuge to get him away from the town without being seen.

When the party arrived at Llanerchymedd, the 'rabble', as the protestors were referred to by the Magistrates, tried to free the prisoner but their efforts were thwarted by that village's own Special Constables.

On the very same day as the prisoner arrived at Beaumaris, the whereabouts of the *Wellington's* rudder was discovered, and the men charged with returning it to the port abandoned their task when they were pelted with stones and pieces of smelter slag by the protestors. This prompted the Reverend Jones, one of the two magistrates, to write to the Marquess of Anglesey requesting military assistance. Before anything could be done however, the protestors once again took to the streets and the riot took on an ugly aspect when the lives of two of the mine agents, probably Treweek and Roose, were threatened.

The magistrate's request for military assistance eventually reached Sir Robert Peel (who in 1829 was to create the first organized British police force) and he ordered the Lord Lieutenant of Ireland to send to Amlwch a detachment of the troops then under his command. This course of action was thoroughly disapproved of by the Marquess, who considered the deployment of regular troops on the island as nothing short of a disgrace. His concern regarding the situation was such however, that he required the magistrates to keep him informed of the developing situation on a daily basis.

On 6 February, Treweek wrote to John Sanderson, the Marquess' agent, informing him that

> . . . there were 200 or upwards parading the streets through last night, with weapons in their hands, threatening the lives of many in the place. I cannot find that any of the miners have joined them. They are the tradesmen of the place, with the sailors and soldiers. If the Magistrates do not send troops I do not know what the end will be. [69]

A little over a week later, Treweek confirmed that

> . . . the mob is composed of Publicans; Shopkeepers; Builders; Carpenters; Coopers and most of the tradesmen of the place with the sailors, soldiers and others, many of which are returning in consequence of work being slack in other parts. [70]

In a further attempt to ease matters, Treweek arranged with others to hold a meeting at

Amlwch on 18 February to consider the plight of the poor, and to devise means whereby their problems might be eased. It is more than likely that this was on his own initiative, for, despite the opinion of many to the contrary, he was more than a little sympathetic towards the plight of the poor.

At the meeting it was disclosed that out of a total population of almost 5,000, 103 persons were unemployed, a fact which could account for the mineowners' seemingly parsimonious attitude. As a means of creating work for the unemployed, the meeting launched a subscription to enable improvements to be carried out to the harbour. The fact that a small white lighthouse was built on the northern pier in 1817 suggests that part, at least, of the improvement fund may have been used for that purpose. The light, which was intended for vessels bound into the bay, was at a height of 28 feet above the half tide level, which meant that under normal conditions, its light could be seen at a distance of about 4 miles, but, "the mariner should be made aware that with southerly winds this light is sometimes eclipsed until very near the land, occasioned by the smoke from the smelting works rushing down the valley."[71]

Further subscriptions for the improvement of roads and for clothing the poor were launched simultaneously, and the fears of the townspeople were perhaps best summed up by Treweek, when he informed his employers that, "There is a great deal of wheat and barley yet in the island, but report says that it is so poor that it is impossible for the people to eat it. This appears to be the reason of the people being apprehensive of a scarcity, all of the people of the county being entirely on oatmeal."

He went on to express his hope that, "we shall have sufficient to employ the men until harvest come, or something else presents itself."[72]

On the day that the meeting was held, arrangements were being made in Dublin to send no fewer than 164 men of the 45th Regiment to Holyhead. The detachment, under the command of Major Alexander Martin, arrived at Holyhead on the following day, where they rested for a further day before setting off for Amlwch, a march that took them eight hours.

Within two hours of the troops' arrival, the *Wellington's* rudder was restored. An uneasy peace returned to the town, and the rioters were able to do little more than threaten to seek revenge on the magistrates and corn merchants once the soldiers had left. Before any date could be set for the troops' departure, however, Wynne Jones, another of the magistrates, issued a directive to the High Constable requiring him to make it known

> . . . to all the respectable Householders in the Village and Port of Amlwch and within a reasonable distance of the same that they are expected to come forward as Special Constables for the preservation of the Peace of the said Village and Port - and to form a nightly Patrole for 6 months.' The magistrates were then to be furnished with a list of the names of those prepared to come forward, in order that they might be sworn in before the departure of the troops. The directive went on to say that, 'You may also inform the said Householders that it will not be deemed expedient to remove the Troops until one Hundred persons at least have pledged themself for the aforesaid purpose of forming a patrole'. [73]

The detachment of soldiers eventually left Amlwch on 29 March, no doubt to the great relief and satisfaction of both the Marquess and James Treweek.

It was not until 11 April that Treweek was able to report to Sanderson that 4 furnaces had been commissioned at the smelter. Some of the remaining furnaces took longer to prepare, and it would appear that their commissioning was further delayed by a shortage of coal brought about by the fact that very few Masters were prepared to sail during the winter months.[74]

By 1818, however, the smelter was in full operation and once again producing fine copper. The product left the smelter either in the form of plates, each of which weighed a nominal 1cwt (112 pounds),[75] or as copper bowls, each of which weighed an astonishing 6 cwt. It is thought that the bowls were intended for Africa, where they were used as salt pans. It would appear that they were in an unfinished state when they left Amlwch for James Treweek referred to a long standing complaint by their customers, Messrs Newton, Lyon & Co, that the copper bowls supplied by the smelter did not "stand the hammer."[76] All of this suggests that an unusual combination of manufacturing techniques was being employed in the making of the bowls which departed from the usual method of fabricating large vessels from thin metal sheets riveted together. It would seem that the bowls were first cast in a rough mould at Amlwch, and then sent on to the customer where they were beaten into the required shape. The claim that the bowls leaving Amlwch were not able to "stand the hammer" suggests that they cracked during this process, the implication being that the copper was insufficiently ductile because of impurities. This may well have been the case, but a similar effect would have resulted if the copper had become hardened by being overworked under the hammer.

Such was the fame of the Amlwch copper industry by the beginning of the 19th century, that many eminent visitors were drawn there. Some came for no better reason than to view the impressive workings, but others came to widen their scientific knowledge. One such person was the distinguished natural philosopher Michael Faraday, whose scholarly work in the advancement of chemistry was surpassed only by his momentous discoveries in the field of electromagnetic induction and electrolysis.

Apprenticed to a bookbinder at the age of 13, Faraday, a blacksmith's son, became passionately interested in the natural sciences, particularly physics and chemistry, and he avidly read as many as he could of the scientific books he was employed to bind. Having greatly impressed Sir Humphrey Davy, perhaps best remembered for his design of the miners' safety lamp, Faraday was given employment as a laboratory assistant at the Royal Institution. There he assisted Davy with his experiments and where, at the same time, he managed to carry out his own research into chemical analysis.

It was during this period in his life that he and a companion set off, in the summer of 1819, on a walking tour of Wales. Their journey began in the south, where they visited Vivian's copper works in Swansea. They then made their way up through mid Wales to Caernarfon, climbing Cader Idris en route.

Setting off by boat down the Menai Strait on 28 July, the two men were able, on reaching Porthaethwy, to see at first hand the preparations being made to build the suspension bridge over the Menai Strait, which Faraday referred to as Mr Telford's hanging bridge. They were thankful for such a pleasant start to what was to prove to be an extremely long and hot day, during which they planned to walk, without rest or refreshment, the remaining 17 miles across the island to Amlwch. As they approached the town they perceived by their surroundings that they were approaching the mines, for the countryside appeared brown and the roads were mended with slag.

Having partaken of a meal at the Ty Mawr, where they were to spend the night, Faraday walked up to James Treweek's home at Mona Lodge, where he presented a letter of introduction from Morgan, Vivian's agent in Swansea. Treweek immediately arranged for

The ruins of the pumping engine house and chimney at Parys Mountain. Since 1981, when this photograph was taken, the chimney has collapsed.
[Don Williams]

the two to be shown around the smelters that evening and to the mines on the following day.

Faraday's description of the smelters was brief:

> These consisted of a row of reverberatories [77] exactly similar to those used at the Swansea works in which the metal is roasted over and over again. The ore does not come in a crude state to them but is first roasted up at the mountain in kilns by which a great part of the sulphur is separated and then it comes to these works. The metal is not tapped into water here as in Swansea but runs into pigs. It is however granulated after the last step of the refinery process for the use of the makers of brass etc. There are two ranges of refineries at this place, i.e. between the town and the port, one range belongs to the Parys Mine and the other to the Mona Mine of which Captain Irewick (Treweek) is agent. The refineries afford a pleasant walk perfectly free from the strong smell of sulphurous acid so abundant at Swansea and very airy. [78]

Although he did not describe the Amlwch refineries in any great detail, Faraday likened them to those at Vivian's works, of which he had given a good account. [79]

The furnaces at Swansea resembled high bakers' ovens which had an immense fire at one end and a flue at the other, at the top of which there was a hopper containing ore. A normal charge of ore weighed somewhere between 4 to 5 tons and, once in the furnace, it was roasted for between 36 and 48 hours. During this process much of the sulphur and arsenic it contained was given off, and it was these fumes that so plagued the entire countryside surrounding the Swansea works. Faraday's remark about the Amlwch smelter being free from the strong smell of sulphurous acid can be accounted for by the fact that the ore was first calcined elsewhere to rid it of its sulphur content before it was delivered to the smelter.

A later description of the Amlwch smelters [80] relates how the furnaces there used Beecher's reverberatory system. Of the 20 furnaces then in operation there were: 6 roasters, 6 ore furnaces, 3 calciners, 3 precipitates, and 2 refiners; and the processes were carried out in the following order:

1. Ores are first calcined - 3/3½ tons, lasting 12 hours.
2. Calcined ore is then melted, and cast into coarse pigs.
3. The metallic mixture produced by stage 2 is calcined.
4. The calcined coarse metal from stage 3 is melted.
5. The purer metal from stage 4 is calcined.
6. The calcined metal is again melted.
7. The copper from stage 6, (80%-90% pure) is roasted.
8. Coarse, or blistered copper as it was known, was then refined by being first melted gradually and, when molten, its surface was covered with charcoal. A pole, usually of green birchwood, was then thrust into the liquid metal, which, as can be imagined had the most dramatic results. When the molten copper had settled down, a little was removed and allowed to cool before it was tested for purity and ductility.

It was, however, possible to overpole the molten copper, which resulted in it becoming very soft, a condition which could only be corrected by removing the charcoal from its surface and exposing the molten copper to air. Mistakes of that kind on the part of the Smelter were rarely tolerated, and Treweek in one of his letters, described how a man named Davies who was formerly a refiner at the Upper Bank smelting works at Swansea: ". . . was discharged for making 80 tons of Copper that required the second making in consequence of its badness. This gave so great offence that he was not allowed to work in the furnace, and was obliged to accept the situation of a slag brick maker."[81] Harsh punishment indeed.

Such was the usual quality of the Amlwch refined metal however, that the "copper sold from these works commands in the market fully £5 per ton above the market price, on account of its extreme purity and malleability."[82]

After refining, it was the custom at Swansea to cast the refined copper into one inch thick, rectangular cakes, which measured approximately 12 inches x 1 inch, and which weighed a little over 35lbs, somewhat less than those produced at Amlwch. These were made by pouring part of the molten metal into an iron moulding box, which was held together by pins, and when the copper had cooled sufficiently, another equal amount was poured over it. In this way, each layer was separated from its neighbour. This process was repeated as many as eight times and when the mould was full, it was unpinned and the copper cakes separated from each other by a sharp hammer blow. All that then remained to be done was to clean off the edges of the plates and the copper was ready for marketing.

Having completed their tour of the smelters, Faraday and his companion were taken to the port, which Faraday observed as being

. . . a very pretty, useful place. Small as the village is, and so far removed towards the end of the island out of the line of communication between England and Ireland still it has above 5,000 inhabitants and more than 20 vessels belonging to it. It may be imagined then a pretty bustling place and we found every appearance of it being so. There were a number of vessels in the port, some laden with copper or copper slag as ballast, and others unloading out iron from London, Swansea etc, or coals from the North or East. From a small spot beyond the port called the East Indies,[83] we had a very fine view of the north seas and in the distance could perceive the Isle of Man.

Early the following morning the travellers were called upon by Captain Lemin, one of the mine agents, who took them

> . . . along a very dusty, dirty road for when bad it is mended with slag and cinder and as there are always 12 or 14 carts moving backwards and forwards on it, these materials are soon ground into black and disagreeable powder. There are no trams used on these roads or in the mines in consequence of the corrosive effects which the waters from the workings would have upon them and which would destroy them in a short time.

This point had earlier been lost on the mine agents however, for Faraday went on to describe how, having purchased a steam engine, they were embarrassed to find it rendered useless within a very short time by the corrosive nature of the water. In order to overcome the problem they were compelled to neutralise the acidic effect by adding lime to it, and the treated water thus became a precious commodity which was recycled continuously by way of cooling ponds.

Inasmuch as Pennant and Bingley have given us a graphic description of the manner in which the mines were worked above ground, Faraday on the other hand, gives us an insight into the conditions under which the men worked underground and the vivid account of his tour of the mine is such that the author makes no apology for quoting from it at length:

> I stripped off everything but my stockings and boots and took possession of a miner's trousers, shirt and coat all of flannel. Then putting on a thick woollen cap, hanging a candle to my breast button and taking another lighted and garnished with clay in my hand I was ready to descend. Magrath [84] was similarly equipped and we laughed heartily at each other as a sort of prologue to our adventure. We followed Captain Leaman [85] to a small shaft a little distance from the office and in such true miners' style that I verily believe the men themselves did not know us for other than miners. The place we prepared to descend was a small aperture in the earth about 4 ft by 3 ft wide and a ladder appeared at its mouth which descended into the darkness below. Captain Leaman chose this shaft because it was the most comfortable. There were two others but the pump rods worked up and down in one, and in the other we could only descend and ascend in the buckets like lumps of ore. Having taken a lesson how to hold our candles we got on to the ladder. It was not long but on reaching its termination we had to swing around it by a little stage on to a second and from that on to a third, and so on until I lost count of their number. We soon left daylight and were not long before we were well used to the place and could trust so securely to our hands as scarcely to notice a false step though a fall would have led us down 200 or 300 feet without any ceremony or hesitation. At last we began to enter the vein and had to shuffle on in a more irregular manner. A rope ladder occurred here and there in places where the chasm was too crooked to admit a straight one of wood and they felt very curious dangling in the middle of the air and darkness.

In the lucid manner which characterised his lectures, Faraday illustrated how a vein of ore could be likened to a sheet of iron thrust obliquely through a lump of clay, which in this case represented Parys Mountain. Unlike the iron sheet however, the vein of ore was not uniform, for it could vary in thickness from as little as half an inch, to as much as 30 feet, and could extend for miles. Having thus set the scene, the philosopher continued with the narrative:

> Our progress in the vein was at first through very confined passages but on a sudden we entered a place like a large chamber, so large that our light would not reach across it. Here the vein had swelled out into a bunch in the way I just now mentioned and had afforded a very rich mass of ore. Here again it became very narrow and we had in one corner to lay down on our backs and

wriggle in through rough slanting opening not more than 12 or 14 inches wide. The whole mountain being above us and threatening to crush us to pieces. You will understand my Dear Girl[86] we were now in those parts of the veins which had been cleared of ore by the workmen. All, however, above and below to the right and left was not void for if the ore had simply been removed and the place left to itself, working would soon have been stopped. You will remember we were now in the centre of the mountain and its whole weight resting over us, and this weight would long ago have crushed the two sides of the empty veins together if precautions had not been taken to keep the place open and support the mountain. This is done thus. When the miners have excavated the vein so as to leave a free space above them of perhaps 20 feet in height, timber as the trunks of trees are let down to them which they place across the cavity a little distance above their heads so as to form a rough, strong floor, and then on this is placed all the gangue and useless rubbish loosened with the ore, until the space is half full of such parts of the vein been left open as are useful for the conveyance and the workings. In this way a number of what may be called apartments or galleries are formed in the empty part of the vein at the end of which men frequently go on working in a horizontal direction on the edge of the vein, whilst others far below them are extending it in depth.

Proceeding along one of these galleries we came at last to a chasm at the bottom of which we could just see men with lights. Whilst admiring the curious scene the large bucket came rushing past us from above and descended down into the depths. This indeed was the shaft at which we had seen horses and men raising ore above ground for the cobbers.[87] It was intersected in this place by the gallery along which we were proceeding and stopped our progress. The shaft here was not perpendicular but followed the inclination of the vein and the bucket slid up and down against one side which was covered with smooth planks. In a few minutes we saw a bucket come up, and to us strangers it had a very curious appearance. The rope moving on for a long time with no visible means, the empty bucket banging, slipping and tumbling down and the full one suddenly emerging from the darkness beneath into the candlelight and immediately disappearing above are so peculiar in their effect as to irresistibly create some degree of surprise.

We crossed this place on a plank and a rope loosely put over it, and advancing onwards soon after descended again creeping and sliding, tumbling and slipping as before, Captain Leaman giving us the utmost attention in explaining everything. Now at times we began to hear explosions which reverberated throughout the mine in grand style, and we soon came up to two men who were preparing a blast.

By way of preparation for the blasting, the miner first bored a hole some 14 inches to 18 inches into the rock face, using an auger about an inch and a half in diameter. Such augers were lengths of iron bar, the ends of which had been formed into a cruciform shape, and then hardened. As the tool was struck, usually with a 6lb hammer, it was rotated, reducing the rock to a fine powder as it progressed deeper into it.

When the miner was satisfied that a sufficient depth had been reached, he cleared out the hole with a scraper, and placed into it a pre-weighed charge of gunpowder contained in a brown paper bag. A long thin rod, known as a pricker, was then pushed into the bag of powder, and the space surrounding it, within the remaining length of the hole, was packed with small stones, dust and clay, all of which was then tightly rammed with a tool called a stamper. Up until the introduction of bagged gunpowder this particular operation was fraught with danger, for sparks generated by the iron stamper when it struck the rock sometimes ignited the powder prematurely. The resulting explosion had the effect of propelling the stamper out of the hole, much like a harpoon out of a gun, and was unfortunately, the cause of death of many of the miners.

When the plug was finally consolidated, the pricker was withdrawn, leaving a narrow hole down which was pushed a straw or quill filled with gunpowder. A slow fuse leading to the end of the straw was then ignited and the miners in the vicinity, forewarned by a shout of *tân* (fire), retired to a safe place until the dust settled.

To a scientist as meticulous as Faraday, the complacency of the miners in matters of safety must have been appalling, for

> It is astonishing how careless the men become of the peculiar dangers to which they are liable from the frequency with which they meet them. They put their candles anyhow and anywhere, and their powder is treated in the same manner. Magrath, to rest himself whilst the Captain gave directions, sat down on a tub and stuck his candle against its side. We found out afterwards it was what they kept the powder in and it certainly would not have been wonderful if we had all made a grand blast together.

> Here the men were at work on the rock cutting a level to another part of the vein and they are paid so much per foot or yard, but returning a little way and then moving on again we soon came to some who were working out ore. They blast it just as in the former case and it is then carried to the edge of the shaft I before spoke of, and drawn up by the buckets.

The manner in which the Parys miners had to bid for work, followed closely the Cornish method known as Bargain Setting. This took place at two monthly intervals, and followed a detailed inspection of the mine by the underground agents. On the day appointed for the setting, all the miners assembled in the mine yard where the Head Agent, standing in what had once been a pulpit in a nearby chapel, gave precise details of the work to be undertaken in each part of the mine. The spokesman for a team of miners would then call out a price at which his group was prepared to undertake the work. The first bid was usually high, and the setting then took on the form of a Dutch Auction, with the various groups undercutting each others' prices. When the lowest figure was finally arrived at, the agent sealed the bargain by throwing a pebble to the spokesman, whose name was then duly entered in the setting book.

It was not unknown for the competition for work to be so fierce, that bargain takers sometimes ended their two months labour with little or no money to show for their efforts. Worse still were those times, when payment for powder, fuses and candles from the company store, or for tool sharpening at the smithy, resulted in the men ending their contract in debt to the mineowners. It is unlikely that the more experienced miners fell into this trap for, over the years, they developed great skill and judgement in relation to every aspect of their work.

The money the miners earned depended on the quantity and quality of the ore they raised, and this was weighed and assessed once every two weeks by highly competent Assay Masters, as well as by Surface Agents who checked the ore as it was processed above ground. Because of the small sample of ore that was taken to be assayed, it was essential that it truly represented the quality of the whole heap from which it was taken; for it required very little by way of improvement with an 'added' lump of rich ore, to bias the assay in favour of the miner. Attempts to adulterate the assay sample in this way were extremely rare, but not unknown.

In a letter to his nephew,[88] Llew Llwyfo, who had at one time been a miner at Parys Mountain, described how as a youngster, he was employed to barrow samples of ore to the assay office, a job that was considered to be one requiring the utmost trustworthiness.

It was the custom for the ore raised by each group of miners to be carted to a specific site where it was weighed, and from which samples were taken for assay. A representative sample from each heap was then put in a small box, several of which were then placed into a box barrow, the lid of which was locked by an official. The only other key to the box was

A two horse power 'Whimsey' at Parys Mountain with the five sailed pumping windmill and steam pumping house in the background – three power sources on one site.

in the possession of the assayer, thus ensuring that the samples could in no way be tampered with.

On two separate occasions, Llew was stopped on his journey to the assay office by miners who had made copies of the key to the box. In the first instance, the youngster let out such a yell that the man ran away, never to be seen at the mine again. On the second occasion, however, the miner set upon the young man in earnest, and Llew only managed to escape by hitting his assailant with a stone. Llew's constant fear of revenge ended only with the news that the man had been killed whilst working on the construction of the Holyhead breakwater.[89]

Luck did not always favour the company however, for there were times when the vein opened up into what was known as a bunch of good ore, when, according to Faraday

the men earn much money during their month or period of time for they raise an immense quantity of ore rapidly without much trouble and now and then save a hundred pounds very quickly . . . generally, however, things are so managed so as to leave them well though not extravagantly paid. None of these men work more than eight hours a day in the mine. The rest of their time is spent above ground at home, there being sets of workmen who replace each other.

Continuing his journey down into the workings, Faraday found himself at the lowest point in the mine where

. . . all the waters that run from the earth into the excavation are collected together to be pumped up. There was a large quantity in a sort of tank boarded over and containing much copper in solution. The waters it appears had risen a little and they were very particular about them just now because close at hand they were deepening the mine and working at a level below that of the well. We were here in the busy part and the black heads and faces that popped into sight every now and then with a candle before them looked very droll. Some miners were stuck up in a corner over our heads making a roof and they seemed to cling to the rock like bats so that I wondered how they got and remained there, but in a few moments I found we had to go up there too and indeed we managed very well. Difficulties and dangers are in almost every case magnified by distance and diminished by approximation, and I do not think that one place in the world can be better suited to illustrate this than a mine.

Following the example of our Captain and peeping into a small chasm through which a man might by contrivance pass, we found it to be the entrance into a large cavity from 30 to 40 feet wide every way. This had been a fine bunch of ore and there were 6 or 7 men with their candles working in it. We did not go down but putting our lights aside laid our heads to the aperture and viewed this admirable Cimmerian scene for some time with great pleasure, the continual explosion on all sides increasing the effect. This was the lowest part of those workings and was about 370 feet below the surface of the earth.

After a little further progress we came to the pump shaft, an aperture cut down from the surface to this spot. It was 360 feet deep and we could see no daylight up it. Below it was a small well connected with the large one before mentioned and into this were inserted pumps. The first was a lifting pump and raised the water a few feet. Then a forcing pump took it and made it ascend up pipes far away out of sight. The pumps were worked by the steam engine we had seen above being connected with it by beams of wood descending in the shaft and continually rattling up and down in it. In the small part of the shaft left vacant by the pistons, pipes and beams were fixed ladders which ascending from stage to stage conducting to the top and up. There we had to go bathed in the shower of water which was shaken off from all parts of the pump works. After long climbing we came to a part of the shaft where the first forcing pump delivered its water into a little cistern and then another pump of the same construction threw it up to the surface. Still proceeding we at last got a glimpse of daylight above and were soon able to see the pump rods by it. Now the danger of the ascent appeared far greater than before, for the extensive light showing in the well above and something of the depth below made us conscious of our real situation whereas before we only thought of the small spot illuminated by our candles. The agitation of the pump rods was more visible too and appeared greater from being seen over a larger space, and their rattling and thumping was quite in accordance with appearances. But in spite of all things we gained the surface in high glee and came up into the world above at the engine after a residence of about two hours in the queer place below.

   All the miners work in flannel cloaths and from our own feelings we had reason to commend the system. We did not feel at all in-commoded by heat during our stay below though when we came up and began to change we found ourselves in the very highest state of perspiration. The advantage of flannel arises from the little influence moisture has over it and it non adhesion to the skin even though damp or moist.

Faraday's description of the pump shaft, with its rattling timbers, accords well with the illustration shown in the Perran Foundry Company's catalogue of pumping and winding engines, dated 1795; his narrative reveals however, that there were more than the one pump operating in the shaft.

In 1982, part of one of the beams of wood, known as drawing lifts, was recovered from what is thought to have been Cairns shaft, before it was capped as a safety precaution. The timbers, which varied in length, were generally about 18 inches square in section, and as they extended 360 feet down the shaft, their total weight, including that of additional plunger poles and coupling irons, would have been well in excess of 20 tons.

Raising the water to the surface was accomplished in stages, known as lifts. In Cornwall, the depth of each, on average, being about 30 fathoms (180 feet).[90] The fact that wooden pipes were used at Parys Mountain could well have meant that the height of each lift was considerably less however. The very lowest lift was different to those above it, in that the water was drawn upwards by suction, whilst the remaining lifts were accomplished by force pumping, under the weight of the drawing lifts.

The weight of the drawing lifts, which because of their length, was more than that necessary to pump the water, placed great demands on the steam engine. A rather indistinct photograph in Owen Griffith's book, *Mynydd Parys*, of what is now the last remaining engine house at the mines, shows what appears to be a counterbalance located near the top of the shaft. It is unlikely that this would have had any other purpose than to balance the surplus weight of the lifts, thereby permitting the use of a smaller engine.

Closer examination of the photograph however, reveals that the aperture in the engine house wall, intended for the engine's massive rocker beam, has been filled in. In its place there is what appears to be a beam, similar in appearance to a short see-saw mounted transversely on another beam protruding from the engine house wall, from the ends of which are suspended iron rods. This is clear evidence that the original pumping arrangement had been replaced by a dual system, which would have been substantially self balancing, and it may have been a similar arrangement to that described as working in the shaft Faraday ascended.[91]

It is known that at least 4 steam engines were used to de-water the workings at Parys Mountain, although the mines could in no way be described as wet.[92] One of the engines worked the pumps in the Cairns shaft, close to the highest point on the hill, and this was unique at the mine inasmuch that it was wind assisted, the essential machinery being housed in what now appears to be the shell of a conventional windmill. Unlike a typical Anglesey windmill however, it was fitted with five sails, which made it more efficient at extracting the natural power of the wind. The power generated in this way was tranferred

THE CORNISH PUMPING ENGINE,

FOR DRAINING MINES, SUPPLYING TOWNS, &c.

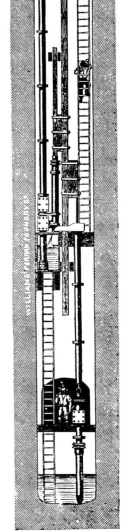

The above illustration clearly shows the usual method of Draining Mines, and notwithstanding all the Improvements in rotatory Engines it is still the most economical method of raising water.

It is of the first importance in Mining operations where it is necessary to employ Machinery for Draining, that the whole should be practically and judiciously laid out.

Very much depends on the constructive proportions of Machinery, and the careful execution of the details to ensure economy, and it is in these essential particulars that **Williams' Perran Foundry Co.** possess such an immense advantage, both from the magnitude and variety of the works they have completed, and their lengthened experience in mining and pumping.

Williams' Perran Foundry Co. continue to devote the greatest attention to make these Engines worthy of the credit they have received from Engineers and others in all parts of the World, and from their abundant manufacturing facilities, are in a position to supply at the shortest possible notice every description of this class of Machinery, and (by a large stock) in many cases to anticipate the wants of their clients.

The Taylor's Engine at the United Mines, Cornwall, was made by the Williams' Perran Foundry Co., and has performed the highest duty registered, having raised 107,000,000 lbs. of water, 1 foot high, per 1 bushel of coal.

Estimates for Engines with Pumps, &c., complete, to suit the various depths and quantities of water to be raised, &c., on application.

A Cornish Pumping Engine as produced by William's Perran Foundry of Perranarworthal, Cornwall.
[Camborne School of Mines]

to the pitwork pumps by means of stout wooden beams which can clearly be seen in one old photograph of the mine.

It was not found necessary to operate the pitwork pumps continuously, and the steam engines were then put to other uses. One for example was used to pump fresh water to the boilers of the other engines, whilst another powered a large lathe from which the pipes used to deliver the mine water, were machined from large logs. Such was the corrosive nature of the mine water that iron pipes would have corroded in a very short space of time, and there was then no practical alternative to the use of wood. The difficulty in effectively sealing the joint between one wooden pipe and another would most probably account for the constant showering Faraday had to suffer as he climbed the ladders up the pumping shaft.

Before the coming of steam engines, the mines were de-watered by horse driven whimseys and windmills[93] and what is thought to be the base of one such windmill still exists close to the Cerrig y Bleiddiau precipitation ponds.

Close to the Cairns pumping shaft there is a flat area quarried out of the hillside, regarding which there is an unusual tale.

It would appear that, by way of celebrating the Coronation of William IV on, 8 September 1831, John Sanderson had the company employees in mind when he wrote to James Treweek informing him that, "a plentiful but plain dinner is to be provided, with a moderate but sufficient allowance of ale to prevent all excess and to ensure an early and peaceable return to the mine and their own homes."

In his reply Treweek informed Sanderson that, "We have bought a very fine Ox and 6 sheep with Bread, Potatoes etc",[94] before advising him that he was catering for no fewer than 1,400 people. What must surely have been the barbeque to end all barbeques appears to have been such a resounding success that the miners thereafter referred to the place as the Oxen Quarry.

Chapter 6
The Francis Map

A second survey of the Bod Ednyfed estate, which was carried out by William Francis in 1828,[95] shows quite clearly the extent to which the port had developed by that time. As with Owen's survey of 1780, Francis included very little information regarding the western side of the harbour, but the care with which he recorded the eastern side is remarkable.

The surveyor was almost certainly the same William Francis who was a retired master mariner and principal of the best known of the local schools of navigation. The school was founded in Parys Lodge Square, where the Captain was assisted in his work by his son and daughter. His daughter Ann later moved to Caernarfon where she established her own highly successful school in which she taught for over 60 years. The full extent to which Captain Francis laid the foundations of Amlwch's acclaimed contribution to the numbers of professionally qualified mariners is difficult to gauge, but the breadth and quality of his teaching was legendary and the numbers of students applying for places far exceeded the small school's capacity. The fees charged for the various levels of instruction were such that the majority of his students would have had to save diligently in order to attend and to sustain them during their time at the school, when they were unable to earn. The very fact that so many young men were prepared to make this investment says a great deal about their personal dedication, and also about the rewards they saw awaiting those who succeeded.

It is unlikely that William Francis was ever trained to be a land surveyor and it was his undoubted familiarity with optical instruments and computation that qualified him for the task.

The map, of which several versions exist, was drawn to a scale of 1 inch to the chain (22 yards), a comparatively large scale which permitted the recording of much detail, thus making it an important research document. Captain Francis carried out his survey using techniques which at that time were in many respects, far more accurate than those being employed by the Government's Ordnance Board in carrying out its own national survey. In order to produce a 1 inch to the mile map of England and Wales, the Board first established a network of trigonometrically determined triangulation points using professional surveyors. These points, although not as accurate as had at first been believed, were then used as references by a number of local surveyors who were required to fill in the topographical details within the triangles. This they did more often than not, by pacing out distances and using nothing more sophisticated than magnetic compasses by way of instruments.[96] Not surprisingly, such basic methods led to quite serious errors.

By way of contrast, William Francis had set out his traverse lines optically, as the very faint lines still to be seen on some of his maps testify. These lines were subdivided into lengths of 1 inch, which corresponded to the use on the ground of a chain composed of 66 links, each of which was exactly 1 foot long. From various points along the chain he then measured and recorded the offset distances to the features he wished to plot.

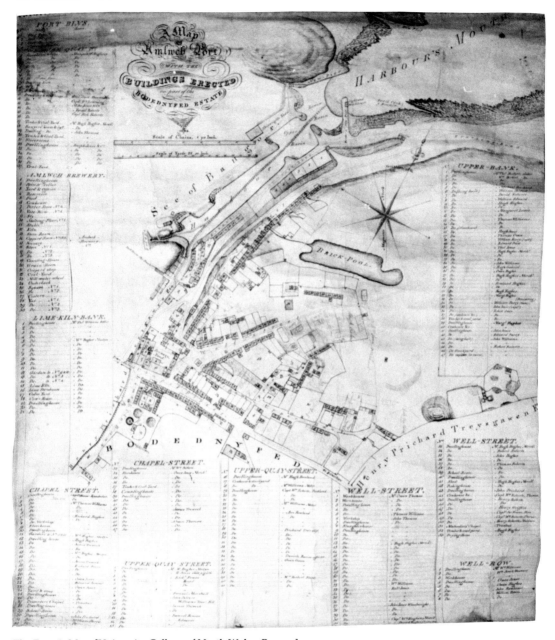

The Francis Map. [University College of North Wales, Bangor]

Whereas the method used by the Captain made it relatively easy to record features on either side of the line accurately, problems arose when it became necessary to change direction, for he did not appear to have an instrument sufficiently good to measure accurately the angle between two successive traverse lines. This resulted in features relating to the same straight line being in the correct spatial relationship to one another, but wrong when related to others measured along separate traverse lines. This was not caused by any carelessness on the surveyor's part, for he was quite clearly a most meticulous man, but rather from the use of an inaccurate instrument, which fact should not detract in any way from his remarkable achievement.

Before embarking on a description of William Francis' map it would be prudent to note those physical changes to the port which had occurred previously. The first reference to actual changes by way of new buildings at the port is in a document [97] recording the payment in 1770 by Nicholas Bayly, of £13 19s 7d to a workman and labourers for the "making of binns and storhouse [sic] at Port Amlwch." The cost was so small, even by 1770 standards, that it is unlikely that the buildings were new. The most likely interpretation therefore is that existing buildings were modified in some way to adapt them to a new role. Bayly's need for a warehouse and bins in which to store the ore before shipment resulted not only from his own operations at the Parys mine but also to store the duty ore he received as payment for Roe & Company's lease of the Mona Mine. As his duty ore amounted to one eighth of the total raised by Roe & Co, it is evident that they also would have needed facilities at the port, probably similar to, but of greater capacity than his.

At that time no fewer than 27 vessels, having an average capacity of 34 tons, were used to ship Bayly's raw copper to the smelters, one such being the 40 ton sloop *Sampson* which he partly owned. Roe & Company's ores on the other hand, were sent to their own smelter, which had been built in 1767 at Liverpool.

The precise location of the new storehouse and bins was not recorded, but according to the Francis map it can be seen that Bayly had leases on several buildings on the east side of the landward end of the harbour. These included a small storehouse next to what was then described as a coal-yard, and the possibility must exist that these were Bayly's original storehouse and bins, access to which was by way of Lower Quay Street. The bins would not have been intended exclusively for the handling of copper ore, for the Parys Mine records show that lead, tin and iron ores were also mined there at that time.

As Roe's mining operations were far more extensive than Bayly's, it follows that their needs at the port would have been greater, and it is almost certainly true to say that there would have been no location likely to satisfy their requirements at its landward end. It must be borne in mind that the eastern side of the harbour was then in its natural state, with the rock face rising steeply from the water's edge, and it is clear therefore that the only practical site for the warehouses would have been on the western side, the approach to which was comparatively easy.

Although little evidence exists to support the theory, it is believed that several buildings and walled compounds, now in ruins on the western side of the port, may well have been first built and used by Roe & Company. Sited alongside the area known as Turkey Shore, their size and location is such as to suggest that their later use by the port's early shipbuilding industry was not their original function.

The next recorded development relating to the port was the building by Bayly, of grain and flour warehouses on its eastern side. These are undoubtedly the six warehouses incorporated into a single building which Francis has shown as belonging to the Marquis of Anglesey. Unless the 160 foot-long quay alongside which the warehouses were built had previously existed to serve the original storehouse and bins it must be assumed that it also was constructed as part of the new development. What is evident however is that the old track which had served Lower Quay Street for well over half a century, was no longer adequate, and a new road had to be constructed down to the quayside. As it left the wharf, the road passed sharply around the northern end of the warehouses and then upwards behind them, from where there was access to some of their upper floors. The road along this section continues to be supported by a series of arches which were accessible from the warehouses, and which were used as storage vaults. Very little now remains of the old buildings apart from their foundations from which it is still possible to gain access to the vaults. The road as it now is connects with Upper Quay Street, but it is evident that when it was first built, it continued upwards behind the Royal Oak and then on to Well Street.

William Francis' map is more than just a record of the way in which Amlwch Port had developed by 1828, it is also an important social document inasmuch that the occupant of each of the properties is named. In those cases where the buildings were used for commercial purposes, the trade of the occupier is also recorded, eg William Jones, weaver; John Jones, wheelwright and Richard Jones, shoemaker. Not unexpectedly, several of the properties were occupied by sea captains, the names of whom appear alongside those of the vessels they commanded. As several of the captains bore the same name, a means had to be found to differentiate between them, and it became common practice in Amlwch to associate each with the vessel he commanded. In this way, one could distinguish between Captain William Roberts (*Portland*), and Captain William Roberts, Master of the *Thomas*; whose homes were in adjoining streets.

One of the little lanes recorded on the Francis map was Lime Kiln Bank (now known in Welsh as Ponc yr Odyn) where there was a combined lime kiln and culm yard, both of which were features of many Welsh ports. Such was the price of coal that few could afford it, and the staple fuel for the majority of households at that time was a mixture of anthracite dust (culm) and clay, pressed into the form of small bricks. Although the bricks did not burn as fiercely as coal, they were nevertheless an excellent substitute.

In order to illustrate the manner in which one industry begets another, one need look no further than the way lime making became associated with a great number of ports in the days of sail. Many of the early 19th century vessels were unstable and difficult to sail when light, and for that reason had to be ballasted. The usual ballasting material was stone, mainly because it was freely available; and many ports had what were known as ballast banks from which supplies of suitable stones could be picked up free of charge. These had been left on the bank by other vessels, which having themselves arrived in ballast would have deposited them there before taking on a paying cargo. Although the stones were free, the fact that they had to be loaded and unloaded meant that time which could have been more profitably used, was lost. For this reason, Masters whose own pay depended on the profitability of their vessels, avoided sailing in ballast whenever possible. This was not the case however when limestone could be used, for there was always a ready market awaiting it at most ports, where it could be calcined to make lime which had many uses, the best known being as a soil conditioner or as a mortar used in building. The former was probably the most important use it was put to, outside the iron and chemical industries.

Lime manufacture is essentially a simple procedure which involves little more than roasting fist sized fragments of limestone in a kiln. An early method of calcining limestone was in large clamps where it was intermixed with fuels such as peat, wood or coal. Care had to be taken in the use of the latter, particularly if it contained a high percentage of sulphur, for the process produced calcium sulphate which disintegrated in air, thereby denying its use as a mortar. When the clamp was complete, and before the fuel was lit, the whole structure was sealed with a thick layer of clay to prevent it losing too much heat. The mixture of stone and fuel was then allowed to burn for a period which, depending on its size, could take anything up to ten days to complete. At the end of the process the kiln was taken apart and the resulting lime taken to a shallow pit where water was thrown over it in a process known as slaking.

By the middle of the 18th century however the clamp kilns were superseded by what became known as draw kilns, which had the added advantage of providing a continuous, large scale process. In Anglesey however, it was usual to calcine limestone in open topped, cup shaped, brick lined kilns measuring about 12 feet in diameter at the top, and about 3 feet at the base. The whole kiln was then contained within a thick walled structure, usually built of stone, which had the added effect of providing insulation. At the base of the kiln there was at least one draw hole through which the calcined stone could be removed, and a later lime kiln built at Amlwch port has three. The kiln head, as the flat floor at the level of the top of the kiln is called, was the place where the large limestone rocks were reduced to the fist sized pieces best suited to the process. It was also the place from which the kiln was loaded with alternate layers of stone and anthracite dust. As the calcined limestone was drawn out of the bottom, additional layers were added at the top to continue the process. In order to facilitate loading it was usual to build lime kilns against steeply rising ground, but the one shown on the Francis map shows a ramp built up to the head from the culm and limestone storage yards below.

According to *Pigot's National and Commercial Directory* there were as many as 21 taverns in Amlwch in 1828, which is not surprising bearing in mind the number of men employed in the mines and the smelters, and the numerous sailors frequenting the port. In most cases the taverns were little more than private dwelling houses adapted to their new, public use, where the quality of the beer often left much to be desired. If local legend is to be believed, some of it was so cloudy that it was the custom to throw the undrinkable dregs which settled at the bottom of the jar, on to tavern floor. From there it flowed out into the gutter where domestic animals, as well as the occasional pig (there are several recorded instances of stray pigs wandering the streets of the town), drank their fill. As a result, many of the creatures spent a good part of their lives in a state of blithe intoxication!

With so many taverns in the town it is not surprising to find that William Francis has recorded the existence of two breweries close to the harbour, the first being a small one in Lower Quay street which was owned by the Marquis of Anglesey and a second, much larger concern was built on the corner of Chapel and Well streets. The site of the larger brewery, previously recorded on Owen's map of 1780, was almost square, with each side measuring about 50 yards.

It is a recognised fact that many well known breweries were first established because of the quality of the local water, and such may have been the case at Amlwch. There the water was drawn from St Elaeth's well, which according to tradition, had curative properties. In his history of Amlwch, Hugh Hughes [98] relates how the well had been a

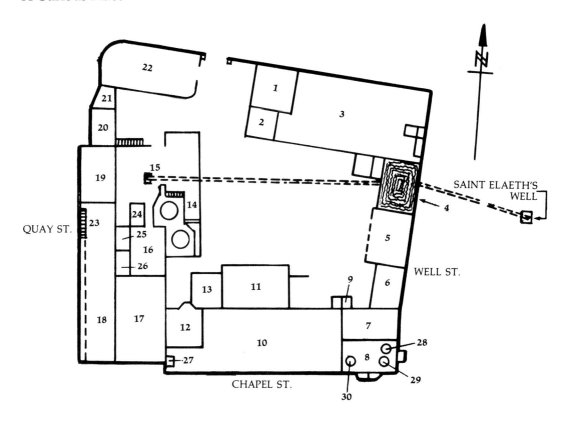

PLAN OF THE AMLWCH BREWERY 1826

Amlwch Brewery, 1826.

1. Dwelling House
2. Spirit Cellar.
3. House Yard & Office.
4. Reservoir.
5. Shed.
6. Cowhouse.
7. Porter Store, No 4.
8. Vats Room.
9. Sty.
10. Malting Floor, No 1.
11. Stable.
12. Kiln.
13. Store Room.
14. Room for Copper No1 & No 2.
15. Brewery.

16. Store, No 1.
17. Store, No 2.
18. Store, No 3.
19. Grain Room.
20. Counting House.
21. Cooper's Shop.
22. Coal Yard.
23. Mill Water Wheel.
24. Underback (Mash Vessel).
25. Square No 1 (Fermentation Vat).
26. Square No 2 (Fermantation Vat).
27. Cistern.
28. Vat No 1.
29. Vat No 2.
30. Vat No 3.

most important spa in ancient times, and one to which people from many countries came to have their health restored by drinking from it. Those who made such a pilgrimage often had a second reason for their visit however, and that was to consult the oracle of the well, which took the form of an eel that had made its home there. The eel supposedly communicated by simply changing its shape, the significance of each change having to be interpreted by an intermediary. It would appear that there were many who professed to have the power of interpretation, for Hughes' final sardonic remark on the subject, claimed that the ancestors of many of his contemporaries had acquired great wealth as a result of their supposed gifts.

The quality of William Francis' work suggests that the man was a perfectionist who was not content with mapping the outline of the many outbuildings comprising the brewery, but also recorded the purpose and shape of each of its rooms. This allows an invaluable insight into the workings of what was undoubtedly the largest brewery ever built in Anglesey.

It is interesting to speculate as to why a brewery should have been built on the site in the first place. It is difficult to believe that it was founded for no better reason than to exploit the reputed magical and curative properties of the water drawn from St Elaeth's well, but if that was indeed the case it would indicate that the commercial opportunism we have come to expect today, came early to the island. It could possibly have been a contributing factor, but it is more reasonable to assume that, as with the majority of manufacturing industries, the factors governing their location are: a ready market for the product which is within easy reach of the works, the availability in the immediate locality of essential raw materials and a constant source of cheap power and labour.

In order to better understand the layout of the Amlwch brewery as it was in William Francis' time, it is important to have a grasp of the principles involved in the brewing process, which have changed comparatively little over the years.

Pliny, the Roman historian was but one who recorded the existence of a fermented drink made from corn and water, but the process is believed to have been known for at least 5,000 years. Over the ages and throughout the world, ingredients which have included straw, rice and potatoes have all been used with varying degrees of success to produce beer of one kind or another. It is interesting to note that the Welsh were clearly no strangers to the delights of beer drinking for the Domesday Book records the fact that it was brewed in Brecon as early as 1086.

In order to produce alcohol it is necessary to have as a basic ingredient, a form of carbohydrate which allows it to be fermented. Traditionally the main ingredient of British beers has been barley, an indigenous cereal which is relatively easy to grow, and one which has been grown in Anglesey for many centuries. The mature grain however is not in a form which lends itself to the brewing process, and it is first necessary to induce a change in its chemical structure in order to facilitate this. The process known as malting requires the grain to be steeped in water, under closely controlled conditions of temperature and humidity, until it germinates. The process takes place on what is known as the malting floor, and the area of the one recorded as room 10 on Francis' map,is approximately 2,400 square feet, which gives a good indication of the enormous quantity of grain which could be malted at any one time. The malting process has traditionally been controlled by the Maltster, who determines the duration of the process, which could take anything between 5 and 11 days to complete. At the end of the period each grain produces a short root and stem, but more importantly, the large complex molecules of which it was composed would

Chapel Street, Amlwch, c1900. The large building on the left was the Amlwch Brewery. The building on the right is the Liverpool Arms.

have been broken down sufficiently to be soluble in water. Taking the malting process beyond its natural limit is counter productive and as a means of arresting it, the grain is then roasted in a kiln [12]. It is at this stage that the potential alcohol content of the beer, its colour and flavour are largely determined. Following the roasting process the grain is then stored to await milling [17 and 18].

Power for the milling process at Amlwch was provided by a water wheel driven by a stream which was one of two which discharged into the harbour, to power which it will be recalled, water was diverted from Afon Amlwch. The culverted leat which delivered the water to the wheel, and then on to its outfall, was unearthed recently when the old brewery site was converted into a children's playground. Among the items unearthed were numerous glass and earthenware bottles bearing the name of the Amlwch Brewery Company. It is probably true to say that the same water wheel provided the motive power for other tasks such as hoisting and driving machinery within the brewery.

When the malt had been milled, the Brewer then mixed it with water in the brewery room [15] to form the mash, which contained all the ingredients necessary to sustain the later fermentation process. The annual output from the brewery is unknown, but its size suggests that it must have been quite considerable. This would have meant that the quantity of clean water necessary to maintain production would have been appreciable. The demand for water was not constant, and was greatest at the start of each brewing sequence. In order to overcome the problem of having to provide such quantities from what was after all little more than a public well, it was found necessary to build a reservoir [4] within the grounds of the brewery. Into this, water from the well was piped slowly but continuously, building up sufficient volume to satisfy each demand for water as it came. From the reservoir the water was piped across the yard to the brewery room where it was used in the mashing stage which took place in a receptacle known as an underback [24].

When the nutriment had been fully extracted from the crushed grain in the underback, it had a residual value as animal feed, and it was for this purpose no doubt, that the brewery had a cowhouse [6].

The wort, as the unfermented liquor was known, was then transferred to the coppers [14] which were, as the name implies, large pans made of rivetted copper sheets. It was at this stage that hops were added to the wort, in order to impart the familiar and characteristic beer flavour to the liquor. Although it is known that hops were used to flavour beers over a thousand years ago, it was not until the 15th century that they came to be used by British brewers. Before that time, British ale was both thick and sweet.

At least four breweries are known to have existed in Amlwch over the years, and the author can recall picking hops from a hedgerow which once formed the boundary of a small brewery at the back of Parys Lodge Square. This could well mean that hops were once grown commercially in the town, but the possibility that it was a self seeded plant must be recognised.

At the time when William Francis surveyed Amlwch Port, many wells in the district were polluted to one degree or another, and it is probably true to say that it was then much safer to drink beer than it was to drink water. This was due to the wort boiling stage of the brewing process which effectively sterilized the liquor, a factor that had not been realised before Pasteur's researches in the mid 19th century.

It is evident that beyond satisfying their customers' thirsts, brewers at the beginning of the 19th century had little thought for their well being and several ingredients were used to flavour the beer, or to enhance its effects, which would be totally unacceptable today. Among these additives were treacle, liquorice, capsicum, cocculus indicus, a mixture of alum and copperas, ginger, slaked lime and linseed. These were intended to promote laxation, wind dispersal caused by indigestion, the inducement of gentle perspiration and stupefaction.[99] Alum and copperas, it should be noted were both by-products of the precipitation process carried out at Mynydd Parys, and slaked lime was a product of the nearby limekiln but there is no evidence to suggest that any of these were ever used at the Amlwch Brewery.

One local product may have been used however, and that was carrageenan (sodium alginate), which was manufactured from seaweed of the same name, the purpose of which was to clarify the beer by precipitating out the proteins present in the wort.

Having separated the cooled wort from the spent hops, which were no doubt sold to local farmers as fertilizer, the liquor was pumped into what would then have been an open fermentation vat [8]. There, added yeast would begin the fermentation process in order to convert the sugar present in the liquor into alcohol.

It was not until Pasteur's researches into bacteriology that much of the technology of the brewing process was fully understood. Although brewers had over the years become increasingly more knowledgeable about those facets of their art which did work, they were correspondingly ignorant of those factors which did not, and which were responsible for the spoiling of very many gallons of otherwise good liquor. In other words, beer making was then very much a hit and miss affair, far removed from the high technology industry it has become today.

It is interesting to note that at some stage, the company diversified its activities, for an earthenware bottle, now in the author's possession, bearing the Amlwch Brewery name, has the inscription 'Ye Olde Brewed English Ginger Beer'.

Another prominent feature of William Francis' map is a very extensive pool referred to as a brickpool, which was located above and behind Upper Quay Street. It is evident that the pool had been formed when the excavation left behind by the removal of brickmaking clay, filled with water. The size of the pool (350 feet x 75 feet approximately) suggests that the industry there was extensive and, if it is assumed that the clay bed was no more than 6 feet thick, it will be seen that no less than 5,830 cubic yards of material were excavated from it. Brick sizes varied enormously across the country during the early 19th century, but if calculations were to be based on the current standard brick size, it can be shown that no fewer than 250,000 bricks were produced at the site. The bricks may have been of firebrick quality, suitable for use in the smelters, but this is thought unlikely for all of those so far found in the locality of the smelter bear the stamp of the Buckley Brickworks on Deeside. One use to which the bricks could possibly have been put to however, was the lining of the beds and sides of early precipitation ponds at Parys Mountain, the remains of which still exist.

What is curious about the brick field is the absence of kilns in which the bricks were roasted, and, as it is most unlikely that they would have been taken elsewhere to be processed because of the nature of the material, one can only conclude that the industry at this particular site had in fact ended well before 1828, when the clay deposit became exhausted.

An unusual feature recorded on one version of the Francis map is the existence on the eastern side of the harbour of a 'tracking road for horses drawing ships out'. The author is unaware of any other recorded instance of seagoing vessels being towed out of harbours by horses, and it may well be that Amlwch was unique in that respect. From the northern end of the harbour the track continued upwards, past and above an inlet referred to as Porth Cwch y Brenin (the creek of the King's Boat), an inlet that was, as the name implies, probably used regularly by a revenue cutter, commissioned to combat the high incidence of smuggling carried out along the coast of Anglesey in the 18th century. Why the vessel was moored outside the harbour can probably be explained by the fact that this location would have provided, at most states of the tide, the best protection for a single, relatively small vessel from the effects of what were only too often, devastating northerly winds.

The map shows that, in 1828, the harbour was very much as it is today, with two exceptions. The first is the existence of a small pier jutting out a short distance into the harbour, close to bin number 3. This has at some time since, been removed to clear the bottle neck it created, and at the same time, to increase the effective length of quay. Its removal prompts the question as to why it should have been built there in the first place, and the most likely reason being that this point represented the outer limit of the port at some stage in its evolution. As it is known that the Parys and Mona mines built a small pier for their convenience in 1782, it is reasonable to assume that this was it.

The second major difference between the map and the port as it is today is found in that section of the harbour lying on the eastern side between the Baulks Pier and the Eastern New Pier, or Watch House Pier as it later became known. The basin there has at some time since 1828 been filled in for reasons that have yet to be discovered.

Chapter 7
Vitriol & Precipitation Works

A most unusual stream, from which no animal would drink and in which no creature could live, flowed from the base of Parys Mountain. This absence of life may have attracted Bronze Age miners to the area but, certainly, the dark green stream caught the attention of the Elizabethans, for in 1579, the Society for the Mineral and Battery Works commissioned a man called Medley to determine its value by experimentation. This he did, by adding a quantity of iron to the water, which he then boiled over a turf fire. When it cooled, the solution separated out into three distinct layers. The top layer, which was green, was referred to as copperas, which, despite its name, was a hydrated sulphate of iron. The middle, white layer, was alum, and the lowest layer, referred to as Earth of Iron, was described by Medley as looking very much like cankered iron, albeit yellow in colour.

Medley then went on to smelt the Earth of Iron in a brick furnace heated by charcoal, and the resultant slag was found to contain no less than 10% pure copper. Despite this, the Society was of the opinion that a commercial undertaking operating along similar lines would not be profitable, and the matter progressed no further.

In 1760, a Doctor Rutty presented to the Royal Society a paper on the medicinal properties of the water. Although he was uncertain of its chemical composition, Rutty was nevertheless able to claim quite categorically that the waters were a cure for galloping consumption, as well as being

> . . . a powerful detergent, repelling, bracing, styptic, cicatrizing, anti scorbutic, and deobstruent medicine, as hath appeared by the notable cures they have effected, not only by external use in inveterate ulcers, the itch, mange scab, tetterous eruptions, dysentries, internal haemorrhages, in gleets, the fluor albus, and diorhea [sic], in the worms, agues, dropsies and jaundice.[101]

For some reason, this panacea for all ills was never exploited, nevertheless an attempt was later made to establish a chemical industry at Amlwch, based on Medley's experiments.

Doctor Joshua Parr, a manufacturing chemist from Carmarthenshire, together with his partners, set up a chemical by-product plant close to Trysglwyn Isaf. This was established in 1803 under the name of the Mona Vitriol Company, and was licensed by the mine owners. Parr's first attempts were directed at producing copperas, which was extensively used in the manufacture of inks and pigments, but his inability to free the compound from the iron oxide it contained, meant that it was of little interest to dyers, who were potentially his best customers.

A very important use to which it could be put was in the manufacture of sulphuric acid, which has arguably been the single most important industrial chemical ever produced. Parr's efforts again came to naught, for a cheaper and more direct method of producing the acid was discovered, using sulphur in place of copperas. This discovery benefitted the mining companies, for the sulphur being recovered locally was sold almost exclusively for that purpose. Because of keen foreign competition, Thomas Williams discovered that he was unable to sell all the sulphur he was producing, and he ventured into the business by building his own sulphuric acid works at Garston, Liverpool. The fact that it was far easier to transport the sulphur from Anglesey to a site close to the market, than it was to transport the sulphuric acid itself, was undoubtedly his reason for choosing not to manufacture it at Amlwch.

Undeterred, Parr and his partners then directed their attention to the extraction of pure copper sulphate, or blue vitriol as it was known, from the mine water but this venture also failed and finally they turned their efforts to the manufacture of alum which, like copperas, was extensively used in the production of dyes and pigments as well as in tanneries, where it was used to dress leather. There were two methods by which alum was then produced, both of which utilized a fine clay-like material known as argillaceous earth, which was found in abundant quantities at Parys Mountain. In the beginning, the process relied on the chemical combination of the earth and sulphuric acid and the difference between the two methods lay in the manner in which the two components of the reaction were brought together.

In the first method, the earth was simply mixed with the acidic water which flowed from the mountain, whereas in the second, the earth was laid over the copper ore as it was calcined in the roasting kilns, where it absorbed the sulphuric acid fumes being generated by the process.

When the chemical reaction was complete, the treated earth was taken to shallow, water filled pits, where it was well stirred. The resulting alum solution was then filtered and concentrated by heating it gently in lead pans, after which it was allowed to cool and crystallise naturally as it dried.

By this process, as much as 1 ton of alum could be produced at the plant each week, and when the local supply of argillaceous earth was exhausted, Parr had it imported from Holyhead and from Dorset. Records show that much of the alum produced at Amlwch was exported to America through the port of Caernarfon.

Doctor Joshua Parr's unnamed partners would appear to have been the Webster brothers, James, George and William who themselves were later to trade as the Mona Vitriol Company at Trysglwyn Isaf. The fact that James, who later became High Sheriff of Anglesey, named his second son, Joshua Parr Webster, indicates that there was a very close affinity between the two families.

Aikin's account of 1797, refers briefly to the fact that "green vitriol and alum, are also made in small quantities by a separate company, but to these works strangers are not admitted."[102] This must have been a reference to the Mona Vitriol Company's operations at Trysglwyn Isaf and it is interesting to note that industrial espionage was, even then, considered to be a serious matter.

Although not specifically mentioned by Aikin, it is evident from an advertisement placed in the *Chester Chronicle* in March, 1799, that the Parys Mining Company had also, until a short time before, been producing vitriol in its Cae'r Pandy Works. The advertisement offered a lease of 21 years on the 37 acre site, on which there were dwelling houses, warehouses, kilns, etc which had previously been used by the owners for the purpose of carrying on vitriol, sulphur and other works.

The alchemists of old had dreamt of being able to transmute a base metal such as lead into gold or silver, and the basis of their belief may have been the fact that a comparatively simple exchange reaction could seemingly change iron into copper. All that was needed to be done to accomplish this was to immerse iron in a blue vitriol (copper sulphate) solution. This resulted in the iron being very rapidly coated with metallic copper. In simplified chemical terms, the iron and copper sulphate solution combined to form copper and iron sulphate solution.

In draining through the ore beds in the mine, rain water, which is naturally slightly acidic, combined with oxygen absorbed from the air to produce an acidic solution of copper sulphate. As this coursed its way through the lower beds of ore, it added further to its copper content, becoming at the same time more acidic. It was this solution that eventually found its way out of the mountain side to attract the attention of the early miners and scientists.

The commercial extraction of copper directly from the mine water was therefore a relatively simple operation to carry out, and was a method that had previously been exploited in the Wicklow mines in Ireland and at Hern Grundt in Hungary.

The great quantities of low grade ore rejected by the 'Copper Ladies', which had been cast on the hill side in vast heaps, were not entirely wasted, for rainwater leached out a certain proportion of the copper compounds they contained. This natural process was accelerated by sparging the water pumped up from the mine over the heaps, which succeeded in enriching the water still further.

A walker on the gentle northern slope of the Parys hill side might be puzzled by a series of what could be described as long ditches, which are bounded on their lower sides by rounded earth banks. The ditches appear to follow the contours of the hill, and are breached only where they are crossed by watercourses flowing down from the spoil heaps above. Their purpose has never been recorded, but it is thought likely that they were built to intercept the mine water, in order that it might be directed into ponds where copper could be recovered from it.

In the mine's early years the copper rich solution was directed into a series of small open ponds built on the hill side itself, where some can still be seen hidden amongst the spoil heaps. Early maps of the workings show that many of the early ponds have since been buried under tons of mine waste. The ponds, each measuring approximately 20 feet x 12 feet, are some 18 inches deep, the floors and sides of which are brick lined. The ponds are connected to each other in cascade fashion, and the passage of water from one to the other was controlled by wooden sluices.

All manner of scrap iron was then thrown into the ponds which were filled to near capacity with the mineral rich waters. By way of assisting the chemical reaction, the contents of the pools were regularly agitated by men using long wooden poles: such work being normally reserved for men who had either been incapacitated or were considered too old to continue working underground.[103] Within a comparatively short time, extending from a few weeks to a few months, depending partly on the acidity and concentration of the salts, and partly on weather conditions, the iron was fully consumed, precipitating a brown sludge on the floor of the pond. When the water was exhausted of its copper content, it was ducted away, leaving the precipitate to drain, before it was sent to the drying kiln, and thence to the smelter.

As the value of the process became more widely appreciated, and as the volume of water raised from the mine increased in line with the underground mining activity, the small ponds dotted around the mountainside became wholly inadequate. Extensive ponds

Precipitation ponds, Parys Mountain. Photograph taken in 1981. [Don Williams]

totalling several acres in area were then constructed wherever there was relatively flat land in the vicinity of the mountain.

The copper content of the mine water depended much on what part of the mine it was pumped from and the most highly concentrated was brought up from the western end of the mountain, under the Great Opencast. This was pumped by one of the mine's steam engines to a level somewhat higher than that of the floor of the opencast. From there it was ducted along wooden launders to small holding ponds, the remains of which are still evident.[104] This was necessary in order to allow the water from the ponds to be ducted under gravity, through the mountainside, to precipitation ponds constructed along the southern boundary of the mine, alongside the road which leads to Trysglwyn Isaf, where the Webster brothers had their Vitriol Works. Early maps show that precipitation ponds once existed on both sides of the road, but those on the northern side have since been buried under thousands of tons of spoil which were tipped over them from the workings above. The level of the ponds was such that water was able to flow from the highest, at the western end, to the vast ochre ponds at the eastern end. As ochre ponds were interspersed with copper precipitation ponds, it must follow that the respective drainage systems were quite independant of each other. From the last of the ochre ponds the water was channelled to the southern Afon Goch, which had its outfall at Dulas.

Another system of copper ponds was built in the hollow of the Mona opencast, which, unlike the totally enclosed Great Opencast, can almost be described as open on its eastern end. From there the spent copper solution was directed to ochre ponds built to the north of the mountain, close to Llaethdy Bach.

As the mine workings became deeper, it was decided to direct the mine water from both the Parys and Mona mines to a joint level, from which it could be channelled away. To do this, a tunnel was driven from the level in a northerly direction towards Llaethdy Bach, along which the minewater could flow under gravity. Although this option must have been extremely costly, it had the advantage of doing away with the great expense of pumping. The outfall led to Dyffryn Adda, where there was already a mill pond serving Melin Adda, a water driven flour mill. It will be recalled that it was the fresh water from this pond that served the Amlwch fulling mill, before finally discharging into the harbour at Amlwch Port.

Copper ponds were, as might be expected, constructed close to the outfall from the joint level, the spent water from which was ducted to ochre ponds and thence to the stream feeding the mill pond. The fact that the stream was polluted by the effluent made little or no difference to the flour mill, but as a fulling mill needed clean water for cloth washing purposes, it must follow that the fulling mill had ceased to function before the opening of the joint level.

A mill later known as Rholdy, was the lower and smaller, of the two water mills known as Melinau Adda. Tradition has it that it was once a fulling mill, but a map dated 1868, shows quite clearly that the mill pool had by then become an ochre pond. When asked about the origin of the name Rholdy, the late Professor Bedwyr Lewis Jones suggested that it might be taken to mean 'roll house'. This could well imply that it was latterly a clay or ochre mill, which used edge rolls to grind ochre for paint making purposes.

So great did the scale of the precipitation industry become, that no less than £9,000 worth of scrap iron was purchased in one 3 year period, and between 1857 and 1924 no less than 19,000 tons of precipitate, yielding about 2,000 tons of fine copper, were produced at Amlwch.[105] Pennant's description of the process relates how the kind of iron used

> . . . was of no moment; old pots, hoops, anchors or any refuse will suffice; but of late, for the convenience of management, the adventurers procure new plates, four feet long, one and a half broad, and three quarters of an inch thick.

It is possible however, that having seen new cast iron plates destined for the floors of the ore burning kilns, Pennant wrongly assumed that they were intended for the precipitation ponds. His observation is unlikely to have been correct for several reasons, the main one being that the process would have gained nothing by the use of purpose made plates, in preference to scrap iron. Secondly, the cost of such plates would have been far greater than the cost of an equal weight of scrap iron, which was readily available. To this can be added the fact that each plate would have weighed approximately 175 lbs, which would have made them very difficult to handle. Indeed there can be little doubt that had the owners been interested in using such plates, they would have purchased thinner ones which, for a given weight, would have cost a little more, but would have had the added advantage of possessing a greater surface area. As the area of iron in direct contact with the mine water was a major factor in determining the time it took to complete the chemical reaction, it would have made economic sense to maximise the area, thereby minimising the time it took to complete the process. This argument is supported to a great degree by Faraday, who remarked on the indifferent quality of the iron used, because that obtained from the ironworks was generally a mixture of iron and slag, in roughly equal measure.

As the chemical reaction took place, the copper content of the mine water diminished, and it was then drained into a second pond, whilst the first was replenished. This process was again repeated, and the water from the second pond fed into a third, and so on to as many as five ponds in succession. The precipitate from the first pond contained the highest percentage of copper, and the fifth the least. Beyond the fifth however, the cost of the iron exceeded the value of the recovered copper, which made further extraction uneconomical.

The precipitate from the first pond normally contained up to 90% copper, the remaining 10% being made up of iron oxide, which had been formed by the oxidation of the iron sulphate solution and other impurities resulting from the dirty condition of the scrap iron.

When the thickness of the precipitate bed was considered to be sufficient, the remaining water was drawn off, and the copper bearing precipitate taken to drying floors where it was left to dry naturally. If it was found necessary however, provision was made to dry the precipitate in coal fired kilns.

The effectiveness of the process can be gauged by Bingley's claim, that for every ton of iron deposited in the ponds, 1,600 lbs of pure copper was recovered from the precipitates at the smelter.

By the end of the fifth precipitation, the original copper sulphate solution had to all practical purposes, become exhausted of its copper content. At the same time, it had been converted into a strong solution of iron sulphate, which because of oxidisation, had by then taken on a yellowish colour. Because of this, the water still had an economic life, for it had one more contribution to make to the sum total of the wealth extracted from the mountain.

Before the iron sulphate solution from the fifth and last of the ponds was released, it was thoroughly agitated, and then ducted into large shallow ponds, where it was allowed to stand. There it became further oxidised by absorbing oxygen from the air and, in time, this settled out as a fine yellow precipitate. This contained no copper, but because of its colour, was marketed as a base material used in the manufacture of paint. Described in one contemporary journal as being of a

. . . strong, brilliant yellow, soft, and so free from impurities , that it requires no treatment before being applied to the purpose, for which it is almost solely used.The golden hue presented by the paper hangings of the best makers of England, and consequently of the world, is obtained through this brightest of yellows.[106]

When it was perceived that the colour of the precipitate was becoming darker as the iron sulphate solution became more oxidised, it was redirected into another pond, where it deposited a precipitate somewhat deeper in colour than the first. As a means of producing ochre of varying colours, the process was repeated several times; each stage resulting in a successively darker precipitate.

After settlement, the ochre was allowed to drain before being taken to covered drying floors where it was allowed to dry out naturally. Coal-fired kilns then completed the drying process and it is thought likely that these were the same as those used to dry the copper precipitate. The damaged remains of the last kiln can still be seen in a building alongside the drying floor at Dyffryn Adda.

The ochre was not always uniform in colour, and it sometimes contained

. . . a large quantity of impurities, but these defects being removed by levigation under a pair of edge running stones in a neighbouring windmill constructed specially for the purpose, the article sells readily for uses to which the precipitated ochres are not applicable. The colour is far less brilliant than that of the former kind described, but there are some branches of painting, both in house decoration and the higher branches of art, to which it affords aid of a valuable nature. Manufacturers of the more refined classes of colour, work it up to a marvellous condition of softness and purity.[107]

The mill referred to, was that at the St Eilian Colour Works, where a few ruined outbuildings and two edge running stones are all that have survived the destruction of the mill itself. One of the three original granite stones, now in the author's possession, is about 2 feet in diameter and 1 foot wide; through the middle of which there is an octagonal hole measuring about 8 inches across flats, through which its axle passed. The fact that the stone has worn very unevenly suggests that it had a floating axle which allowed it to rise and fall as it was being driven. It was usual for two such stones to be located diametrically opposite each other, both of which were driven in a circular path inside a pan containing the raw ochre. The two stones were so positioned along their respective axles that the circular path travelled by one was inside that of its companion. Their combined weight of over 1,000 lbs meant that little time was wasted in reducing the ochre to a fine powder, suitable for mixing into paint. One of the better known products of the St Eilian Colour Works was a speciality known as Venetian Red. This was not a naturally occurring colour, for it could only be produced by roasting the ochre at a temperature higher than that needed for drying.

Part of the iron oxide produced in the ponds was sent to gas works, where it was used as a gas purifier. This was discontinued for a while, when a prodigious amount of naturally occurring iron oxide of good quality was discovered at the mine.

At the end of its life, the spent mine water was released into two streams, one being the Afon Amlwch to the north, and the other to the original Afon Goch which flowed from the south side of the mountain to the sea at Dulas. Because the streams' colour was similar to that of beer, one wag claimed that if their taste was as good as their colour, he would stop both in their tracks, for a short while at least.

Chapter 8
Later Smelting

Britain's expanding world trade meant that an increasing number of vessels were crossing the warmer oceans, where the timbers of many became infested by the notorious teredo worm. Teredo Navalis is no ordinary worm, it can grow to a length of 3 feet, and at that length, its body is about 1 inch in diameter. The havoc even one of these creatures could create by boring its way through a vessel's wooden planking, using a peculiar drill-like arrangement at its head, can readily be imagined. In this way, countless wooden vessels were rapidly and totally destroyed by the worm, and in such cases there was no recourse to insurance as policies specifically excluded loss by this means.[108] By way of preventing infestation, it became the practice by the 1760s, to sheath the hulls of admiralty vessels with thin copper sheets and by 1783, the technique had been extended to merchant vessels sailing out of home waters. By that time also, the practice had been extended to most of the continental navies and Thomas Williams was instrumental in supplying the various governments with the necessary copper plates.

In July 1822, Sanderson was prompted to inform Treweek that he had received hints from various quarters, that the Anglesey copper was not so well thought of for sheathing purposes as that which was made from Cornish ores. Its objectionable quality, as he put it, was supposedly due to the quality of the iron used in the precipitation process. He was loathe to blame William Morgan for this however, and went on to suggest that as bushel iron was undoubtedly better than scull iron for precipitation purposes, it might, notwithstanding the price, be better to confine their purchases to the former.

In his reply, Treweek ventured to disagree with Sanderson by stating that it was foolish to fancy that the iron could have had a good or bad effect on the copper, but he nevertheless went on to state that both he and Morgan were of the opinion that scull iron was the best in quality, and would be by far the cheapest if it could be obtained in a clean state. At that time iron for the precipitation ponds was being imported in large quantities from both London and Dublin, and according to Treweek three kinds were normally used, in the following ratios– cast iron $1/7$, scull iron $1/7$ and bushell iron $5/7$ of the total.

The hints referred to by Sanderson were later substantiated when a surveyor called in to investigate the decay in the hull timbers of the brig *Deveron*, reported that the problem resulted either from some imperfection in the manufacture of the sheathing, or in the basic raw material from which it was made. Further investigation revealed that the sheets had been manufactured by Newton, Lyons & Co, from copper supplied by the Amlwch smelter. The probability that the copper had been smelted from precipitated ore containing an unacceptable level of iron compounds, was put forward as an explanation for what would appear to have been an unusual deviation from the norm.

Despite the aborted strike of 1819, manpower problems at the smelter did not disappear altogether, for they resurfaced some 6 years later when Treweek had to report that there was yet again, serious discontent amongst the smelters. This came about by the imposition of long working hours in what was undoubtedly, a harsh environment, for what were claimed to be poor wages. Another cause for discontent lay in the fact that although the practice of Sunday working had by then been discontinued at the Swansea smelters, it continued to be the custom at Amlwch and Treweek, a godly man, had the courage to suggest to his employers that it was time for a change at Amlwch too.[109]

The returns of the actual quantity of copper produced by the Mona smelter in the year ending in mid June 1825, revealed that the amount fell far short of what could have been expected, on the basis of the assays that had been carried out. Sanderson was greatly disturbed by the revelation, and he charged Treweek with the task of investigating the matter fully.

Having allowed Treweek two months in which to complete his enquiries, Sanderson wrote a letter, in which he expressed his own views on the matter. Its tone and content say much about the writer's character and thoroughness, but the document is perhaps more important for its illustration of the relationship between master and servant at that time:

> I have been waiting anxiously for your report on the subject of the investigation that has been going on for some time past relative to the Smelting house deficiency of metal in the year ending 30th of June last, and also as to the result of your further enquiry embracing the operations of the quarter ending on the 30th of September following.
>
> It is necessary that I should receive the information before other measures affecting the late management of the Smelting Department can be proposed and determined upon.
>
> We have too much reason to believe that the enormous evil which has occurred has arisen from remissness or want of power in the smelting Agent, or from wilful misconduct of the overseers and workmen of the department.
>
> It is not possible that we can impute to ignorance that which never occurred before in the like operations, with the like materials and means; and it is probably now manifest that it was not matters of mistake or accident, since you have already ascertained that besides the two distinct assays by Mr Webster on charging and discharging the calciners, and the established and accurate check upon the quantity of ores delivered at the Smelting Yard - I say you have already ascertained by means of a third assay, recently made by another hand, that the two former assays were correct. But in proof also of the quantity of ore smelted, there is the striking fact that the full amount of expence (sic) has been incurred that would have been calculated upon had the furnaces' produce answered that of the assay, with the surplus accruing upon all former occasions. You have likewise proved the accuracy of the accounts of shipments, and I suppose by this time, you know that the stocks, including furnace bottoms, both at the beginning and end of the year have been correctly taken.
>
> The question then resolves itself into this: that the Overseers, and Furnace Men are the principal instruments of this most shameful defalcation. We have learnt since the discovery was made, that these men had got above the control of Mr Morgan, who is, himself, distinctly blameable for not having directed the fact of his own want of authority in time to prevent the evil complained of.
>
> What I had meant to have undertaken myself, had your investigations been completed in time, to have admitted of my going to Amlwch this week. I must now leave in your hands with such hints as I conceive may be of use to you in your progress - I would recommend that every person connected with the work - Overseers and Furnace Men - should be separately interrogated upon the following, amongst other points that may occur to you.
>
> 1. Whether any, and what difference has taken place in the last year in the mode of charging the furnaces.
> 2. In respect of consumption of coal.
> 3. As to time allotted to fusion.
> 4. As to number of runnings.

5. Particularly as to strict observance of the proper hour for tapping.

6. In mixtures of ores etc.

Should anything come out of this course of enquiry to throw light upon the business, and to exculpate the men, the blame may yet fall upon other heads than theirs.

I have not touched upon embezzlement of metal in its rough or refined state, but I nevertheless think that possible in a very relaxed state of management, and to a great extent systematically pursued; it may be right therefore to take some steps on this suggestion.

In a former letter I intimated that a Reward for discovery, and on detection of a conspiracy or other process of knavery, might be worth a trial.

Whether the men meant merely spite towards Mr Morgan, or from whatever other cause the deficiency of metal has arisen, it has produced the effect of a robbery of their employers property to a great amount. It has done more than this, it has given a character of uncertainty and risk to the Concern which it never bore before. In the meantime every Agent in any way connected with it must feel himself more or less stigmatized by the transaction.

If the individuals who are more directly implicated cannot be found out, the business must at all events be removed and replaced by others, on whom no suspicion falls, and with respect to Mr Morgan, other reasons would induce me to propose some change, altho' it were proved that he neither foresaw the evil complained of, nor could prevent them if he did.

We all know that he wants proper influence amongst the workmen, and we know too that it is certain to expect his receiving a proper assistant. These are two strong reasons for engaging a separate Refiner to take charge at least of one of the Works. A third reason may be urged in favour of this measure, Mr Morgan is of an age at which it may be calculated that his ability to conduct the Works as they ought to be conducted, will fail; and we must also contemplate the embarrassed situation we should be in if we left ourselves, at this period, without a competent person to succeed him. For this reason I have lately made enquiry through Messrs Newton, Lyon & Co. about a Refiner, and the answer they give is so satisfactory that I am much inclined to recommend an engagement of the person who is alluded to by Mr Beavan - But I wish first to receive your opinion upon that particular point, and also as to the consequent arrangement to be made with Mr Morgan, as well as with respect to the precise footing of the new agent.

If we engage the latter as a Refiner and Superintendent of ore furnaces without general management, Mr Morgan might retain his present situation and emoluments, especially if he would give the Refiner the benefit of his experience; or otherwise we might feel ourselves obliged to detach Mona from Mr Morgan's superintendence altogether.'[110]

Although Treweek investigated the alleged embezzlement thoroughly, the matter remained unresolved, and it is evident that the whole affair had left the ageing William Morgan completely demoralized.

Matters improved considerably by 1825, so much so that Sanderson was pleased to note that the works were then able to smelt more economically than had been the case under the Vivians, during their time at Amlwch. In order to smelt even more effectively he proposed that both he and Treweek should go to Swansea on what was to be little more than a spying mission.[111] The arrangements were that the two were to travel separately to Swansea where they would meet, but that it would be "best not to appear together in matters relating to smelting operations", as Treweek's acquaintances there would probably be more communicative if he was alone with them! From Swansea, Sanderson proposed that they should then go on to Pembrey, or perhaps Llanelli, to discuss with a Mr Gaunt the feasibility of smelting low grade ores in that district. The reason he gave for suggesting the trip was to "get quit of such ores (below 1%) as we cannot smelt at Amlwch to profit, and thus provide a return freight for the vessels carrying coals from S Wales by which

Amlwch Port showing the inclined plane leading from the Smelter to the quayside. The New Haven public house is on the right.

means we may obtain our supplies at a reduced freight, and at the same time, enable the traders to make a more profitable voyage." [112] In reply Treweek, at his most methodical best, stated that he had already prepared a list of questions he proposed to ask. Nothing would seem to have come of the proposed visit to Pembrey, but it would appear that the visit to Swansea was not all it might have been, for matters at the smelter deteriorated yet again, and for which, William Morgan bore much of the blame. Sanderson's declared intention to replace him as the manager of the Mona smelter, did not come about until 1826, when Morgan had all but lost interest in his job and was delegating much of it to a subordinate.[113]

As the two smelters were operated jointly, it must be assumed that the Parys concern had agreed to Morgan's replacement, albeit reluctantly, for he had indeed served the Hughes family well over many years. Despite Sanderson's low opinion of his managerial capabilities, and possibly because of intercession on the part of the Hughes family, Morgan continued at the smelters in an advisory capacity. Ironically, the smelting methods used by William Rees, his successor, were singularly unsuccessful from the start. For this, he blamed the furnacemen, and he suggested that they should be replaced by others from South Wales, who were familiar with his methods. As time went on, it became increasingly evident that his methods were at fault, and as a result, the cost of smelting under his direction rose by 25%, over those in Morgan's time, a fact that no doubt gave the latter a great deal of quiet satisfaction. Understandably perhaps, the relationship between the two men never improved, a fact which earned them a rebuke from Sanderson, who urged them to work hand in hand for the benefit of both works.[114]

One matter on which they both agreed however, related to the smelting of copper bearing peat from the turbary belonging to James Webster of the Mona Vitriol Works. It would appear that the peat was far from suitable, and both men were of the opinion that "Mr Webster's peat smells very stiff - it will not do well with our ores, having tried three charges of it, which took more coal and longer time than our ores." [115]

It will be recalled how Faraday had described the movement of as many as 14 carts, to and from the mountain. These not only brought the ore down to the smelters, but on their return journeys, they took coal up to the steam engines, and iron for the precipitation ponds. Two roads had been built to accommodate this traffic, and both converged at the cross roads known as Grogan Goch and it was on the north eastern corner of these crossroads that the earliest weighbridge was located.

The cartage business had been a monopoly held by William Hughes of Madyn Dysw [116] since 1811. He was, by all accounts, a very efficient contractor, but Sanderson nevertheless believed that the transportation costs could be substantially reduced, if a railway was built to connect the mine directly to the smelter and the port.

Despite objections by Treweek (who was by then related by marriage to the Hughes family), Sanderson commissioned Charles Vignoles, a noted civil engineer, to report on the feasibility of such a scheme. Vignoles spent a week at Amlwch carrying out a detailed survey and in March, 1828 he reported that he was,

> of the opinion that the formation of an edge railroad on the most approved modern principle laid down on Self Acting Inclined Planes and intermediate levels; and the transport of copper ore, coal etc, thereon, in proper waggons, would be followed by a most important diminution of expence, compared with the present mode of transporting those materials. So considerable would be the gain that the necessary cost of forming the railway etc, might be repaid in less than three

years, by appropriating only the difference between the expence of the present and the proposed method of carriage.

From his detailed report it is possible to determine the line Vignoles' railway was to take, and it is clear that it was his intention to construct it in as straight a line as possible from the foot of the mountain to the smelter. Two inclined planes were to be incorporated into the line, which would have allowed the heavier ore waggons going down to the smelter to draw the lighter ones on their way up, without the additional expense of a steam engine.

The railway was never completed, but hitherto it had been thought that it had not even been started; and that a reference by Treweek to the start of a railway, referred to the incline that worked between the port and the smelter. This was probably not the case however, for the 1886 edition of the Ordnance Survey map shows a narrow track, bounded on either side by a wall, leading towards the mountain from the back of Machine Street. This lay almost directly on the line of Vignoles' proposed track and, as it would appear to have had no other purpose, it could well have been the start of the mountain railroad.

Chapter 9
Chemicals

Sulphuric acid is widely recognised as being the most important of all industrial chemicals. Manufactories producing it are known to have existed as early as 1736, all of which depended on burning brimstone (sulphur) in the presence of nitre (potassium nitrate), in a vessel containing water in order to produce the acid. The water absorbed the fumes readily, forming dilute sulphuric acid as it did so, and this in turn was further concentrated by distillation. Early containers used in the process were made of glass, but with the later discovery that lead was resistant to dilute sulphuric acid, a chemist named John Roebuck devised what became known as the lead chamber process, in which the glass vessels were replaced by small chambers fabricated from sheet lead. The floor of each chamber contained water to a depth of about 4 inches, and over the course of a month or so, during which there were several firings of the brimstone and nitre mixture, the water became increasingly more acidified. When the process was complete, the dilute acid was drawn off for further concentration, and the process repeated.

It will be recalled how by calcining the pyritic ores from Parys Mountain it was possible to recover the sulphur they contained, and one important development in the manufacture of sulphuric acid was the omission of that stage by using raw pyrites in place of the sulphur. By omitting one complete stage in the manufacturing process the new method was clearly very much cheaper than the old. The originator of the pyritic process was an enterprising manufacturing chemist called Charles Henry Hills,[117] who owned a chemical works at Deptford in London.

There can be no doubt that it was the abundant availability of cheap sulphur that first attracted C H Hills to Amlwch, where, in 1840,[118] he established a chemical works in which to produce artificial fertilizers. Unfortunately, very little indeed is known of his early industrial activities in the town, apart from the fact that his first works were located on the exposed headland at Llam Carw, to the north east of the harbour. The 1866 edition of the Ordnance Survey map of the area shows what was then remaining of the works, which would appear to have been a group of isolated buildings on a site covering an area of about 4 acres. Apart from a great deal of fine cinder and clinker which can be found around the site, very little now remains of the chemical works itself apart from the remains of a small dam built to contain the waters of a stream which had its outfall in the nearby creek known as Porth Llam Carw.

It would appear that at one time or another, an attempt was made to widen the creek, for it is evident that the rocks close to the low water level have been worked to form a narrow, flat platform, close to the mouth of a small cave. It is unlikely that these alterations were carried out by Hills as part of his development of the site as close inspection of the cave reveals evidence of copper ores.

What little documentary evidence so far discovered relating to Hills' activities in Amlwch dates from late September 1860, when he sought an agreement with the Mona Mine Company, which would allow him to calcine their ores for them:

Having made a trial of the copper ore from the Mona Mine at my works at Amlwch and finding that it can be exceedingly well calcined in my kilns, I beg to make you the following proposal viz.

I will erect sufficient vitriol chambers and kilns at my works, and agree to calcine the whole of the ores raised at Mona Mine (except smalls etc.) in such a manner as to make them fit for smelting. If you prefer having the ores calcined at the Smelting Works I have no objection to erect the necessary plant there instead of at my own works, if one of the sheds and a part of the late Parys Mine yard (now unoccupied) be granted to me for this purpose - The advantage to your Works will be the having the ores calcined and rendered fit for smelting in the best possible mode without any of the delay, waste, uncertainty and frequent failure of the present system of calcination in heaps at the mine, and with as near as I can calculate effect a saving of 3/6d per ton of ore.[119]

Before entering into an agreement with Hills however, Evan Evans who was the mining company's agent at Amlwch, advised his employers that before closing any agreement,

. . . it should be strictly understood that Mr Hills is not to manufacture Salt Cake on the premises as the smoke or vapour would be a source of intolerable nuisance to the workmen and to the inhabitants of the houses around.[120]

There would not appear to have been any intention on Hills' part to manufacture salt cake which was the name given at that time to an impure form of sodium sulphate at that time but, as this was a most noxious by product of several industrial processes, it was undoubtedly a good point to make.[121]

In the same letter Evans, commenting on one of the proposed sites for the new works said

. . . this would be the most convenient spot unless the place chosen by Mr Hills would be more convenient for the transit of the Sulphuric Acid to Llam Carw which Mr Hills told me he intended to do by laying down leaden pipes.

It is highly unlikely, for obvious reasons, that it was Hills' intention to pump dilute sulphuric acid from the new calcining works to Llam Carw, and it must be assumed therefore that his choice of site was such that the acid could flow from there to the works under gravity. If this was the case it is likely that the site under consideration was located somewhere in the vicinity of the northern end of Upper Quay Street, where there would have been an adequate supply of essential fresh water from the old brickpool, and from where the dilute acid could have been piped under gravity to Llam Carw.

By way of further convincing the mining company of the worth of his proposal, Hills offered to calcine a batch of ore for them, and in a letter to Legg,[122] the Marquess' agent, Evan Evans referred to

. . . the small parcel Mr Hills calcined at Llam Carw as a specimen, and he (William Hughes, the smelter) says that positively he never would wish to have ores better calcined than that was - far superior to the ores calcined in the mine kilns. William Hughes seems quite satisfied that Mr Hills mode of calcining under proper attention cannot fail giving every satisfaction.

An agreement was eventually arrived at, but it would appear that the new plant was not commissioned until the middle of June 1861 when Legg had to write directly to Hills to complain about the escape of smoke from the calciners, which he insisted, called for an immediate remedy. In his reply Hills stated that the problem resulted from the fact that the draft pipes had been incorrectly fitted, which caused the sulphurous gas to escape from the front of the kiln instead of passing into the lead chambers.

As the chemical works prospered, Hills' dependence on shipping for the importation of certain raw materials, and the exportation of finished products grew accordingly, and it was for this reason no doubt, that he was elected on to the Amlwch Harbour Board of Trustees. In common with others on the Board he was also a shareowner in several vessels associated with the port, one such being the *Charlotte Maule*, managed by local Captain John German, as well as the *Eilian Hill* launched from the yard of William Thomas & Sons in 1881.

The diminishing output from the mines meant that the amount of sulphur being produced by Hills was inadequate for his needs, and the Amlwch Harbourmaster's logbook for 17 January 1887,[123] records the arrival of the French brig *Edmond*, from Huelva with a cargo of Spanish sulphur for the firm. Amongst other raw materials recorded as having arrived for Hills were two cargoes of ground phosphate from Antwerp, the first by the *SS County of Lancaster*, and the second delivery by the locally built iron schooner, *Mary Catherine*. It is evident that Hills was using the sulphuric acid he was manufacturing to treat the phosphate rock to make fertilizer.

Under the heading *Opinion of the Press,* a local Welsh language newspaper dated September 1889, carried an advertisement in the guise of an editorial, praising the merits of Hills' fertilizers. The stilted manner in which the article was written suggests that the author had translated directly from what would now be known as a press release, but it is nevertheless, an important record of the products then being manufactured by the firm:

> One of the long established Works, which bear a high reputation, and in which the utmost confidence can be placed is that of Henry Hills & Son, of Newcastle upon Tyne and Amlwch, Anglesey. This factory has been established for over 50 years,[124] and during that time it has become noted for its fertilizers. It has been particularly careful to keep ahead of the times, and to profit by all the latest discoveries, without neglecting anything that would have added to the efficacy of its products. We believe that Henry Hills & Son's fertilizers are the best obtainable.
>
> This firm has produced Nitro Phosphate for the past 36 years, and as a general fertilizer for all kinds of crops, it has given the utmost satisfaction. Their Bone Manure has also proved to be made of the best ingredients, and is used by many hundreds of farmers.
>
> The Company's Corn and Grass Manure, which has been prepared especially for corn and hay crops by containing more Nitrogen and Ammonia than the Nitro Phosphate, which these crops need.
>
> The firm's Dissolved Bone Manure is guaranteed to be pure Bone Phosphate, and is available in a form suited to drill sowing.
>
> The Potato Fertilizer, which has been formulated expressly for potato crops contains more essential elements than the other products, and excellent yields have resulted from the use of this product.
>
> There is high praise indeed for the all purpose Phospho - Peruvian Guano, which is in great demand for Corn and Grass applications, and which can also be used mixed with Superphosphate for crops such as Turnips and Parsnips. The Superphosphate will also give the utmost satisfaction when mixed with natural farm manure.

The article went on to name three chief public analysts who fully endorsed the excellence of the fertilizers, and to state that testimonials had been received from innumerable farmers countrywide. In conclusion, and in time honoured fashion, the author exhorted his reader friends to put Hills' fertilizers to the test!

It is evident that some time before 1893, Hills had extended their ore calcining operations by entering into full scale smelting, for in that year the local newspaper reported that the roof of their smelting house had been set on fire when molten copper had accidentally flowed on to a mound of coal! [125] Unfortunately nothing more is known of this facet of the firm's business, but it would appear to have ended before 1897, because after that date the former smelter complex was invariably referred to as Hills' Chemical Works or, in Welsh, Gwaith Hills.

Under the enlightened management of Lewis Hughes the firm continued to prosper and became unusually busy during the early months of 1898, when it was found necessary to employ additional labour to allow the works to operate on a 24 hour basis. The scale of the boom can be gauged from the fact that six vessels, three of them steamers, delivered raw material to the works in the first week of February and the local newspaper correspondent reported his delight on seeing the liveliness in the town where many of the unemployed had been delivered from near starvation by the firm's prosperity. The boom would appear to have continued into the following year, when according to the same correspondent, dozens of large vessels continued to deliver raw materials to the works, resulting in road traffic resembling that to be seen in Liverpool's famous Lime Street! [126]

When, and under what circumstances the firm closed down has not been discovered, but it is evident that its undoubted success over a period of at least 60 years, met the needs of a great many of the town's families who would otherwise have been much the poorer, following the decline in the mining industry.

Chapter 10
Tobacco

It is perhaps not surprising that the heavy nature of the industries such as those which were established in Amlwch in the 19th century, should have generated a local tobacco industry, for this was the pattern already set in the larger centres of shipping and heavy industry such as Liverpool, Bristol and Glasgow.

The first documentary reference to tobacco processing in the town appears in *Slater's National & Commercial Directory* of 1849, when Morgans and Jones of Bank Street, were listed as manufacturers of tobacco and snuff.[127] In the directory's 1850 edition however, the firm appears under the name of Edward Morgans [*sic*] only.

By 1868, another tobacco firm owned by Edward M Hughes had been established in Methusalem Street, now known as Mona Street. By that time, Edward Morgan's business address had changed from Bank Street to Market Place. This does not necessarily mean that the firm had relocated, for it is evident that several of the town's streets were renamed, sometimes more than once, over the years.

Both firms were again listed in the 1880 directory, in which Edward Morgan (not Morgans) claimed to be the 'original manufacturer of the celebrated Amlwch tobaccos'. Edward Morgan Hughes on the other hand, not only claimed to be the manufacturer of the celebrated Amlwch tobaccos, but also described himself as being a tobacco cutter, snuff grinder and cigar importer, as well as being the supplier of fancy tobaccos such as *The Old Favourite* and the *Cambrian Smoking Mixture*. In the same edition, the firm of William Mostyn & Co, described as "Tobacco Manufacturers of Madyn Works [128] and Petters Street", appeared for the first time. By 1910 however, this latest company had changed hands, and was then in the ownership of Hugh Owen and Sons.

Unlike the major tobacco manufacturing centres mentioned earlier, there is nothing, despite the extent of the local industry, to indicate that raw tobacco was ever imported into Amlwch directly from abroad. In later years, it was customary for the local manufacturers to purchase their raw material from leaf merchants in Liverpool and London, and it is probably true to say that this had always been the case.

Although Virginia and Empire grown leaves were used in the manufacture of Amlwch tobaccos, preference was usually given to the latter, for the simple reason that they carried a reduced rate of customs duty. This reflected the government policy of encouraging the development of trade within the British Empire, and tobacco leaves from Rhodesia, Nyasaland, India and Canada made up the bulk of those used.

In order to provide a product of consistent quality, it was usual for the manufacturers to blend their products using leaves obtained from more than one source and, by way of enabling them to determine the proportions required of each, it was the custom for the leaf merchants to supply generous free samples beforehand. Depending on the quantities required for production, the raw tobacco was delivered either in bales of 220lbs, cases of 440lbs or in half hogsheads weighing 880lbs. The large, yellowish Canadian tobacco leaves

A tobacco blender at Edward Morgan's tobacco works, Amlwch.

for example, were invariably delivered by the case, sometimes referred to as a quarter hogshead; whilst the smaller and darker African leaves were bought by the bale. The cheapest leaves of all to purchase, were those from India.

As delivered, the leaves were dry and brittle, and those destined to be made into snuff (which was known locally as *snisin* – sneezing) were taken as they were to a snuff mill, which is best described as a large mechanized version of a chemist's mortar and pestle. There, in the *felin snisin*, the leaves were ground into a fine powder which, depending on the proclivities of the user, was either sniffed up the nostrils or rubbed on the gums. By way of catering for those with more unusual tastes, and ladies in particular, some snuffs were artificially, but quite legally, flavoured and scented. If legend is to be believed however, some was quite shamefully adulterated.

It would appear that one snuff maker (who was also a lay preacher) had come to Amlwch to preach one Sunday and, on his way home, he was seen to make a detour to a heap of ochre where he helped himself to a generous amount. The reason for this was not hard to fathom, for the particular shade of ochre he had taken was identical to that of the snuff he was making. It was believed locally that it was as a result of this discovery that legislation was introduced making it illegal to adulterate snuff with ochre or other earths.

Edward Morgan & Company's Tobacco Works, Bull Bay Road, Amlwch. This building was demolished to make way for the new A5025 road.

In order to make leaves intended for other products such as chewing and smoking tobaccos easier to handle, it was necessary to restore to them a measure of their former elasticity by dampening them with water. This was done after the blender had weighed out the appropriate amounts of the various leaves needed to make his mixture. To do this, the leaves were spread out in a single layer on low wooden staging, the surface of which sloped gently towards one end. There they were sprinkled with water, using nothing more sophisticated than a garden watering can. When this was done, another layer was placed on top of the first, and the procedure repeated as many times as were necessary to treat the whole batch.

As duty on the tobacco was determined by its weight when it left the works, it was essential that its moisture content was carefully regulated within certain limits prescribed by HM Customs. For that reason the exact quantity of water necessary to dampen a given weight of leaves had to be accurately determined, and any that failed to be absorbed ran down to one end of the staging where it was collected and re-circulated. At the end of this simple but vitally important first stage, the leaves were sufficiently pliable to be handled with ease.

Twist, as one type of tobacco was known, was so called after the process by which it was produced, a method which bore little or no similarity to the way other tobaccos were manufactured. In a manner similar in many respects to the way hemp or sisal can be wound to make rope, tobacco leaves can be wound to form long rope like lengths known as twists. This was done by a machine which not only imparted a twist to the leaves but, at the same time, gathered the resulting twist onto a large spool, much like cable on a drum. When the batch was complete, lengths of the twist, each weighing 1 pound, were then taken off and re-wound on to bobbins, forming coils about 5 inches long and 4 inches in diameter. In order to keep their shape when they were removed from the winding bobbin, each coil was tied with twine before the outer layers were liberally coated with olive oil. An outer wrapping of greaseproof paper was then placed around each coil, and a length of thin sisal rope tightly wound around the outside. When the whole batch had been prepared in this way, the coils were placed in rows on the base plate of a screw press; and when this was full, a steel plate was placed over the coils, and the procedure repeated. In this way, several layers were built up, one on top of the other, until the press was full.

On the side of the press there was a wheel similar to a ship's steering wheel which, when turned, acted through bevel gears and a worm to exert considerable pressure on the several layers of coiled tobacco in the press. As the wheel was turned a little at a time over a period of days, the coils of tobacco gradually became more compressed. The binding rope prevented the coils from being flattened, and when these were uncoiled, they resembled long lengths of square liquorice. Only the lower layers were removed from the press; the remainder being replaced in their original order, and one or more layers added to the top as required. The twist became progressively darker as it worked its way down to the lowest layers, by which time it was deemed to be ready for sale. It was usual for the twists to be sold to the tobacconist in this form, and it was he who cut it into the appropriate lengths for the customer. One reason for the popularity of twist was its reputation for being long lasting, and although it was bought mainly for chewing, there were many who were happy enough to whittle away at the hard plug with their penknives in order to fill their pipes.

Another type of tobacco manufactured at Amlwch was known as shag which was intended mainly for smoking, but was also used for chewing by many of its devotees. From the damping staging the tobacco was taken to an extremely sharp mechanical guillotine where it was sliced into thin shreds. Such was the nature of the tobacco that the 12 inch wide blade of the guillotine soon lost its edge, and had to be resharpened every half an hour or so and, despite being 10 inches long when new, its life was rather limited as a result. The resulting tobacco, much of which was compacted by the guillotine, was then placed on warmed plates where it was partly dried, a process known as stoving. This enabled it to be separated into the long strands with which most people are familiar. A sample of the tobacco was then taken to be tested for water content, for under no circumstance could the upper limit prescribed by HM Customs be exceeded. The finished tobacco was then weighed out into $1/2$ or 1 ounce quantities by a weigher, who passed them on to be packed into cylinders. This method of packing was employed by all of the local manufacturers, but whether it was unique to Amlwch is not known. The packer had at hand a pile of inner greaseproof wrappers, and a pile of paper outer wrappers bearing the names of the tobacco and its manufacturer. The weighed tobacco was then hand rolled into a cylinder formed by the two wrappers. The tube of loose tobacco, looking very much like a very fat cigarette, was then slipped into a hole bored through the centre of a hardwood hand bobbin. The wrappers, protruding equally from either end of the hole were then expertly and very neatly turned in towards the middle, and the sealed pack ejected in one deft move.

Chewing tobacco, referred to locally as *tsioin*, was extremely popular and, however disagreeable the subject might be, the following description by Robert Roberts of the precentor of the church at Amlwch, gives an amusing account of the tribulations of one of the habit's devotees:

> Our precentor, Wil Dafydd was not quite so ignorant of music as Owen Hughes, but being an inveterate chewer of tobacco, it involved too great a sacrifice to take the quid out of his mouth while singing; hence much of his attention was engaged in so shaping his mouth as to enable him to sing with force and effect and at the same time keep the super abundant juices of the weed from overflowing. His contortions of face during this struggle, often vain as it proved, were too much for one's gravity. [129]

It was widely believed that tobacco had curative properties, as the following rhyme written in praise of Edward Morgan's *Hen Wlad* (The Old Country) tobacco clearly demonstrates:

> I Amlwch am dobaco,
> Aed Gwyddel, Sais a Chymro,
> Ac yno gan E Morgan fad,
> Y mae'r *Hen Wlad* diguro.
>
> At buro'r awyr sylwch,
> A lladd clefydau coeliwch,
> Ni cheir drwy'r byd, does neb a wad,
> Fel mwg *Hen Wlad* o Amlwch.
>
> Ei glod a gân lafurwr,
> A thystio wnai pregethwr,
> Nid oes tebyg i'r *Hen Wlad*,
> Am roi mwynhad i'r smygwr.

The supposed healing and purifying properties of tobacco smoke were widely believed in, and it was not unheard of for parents to place a well chewed *sigyn* (quid) into a child's ear to alleviate earache, or to apply it to an open wound where it was intended to stem bleeding and act as an antiseptic. Folk cures such as these were extended even to animals, for it was common practice locally to use tobacco to de-worm horses. The usual dose was a 1 ounce pack of shag, which because of its bitter taste would not normally be ingested voluntarily, and the farrier had to resort to pulling the horse's tongue sideways out of its mouth in order to place the dose where the poor creature had no choice but to swallow it. The technique also ensured that the farrier's fingers were not lost in the process.

Towards the end of the company's manufacturing life, E Morgan & Co were processing about 200lbs of tobacco a day, the greater part of which was sold for 8d an ounce in the early 1930s. This price remained constant for many years, but two of the firm's best known shags, *Pride of Wales* and *Baco'r Aelwyd* differed slightly in price, a variation which may have reflected the difference in the cost of packaging what was in every other respect, the same tobacco!

The only cigarettes which appear to have been made at Amlwch were manufactured by E Morgan Hughes & Co. These were sold under the name of *Welsh Terriers* but, as cigarette smoking increased in popularity, competition from the larger tobacco companies grew more intense, and the company reverted to the production of twists and shags, for which a steady local market remained.

Hugh Owen and Sons, known at one stage as the Amlwch Tobacco Co, were the first to cease production and they were followed by E Morgan Hughes and Co, who managed to continue trading as distributors until the 1950s.

Messrs E Morgan and Company, the first and last of the Amlwch tobacco manufacturers, ceased production of their own brands in the late 1940s, but continued in business as wholesale tobacco merchants until 1985.

Chapter 11
The Port

The importance of shipping to the effective running of the mines is self evident, and until the arrival in Amlwch of the railway in 1867, the several mining companies were dependent on vessels drawn from the Irish Sea coastal trade.

Sir Nicholas Bayly had bought shares in the sloop *Sampson* in March 1773 however, which would appear to have been employed mainly in the London trade, plying between Amlwch, Caernarfon and Southwark's Pickle Herring Dock. In a printed notice, her Master, Richard Hughes, described the vessel as one of the constant traders which possessed "good accommodations for passengers".[130]

Although the Parys company had a few vessels of its own by 1782, it is generally true to say that the mining companies shied away from any great involvement in shipping. In 1788, however, several investors who were in one way or another associated with the mines or the smelters, formed the Amlwch Shipping Company,[131] which traded to and from the port continuously for at least 30 years.[132]

The mines were then at their zenith and the quantities of ore, sulphur and fine copper passing out of the port, as well as the prodigious amounts of coal then being imported, meant that the existing facilities were woefully inadequate. The increasing need for additional quays, as well as dockside storage which could accommodate ore, coal, slag and imported scrap iron, meant that bold and imaginative steps had to be taken to solve the problem. The proposals were such however that it was necessary to petition Parliament before work could begin, and on 21 June, 1793 an Act was passed which permitted the ". . . enlargement, deepening, cleansing, improvement and regulation of the harbour".

The reasons for its enactment are given in the preamble to the Act:

Whereas the harbour of Amlwch, in the Isle of Anglesey, is inadequate to the Occasions of the Trade carried on there, and in certain Winds does not allow Safety for Vessels lying therein, for Want of a Pier and other necessary Works: And whereas the said harbor is capable of being rendered safe and commodious, and, if the same was effectually improved and regulated, it would not only be beneficial to the Trade and Commerce of the said Isle, but would, in Cases of strong Westwardly Winds, be very useful as a Retreat for Ships.

The regulation of the Harbour was delegated to a Board of Trustees, amongst whom were Thomas Williams, Edward Hughes and Sir Nicholas Bayly's successor, Lord Uxbridge. Others who resided within a radius of 5 miles of the port were also qualified to become Trustees, provided they either possessed real estate to the annual value of £20, or had personal property amounting to no less than £300.

The power given to the Trustees by the Act was comprehensive, and which included the right to raise funds by borrowing, or by levying rates and duties from the owners of vessels using the port. There were exceptions however, and these included the King's warships, vessels employed solely for fishing, or any vessel of a burthen not exceeding 15 tons, laden with limestone or ballast.

The Trust's primary task was to improve the eastern side of the port which was, to a large degree, still in its natural state, and for that reason presented a daunting problem. The ultimate solution however was one that might have been expected from men who were miners first and foremost.

To the north of the new grain and flour warehouses the rock face rose steeply from the water's edge and it was here, despite the obvious difficulties, that the Trust decided to create a flat platform out of the solid rock. By cutting into the rock face, a level floor some 400 feet long and 60 feet wide, was created at a level about 3 feet below that of the original quay built alongside the grain warehouses.

This meant that a great deal of additional rock had to be excavated, and it has been calculated that something in excess of 20,000 tons had to be blasted and removed in order to complete the work. Some of the stone produced in this way was used to build a small pier, as well as to face the dock wall alongside which the ships would berth. The large stones used for this purpose were laid with their long sides vertical, a feature which is rarely met with in Anglesey, but which is reminiscent of the Cornish method of harbour construction. This suggests that the work was carried out under the direction of a Cornishman, many of whom had migrated to Amlwch in search of work at the mines. Tons of the remaining stone quarried from the rock face were used to build the thick walls of the bins, and it is possible that some was used to construct the many conical, ore burning kilns described by Lentin.

Such was the expense involved in developing the eastern side of the port, that the Trust must, for some reason, have dismissed the idea of further improving the western side belonging to the See of Bangor, where ground conditions were far more favourable. One possible reason may lie in the fact that the disruption which would have been brought about by new works would have exacerbated the port's problems without adding greatly to their solution. When all things are considered, it is clear that the Trust had little or no option but to concentrate their efforts where they did.

At the top of the excavated rock face, on average some 35 feet above the level of newly formed quay, a road was built which gave direct access to Llam Carw, where Charles Hills had his works. This may not have been its main purpose however, for it was also used by carters to deliver their loads of ore directly into the quayside bins without causing any additional congestion on the quay itself. This was achieved by means of wooden chutes attached to the rock face, down which the ore was tipped. There were several such chutes, but only one now remains, and that in a very decayed condition.

According to the Francis map there were originally six bins, three of which were for the storage of slag, iron and coal, and were open, whilst the remaining three, intended for the storage of copper ore, were roofed over. These have subsequently been sub-divided to increase their number to eight.

Photographs taken at a later date show that a section of the road was supported by a small six arch viaduct which had been built across a stream flowing into the harbour from the brick pool above.[133] The new road cut right across the one previously built to serve the new grain warehouses, but at a level some 6 feet below it. This was quite clearly done to provide a more direct route to the quay without having to first pass along Well Street.

The harsh weather conditions which prevailed in the Irish Sea meant that vessels were frequently damaged, and reports of dismastment and other structural damage to the vessels were commonplace. In such cases it was usual for coastal sailing vessels to put into the nearest port for repairs. In the absence of an established shipwrights' yard however, ship repairs were often carried out by a loose federation of craftsmen, but as work became more plentiful, such *ad hoc* arrangements gave way to a more structured system using purpose built workshops and facilities which had the capacity to provide specialised services. How far the industry had developed in this sense at Amlwch before the coming of James Treweek is difficult to discover.

One example of the ill effects of bad weather concerned the vessel *Marchioness of Anglesea*. Under the command of Evan Hughes, a local man, she sailed from Liverpool bound for Amlwch on 10 April, 1818 with a cargo of coal, bricks and general merchandise.[134] On board were 12 passengers, in addition to her crew of 6, and when the vessel was almost within sight of her destination, she was overtaken by a fierce easterly gale and driven ashore at Llys Dulas. There her Master, four crew members and 10 passengers were drowned, one of whom was the wife of the renowned Anglesey preacher, John Elias. The survivors, which included a boy member of the crew, had very wisely climbed the ship's rigging, and were rescued early on the following morning. Before any salvage operations could be put in hand however, much of the general merchandise on board was plundered, which despite being a punishable offence under the law, was according to Treweek, a practice nevertheless resorted to by many. The greater part of the coal and bricks intended for the mine and the smelters were recovered however, no doubt much to Treweek's relief.

As often happened, the vessel was refloated, and unless at some stage she was replaced by another bearing the same name, she continued to appear in the Amlwch shipping lists for a further 27 years.

The weather frequently added to the port's problems, particularly in the winter months, and Treweek was at times driven to the point of desperation when much needed commodities failed to arrive. In a letter to Sanderson in March 1817, he informed him that

> . . . we have been sadly put to it this month for lack of powder - have borrowed and bought all we could get throughout the island. The vessels being kept away by contrary winds, however they have arrived at last and we have a good stock of powder, enough to carry us through the winter.

From 1786 onwards, records of vessels built at Amlwch are contained in the Port of Beaumaris Registers of Shipping. It may not be true to say that all vessels built at Amlwch were registered at Beaumaris however, for it was permitted to do so at another port, but it is thought that this would have been highly unlikely.

The registers show that as many as 29 vessels were built in Anglesey between 1786 and 1825, some of which are known to have been active in the Amlwch copper trade, but only two are recorded as having been built at the port. The first was a 15 ton sloop called *Lovely Nancy*, built in 1788, which was followed in 1791 by an altogether smaller vessel the *Swallow*, registered as a 7 ton sloop.

Clearly there was no great tradition of shipbuilding at the port, even during the period of greatest activity at the mines. One explanation for this can be found in the physical nature of the harbour where berths had been hard won at great cost, and where a suitable location for a shipyard would have been difficult, if not impossible to come by. Another, perhaps more likely explanation lies in the fact that ship repairing was much more lucrative than shipbuilding, and would consequently have taken precedence over it.

Whatever Treweek's financial standing may have been on his arrival at Amlwch, it is evident that his salary at the mine far exceeded that which was needed to support his growing family for, in a comparatively short time, he had accumulated sufficient capital to invest in a business venture of his own. The fact that his duties brought him into close contact with the workings of the port meant that he was well placed to recognise the opportunities which existed there, and it was there that he first entered business on his own account.

The first reference to the enterprise occurs in the mineowners reply to a petition sent to them in 1822 by local coal merchants complaining about the incursion into their trade by Treweek's 18 year old son Nicholas. In their reply, the owners stated that whereas they did not permit their agents to traffic in articles for the supply of the workmen, it was not within their power to prevent Mr Treweek's son from setting up as a coal merchant or indeed in any other line of business in which he believed he could survive. [135]

Some three years later, James Treweek decided, in common with many other people in Wales at that time, to invest in a brand new vessel of his own, which he commissioned his son to build. As he had been a coal merchant some three years previously, it is unlikely that Nicholas had qualified as a shipwright and it is believed that the supervision of the work was entrusted to a local man. The first vessel to leave yard was the 68 ton sloop *Unity* in 1825. What purpose Treweek had in mind for the vessel is unknown, and the little knowledge that we have about her early voyages gives no clue as to whether she had been built to satisfy the rigorous demands of the copper trade, or was simply an ordinary coaster. Her early voyages, under the command of Robert Jones of Amlwch, were to Chester, Swansea and Liverpool and could have been for either purpose.

The *Marquis of Anglesea* launched in 1826 was the second vessel to leave the yard. She had a long and successful career which could have ended when she sank in 1865, were it not for the fact that she was sold as a wreck to Owen Roberts, a ship's carpenter from Pwllheli. Under his supervision she was refloated and taken to her owner's home port where she was beached and rebuilt. The refurbished vessel worked out of Pwllheli until 1908 when she was sold to a Liverpool owner and the last report of her was that she was still giving sterling service in 1917, as a barge on the River Thames. The fact that she was then almost a hundred years old testifies to the quality of her construction.

In 1827, the yard launched its third vessel, the *Margaret* which was a 43 ton sloop built for a local owner, but a further two years were to elapse before the next vessel, a 17 ton smack called the *Eleanor* was built there. The registered builder of the new vessel was Francis Treweek, who was then 18 years old and, as no reference was made in the records to his elder brother, it must be assumed that the venture was his alone.

In 1823, the Parys concern departed from its policy of depending solely on outside interests by purchasing the *Hero*, a 90 ton schooner built at Chelmsford. The vessel's Captain John Evans, had served in the Napoleonic Wars and was for a time a prisoner of the French. His integrity and outspokenness were legend, and there can be little doubt that he was a most able and conscientious servant.

The *Hero's* maiden voyage from London was with one of many cargoes of scrap iron for the precipitation ponds, consigned by Robert Webster, a relative of the two brothers who owned the Mona Vitriol Works at Trysglwyn Isaf.

In the belief that the *Hero* was an excellent vessel, the company initially sailed her without insurance; but within two years part of her hull had decayed and had to be replaced. She nevertheless continued to serve the company well, surviving storms which brought about the loss of many of her contemporaries.

It is evident that Captain Evans had his reservations concerning the integrity of the

Treweek family, for in 1827 he wrote to John Sanderson, agent to the Earl of Uxbridge, stating that

> . . . I scarcely ever get an article for the use of the vessel but from Mr Treweek's stores - I cannot but observe that I never have an insight of the particulars which the *Hero* has had from his stores, indeed the idea strikes me very forcibly touching the necessity for such a step when I consider that justice should be the generous maxim of upright Britons, indeed Sir I could not add the above hint, without being justified in my observations with respect to private accounts with Mr Treweek.

What Evans was complaining of was his inability to verify the expenditure that had been incurred on his vessel whilst it was being maintained by the Treweek yard; the clear assertion being that items or services charged against her account had not been supplied, and that the bills were approved for payment without verification, presumably by James Treweek himself.[136]

Hard use over a period of over 30 years took its toll of the little vessel however, and in 1854, some 14 years after the death of Captain Evans, a local surveyor recommended that for an estimated outlay of £332 she could be refitted to a standard which would extend her life for many years to come.[137]

During his lifetime, Captain Evans was never averse to air the injustices he had to suffer, and one of his most persistent complaints related to the undue delays he had to endure whilst at Amlwch Port. This was a problem that had long been recognised by both Treweek and Sanderson, and from time to time, petitions were received from Masters in the copper trade, for an increase in the freightage rates, because of the delays.

At the root of the problem was the fact that the port was much too confined for the volume of trade it had to handle, and that freight was generally allocated on a first come, first served, basis. In countering one such petition, Sanderson maintained that the Masters should be made to realise that the delays were chiefly of their own making, inasmuch that if there were fewer vessels in the trade, the delays would be minimised. This he claimed, would consequently result in more frequent sailings, and greater profits for the shipowners.

One problem which the Harbour Trustees had to address, was that of damage frequently caused to both the fabric of the harbour and the vessels within, by high seas resulting from strong northerly winds. Over the years, several attempts had been made to minimise this effect by constructing piers part way across the width of the port. These had not been entirely successful however and the Trustees were faced with the problem of finding a way to close off the port when needed.

They chose to solve the problem by building two short piers opposite each other, across which could be drawn no fewer than 13 long baulks of timber; which were then lowered into slots, one on top of the other, to form a barrier. As might be imagined, this required a great deal of effort, and the Harbour Rules made provision for this by stipulating that the Master of each vessel within the port should provide as many as two-thirds of its crew members for this purpose. Failure to comply with such an order meant that the Harbour Master was empowered to engage others to do the work, and to recharge the cost to the defaulting Master.

By way of warning vessels wishing to enter the port, that the baulks were down, and that access was denied to them, a signalling system comprising of a flag and a ball were raised on a pole on the headland at Llam Carw. These were frequently ignored however, as the Harbourmaster's log records numerous instances of vessels entering the outer basin, "contrary to the rules of the harbour".

The Treweek family's shipbuilding concern continued apace with the launching in 1830, of the largest vessel ever built at Amlwch, the 130 ton wooden brigantine *James and Jane*. It is significant that the new vessel, named in honour of their parents, was recorded as having been built jointly by the Treweek Brothers, which probably meant that they were by then full business partners. The ship built for John Hughes, an Amlwch owner, who would also appear to have been her first Master, barely survived to be ten years old, for she foundered in the Bay of Biscay in 1840.

The launching of a new vessel was an event eagerly awaited by the local people for it was invariably the occasion for great celebration. It was not unusual for hundreds of people to turn up on the day to view the scene from the several vantage points overlooking the port; and children were given the day off from school to witness the spectacle with their families and friends.

Before the launching ceremony, the vessel was raised off the blocks on which it had been built, and then carefully lowered on to a specially prepared slipway down which it would slide into the sea.

For the naming ceremony, or the christening as it was known locally, the vessel was dressed overall in flags and bunting with a pennant bearing the ship's name flying from the highest mast. The honour of naming the vessel was frequently given to a young lady member of the new owner's family, and she would have been assisted in her task by a 'volunteer' crew consisting of several local youngsters who were permitted to remain on board for the launching.

Following the event it was usual for the owners and builders to partake of a celebratory meal at a nearby hostelry, whilst the yard workers partook at another, where the celebrations were a little more boisterous no doubt.

The brothers' next vessel, the *Amlwch Packet*, a 37 ton smack, built for Thomas Jones of Bangor, was launched in 1832, a year that marked Francis' premature death, at the age of 21. The company nevertheless continued to trade under the name of Treweek Brothers, and in 1834 launched its seventh vessel, the diminutive *Sarah*, an 18 ton smack built for a local buyer. This reversion to building small vessels after the relatively large *James and Jane*, suggests that the yard was otherwise engaged in ship repairing and it was not until 1836 that it turned out two further sloops, the 28 ton *Cymraes* and the 72 ton *Jane and Margaret*. The *Cymraes* was the first recorded Amlwch built vessel to bear a Welsh name, and she was originally under the command of Thomas Hughes of Penrhoslligwy, who owned a quarter share in her, but by 1879 her connections with Anglesey were severed when she became the property of a Norwich owner.

The Treweek yard boasted a three storeyed building which housed the counting house, a carpenters' shop, a smithy and a sail loft. The back of the building had been built hard up against the rock face and was accessible at first floor level from the slag dump above.

Thomas Hughes was clearly very satisfied with the *Cymraes* for he returned to the Treweek yard for another vessel. The *Marianne* a 72 ton sloop, probably built to the same specification as the *Jane and Margaret*, was launched in 1839, but of this vessel Thomas Hughes owned but 2 ounces.

This curious unit of share ownership reflects the division of the imperial one pound weight into 16 equal parts known as ounces. An owner who possessed 2 ounces therefore owned an eighth share in that vessel. Because of the increasingly high cost of shipping, and the subsequent increase in the number of people who owned shares in them, the division was not confined to whole ounces, and there are many instances of people owning as little as a single quarter ounce share.

It would appear that Nicholas Treweek had ambitions beyond the building and repairing of vessels, for in 1840 the yard launched a 46 ton schooner called the *Economy*. The owners were Treweek and Company, which had no doubt been formed to exploit the ever increasing coastal trade with the developing townships on Merseyside and elsewhere. He later discontinued the use of Treweek Brothers as the name of the shipyard, and it is his name only which appears in the shipping register as the builder of the 62 ton schooner *Catherine*, which left the yard in 1842. The vessel's registered owner was given as James Treweek who could have been either the builder's father or his brother, who was two years his junior.

In the very same year as saw the launch of the *Catherine*, Treweek built a 74 ton schooner the *Mary* in his new yard at Hirael in Bangor. What purpose he had in mind when he founded this new venture is not known, for the *Mary* was the only vessel he built there.

What is clear however is that for some reason, Treweek's interest in the Amlwch yard was waning, for at the age of 40 he took a post as the Liverpool based forwarding agent for the Mona Mine. Before his departure however he oversaw the building of a 20 ton smack named *Cymro*, which was the 14th vessel to leave the yard when it was launched in 1844.

During his sojourn in Liverpool, Nicholas Treweek was in daily contact with numerous shipping interests. As a result, he was able to profit from their relationships: for in the ten years between 1845 and 1855 he had gained a financial interest in no fewer than 49 vessels, ranging from large full rigged ships to small coasting ketches.

At that time a great deal of interest was shown by British shipowners in North American built vessels, and Treweek was no exception. The relatively cheap locally grown timbers of the eastern seaboard meant that the vessels built there were exceedingly good value, and it was not unusual for purchasers to load their new vessels with timber on their maiden voyage across the Atlantic. The profit from the sale of the timber often went a long way towards meeting the vessel's original cost.

Amongst the Canadian vessels owned by Treweek were the 712 ton *Arethusa*, built in Quebec in 1845, and the 996 ton *Recruit,* built in New Brunswick in 1852, both of which he then used in the rapidly developing, and profitable, Australian trade routes. Two other similar ships were the 860 ton Quebec built *Helen*, and a 632 ton barque which he registered at Beaumaris in April 1851, as the *Anglesea*.

The yard, which had a monopoly of ship building and repair at Amlwch, continued in business during his absence, although strangely enough, no vessels were built there during that period. Treweek was forced to relinquish his post at Liverpool due to ill health, and he retired to his farm at Bod Ednyfed in Amlwch. Despite a holiday in his native Cornwall, during which it was hoped his health would be restored, Treweek disposed of his shipping interests to members of his immediate family. He retained his interest in the Amlwch shipyard however, for the development of which he had devised a most ambitious and costly plan.

His decision to establish a totally new yard on the eastern side of the harbour may probably have come about by his desire to build iron vessels or, alternatively, that he had seen the advantages to be gained in owning a dry dock in which he could repair ships. As there was no way that either of these two objectives could be accomplished on the western side of the harbour where his yard was situated, his interest focused on the opposite shore

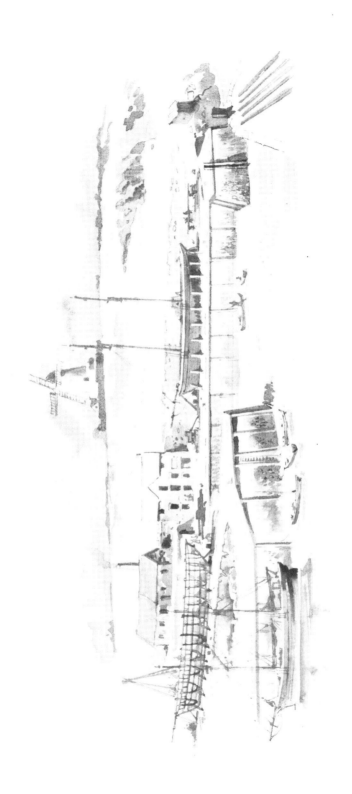

The schooner *Charles* (right) almost completed with *Holy Wath* (left) in the frame at Iard Ochr Draw, Amlwch Port, 1871.

where there was room to expand alongside the small inlet known as Porth Cwch y Brenin, which had the potential to be enlarged to create a dry dock.

In a similar way to that used to create the eastern quay, the rock was blasted away to form a 20 feet wide flat floor, the eastern side of which rose almost vertically to a height of about 35 feet. Because of the natural slope of the rock however, the dock wall on the seaward side was only about 15 feet high and, alongside this, Treweek built a new slipway using the excavated rock, which was also used to build walls which both retained and protected the new yard.

As with other conventional dry docks, the vessel entered in at high water and, as the tide receded, it settled on to a series of blocks laid down along the centre of the dock floor. When the tide was at its lowest, the floor of the dock was dry and two massive wooden gates were then swung across the entrance to seal it. The obvious advantage of a dry dock is that vessels can be worked on continuously whatever the state of the tide, and in the case of major alterations such as lengthening, without the need to draw the vessel completely out of the water.[138]

One of the many captains employed in Nicholas Treweek's fleet was a young man named William Thomas. Born at Cae Pant, a smallholding less than 2 miles from Amlwch Port, William ran away to sea when he was but 12 years old, and for many years his family had no idea of his whereabouts. There is no record of what he did or where he went during his early years at sea, but it is probably safe to assume that he was not sailing in the coastal trade for, had that been so, he would certainly have been recognised by the many local men who were similarly employed, and who would without doubt have carried news of him to his parents.

Whatever his training, it is clear that it benefited him greatly as a man, for by the age of 23 he was sufficiently well qualified to convince Nicholas Treweek that he should give him command of his 97 ton Canadian built schooner *Red*.

A shipping mania akin to the canal and railway manias experienced elsewhere in the country, had swept Wales by the middle of the 19th century. Amongst those with money to invest in ships were preachers, chemists, shopkeepers and farmers such as the Thomas family of Cae Pant. By 1849, William and his father Lewis, together with a third member of the family, became the owners of the 123 ton Canadian built brigantine *Clyde*. William, who was by then 27 years old, was appointed Master, and he remained in command until 1851, when it was transferred to his brother John.

Captain Thomas' next command was of the 85 ton schooner *Kendal Castle*, built at Frodsham in 1839, in which both he and Nicholas Treweek had shares. He retained his command until 1854, when he bought the 99 ton schooner *Anglesea Lass*, newly built at Rhyl and the command of the *Kendal Castle* passed to his brother John.

Increased competition brought with it a demand for faster vessels, which in turn gave rise to many changes in ship design, perhaps the most significant of which being the use of iron as a replacement for wood in their construction. Such had been the demand in Europe for suitable shipbuilding wood that it became both scarce and expensive. Indeed it was this that made North American built vessels such an attractive proposition to shipowners like Nicholas Treweek and the Thomas family.

Shipwrights were at the same time, anxious to find an alternative construction material because the demand was for ever larger vessels, and the inherent weakness of wood limited the size of vessel which could be economically built of it. Although canal barges had been built of iron as early as 1787, its use for shipbuilding was initially confined to vessels intended for nothing more taxing than river and estuary work. The progression to its use in the construction of seagoing ships, which came some while later, occurred in two stages.

The first was confined to the replacement of the vessel's wooden frames by those fabricated from rolled iron sections, on to which the usual form of wooden cladding was attached. Not only were these frames both lighter and stronger than the massive wooden frames they replaced, they also allowed the vessel's carrying capacity to be increased. The second phase of the development took place when the traditional wooden cladding forming the ship's hull, was replaced with rolled iron plates riveted to the frames.

The two vessels best known as fine examples of the early use of iron in shipbuilding are Brunel's *Great Britain* and *Great Eastern*. The former has since been restored and now lies in the very dock in which she was built at Bristol, following an epic voyage from the Falkland Islands where she had been abandoned as a hulk. The 32,000 ton *Great Eastern* was by far the largest vessel ever built when she was launched in 1858, one year before the first iron vessel to be built in North Wales was launched at Amlwch.

In 1859, a local newspaper reported that

> . . . this thriving little port is full of bustle, being crowded with shipping, discharging and receiving cargoes, and the shipbuilding yard of Mr Treweek busily occupied with a fine schooner in wood nearly completed, and another in iron - the first of that material ever constructed in North Wales.

The wooden schooner referred to was the 93 ton vessel *Alliance* which was launched in March 1858 for Messrs Palmer & Co of Amlwch, and the iron vessel was the *Mary Catherine*.

One report of the celebrations held to mark the launching of the *Mary Catherine*, caught the mood of the event:

> On Friday there was launched from the building yard of Messrs Hughes, Thomas and Co, at Amlwch, a beautifully modelled iron schooner, named the MARY CATHERINE, of about 160 tons, to be commanded by Captain John German, late of the schooner JOHN MORGAN. The builders were warmly congratulated on this their first and successful attempt at iron-ship building, and on the noble appearance of the ship on the water, which looked a perfect yacht. In the afternoon the builders and the owners, with a few friends, celebrated the event by partaking of a substantial dinner at Parry's Vaults. All the workmen in the employ were also entertained to a dinner at the Britannia Inn.

The Beaumaris Registers show that the shipbuilders were indeed Hughes, Thomas & Co, and although the vessel was built in Treweek's new yard, his name appears nowhere in the registers. This anomaly could be explained by the fact that it was often the custom to refer to those who commissioned new vessels, as shipbuilders. If that was indeed the case with the *Mary Catherine*, the likelihood is that Hughes, Thomas & Co commissioned the vessel as a speculative venture, and then went on to sell it to the registered owners, Jones & Co of Amlwch, before it was completed.

There is no reason to suppose that Treweek had personally acquired the expertise necessary to either design or direct the building of iron ships whilst he was in Liverpool. His first priority would therefore have been to appoint a well qualified and experienced yard manager, who would not only have possessed the necessary expertise to design the vessel, but also to advise regarding the specialist craftsmen and machinery required to carry out the work. As she was the first vessel of her kind to be built in North Wales it is thought likely that specialist craftsmen were recruited on Merseyside, where there were at that time, several well established builders of iron ships. The vessel was originally designed as a topsail schooner, but she was later re-rigged as a ketch. Her two bulkheads gave her enormous strength and she served her owners well, giving splendid service as a coaster, sailing to most of the principal British and continental ports over a period of almost 60 years. The quality of her construction can have had no better testimony than the fact that she was bought when 30 years old by Captain Thomas' sons William and Lewis, who were noted for their discernment in such matters.

By 1916 however the *Mary Catherine* had been sold to Bert's Barges Ltd, of Liverpool, who converted her into a barge, which might be thought of as an unfitting end to a vessel once described as being of noble appearance. Her useful life however continued until 1939 when in her 82nd year she was broken up for scrap.

Unfortunately there is no information available regarding the ship repair business generated by Treweek's new yard at Amlwch, but what is known is that a further three vessels were built there, the *Sea Queen*, the 99 ton iron built schooner *Princess of Wales* and the *Perseverance*.

It would appear that the Treweek's old yard was disposed of almost immediately after the establishment of the new yard for, in 1859, the new owner, William Cox Paynter, launched the *Charles Edwin*, a 94 ton wooden schooner built for Dyer & Co, of Amlwch. The new owner, Captain C B Dyer was one of the Cornish agents who had charge of the Mona mine following the death of James Treweek and who may well have had a family connection with Charles Dyer, the shipbuilder of Sunny Corner near Truro. This has not been confirmed however, but the fact that the first ever vessel to leave the latter's yard was the *Florence Vivian*, indicates a link with the Vivians, who it will be recalled, were Lord Uxbridge's partners in the new Mona Mine Company.

Wednesday 26 October, 1859 was the day on which Anglesey experienced one of its worst ever storms, and its worst ever shipwreck, with the loss of the auxiliary clipper *Royal Charter* at Moelfre, some 6 miles along the coast from Amlwch. The vessel was on passage from Melbourne to Liverpool with about 400 passengers aboard, many of whom were gold miners and their families returning home having made their fortunes in the Australian

Paynter's sawmill

goldfields. Departure from Melbourne had been on the 26 August, and the voyage eastward around Cape Horn had been uneventful; and the ship's unbroken record for completing the voyage in under 60 days, seemed to be safe yet again. Despite the worsening weather, many of her passengers took the opportunity of going up on deck as she passed Holyhead, to view Brunel's mighty *Great Eastern* anchored outside the breakwater. As she rounded the northern coastline of Anglesey however, the weather deteriorated, and she was driven on to the rocks at Moelfre with the loss of 387 lives.

The harbourmaster at Amlwch would have been aware of the worsening weather conditions, and there can be little doubt that he would have made every effort to drop the baulks across the harbour entrance, for there were several vessels from which he could press the required number of crew members to man the crab winches. Whether he succeeded or not is not recorded, but one newspaper reported that the waves were so powerful, and running so high as they surged down the harbour, that they demolished a landing stage and a warehouse belonging to the Amlwch Steamship Company, sweeping its entire contents into the sea.

Few if any vessels were left undamaged; those whose moorings had been broken were driven down the harbour with such force that they crashed into an iron bridge at the foot of the inclined plane, lifting it bodily off its abutments and destroying it completely.

Unable to enter the harbour, the brig *Agnes* was left at the mercy of the powerful onshore wind, and was driven relentlessly on to the rocks at its entrance, where two of her crew were drowned. The remainder were saved however, and their rescue was described as being nothing short of miraculous.

Deserving of perhaps more than the two lines afforded it in the local newspaper, was the report of the loss in the same storm, of the Amlwch vessel *Kendal Castle* and of the drowning of Captain William Thomas' brother John.

The same newspaper also recorded in the barest detail, how a vessel which was nearing completion at an unnamed Amlwch shipyard was swept off its blocks by the waves, and completely destroyed. The fact that Cox Paynter's yard faced the open sea at the entrance to the harbour, and had little or no protection from the waves, suggests that the incident occurred there, and not at Treweek's new yard which had the benefit of some protection from northerly seas. The very fact that the Treweek yard launched the *Grace Evans* some time during the same month would appear to support this theory.

Captain William Thomas was quite evidently an astute businessman, who had over the years, gained a great deal financially from his business enterprises; but there is one aspect of his life which is shrouded in mystery, and which concerns his activities during the time of the American Civil War.

One Thomas family legend has it that he was in some unspecified way, personally involved in the war. By way of reward for his contribution he was given a tract of land which subsequently formed part of the Anglo-American oilfield. This it is claimed, was eventually sold for a considerable sum. Although no evidence can be found to substantiate the claim that Captain Thomas visited North America during the conflict, the possibility that he did so cannot be dismissed.

A second, equally colourful account appears in *Enwogion Mon*,[139] which describes how the Captain, having sailed into an American port during the war was pressed into service aboard a warship, a deed for which he was ultimately well rewarded. This second account may well have had some basis in fact, for there is evidence to show that several sailors from Anglesey and the neighbouring County of Caernarfon were pressed into service on board the Confederate warship *Alabama*, when that vessel captured or sank their own ships.

One such man was 'Captain' Sam Roberts of Groeslon, near Caernarfon, who, having emigrated to Australia as a young man, was serving on board a vessel sailing out of Melbourne for Boston, Massachusetts, when it was intercepted by the *Alabama*, and he was captured. On board the warship were another 48 prisoners detained in a similar fashion, who as time went by, were pressed into service as mercenaries, to replace those killed in action. Such was the *Alabama's* success as a raider that Sam Roberts went on to claim that during the thirteen months he served aboard her, he had earned somewhere between £2,000 and £3,000 in prize money. He was unable to collect his entitlement however, for he took the first opportunity to escape when the vessel put into Capetown.

Captain Thomas' name however, does not appear amongst those known to have been aboard the *Alabama* at that time.

The old adage that there is no smoke without fire, suggests that some credibility should be given to the legends that the Captain's fortune was in some way associated with the American Civil War. Bearing in mind the sailor's penchant for spinning yarns however, it is difficult to understand why he chose not to discuss what was undoubtedly a great adventure – unless of course, he had very good reasons for keeping quiet.

Surprising as it may seem that there should have been any association at all between Gwynedd and the *Alabama*, it may come as an even greater surprise to learn that the two were even more closely associated before the warship began her notorious career as an armed raider.

Captain Thomas' business activities meant that he was very familiar with the ports of Liverpool and Holyhead; and he may also have been aware that they were both the focus of international espionage.

The Confederate States realised fairly early on in the conflict that their survival depended greatly on their continued ability to export cotton, for which there was a world-wide demand. Nowhere was this demand greater than in Britain, where the raw material was spun and woven into cheap garments for domestic use, and for exportation to the far corners of the empire. The continuity of trade was therefore of paramount importance to both the producers and the buyers. Over the years a great affinity had developed between the cotton traders on both sides of the Atlantic, and in Lancashire particularly there was a great deal of sympathy for the rebel cause.

In order to frustrate trade between the southern States and the rest of the world President Lincoln ordered in April 1861, a blockade of all southern State ports. As a means of countering this, the Confederate Navy was desperately anxious to procure fast warships of its own, which could be used to run the gauntlet, and harass the enemy on the high seas. To this end several of its serving officers were sent to Britain with the necessary authority to commission new vessels, and to purchase any others which they considered suitable. In pursuit of this policy, Captain James D Bulloch CSN, was sent to Britain later in 1861 to act as the Confederate Naval Commissioner.

Bulloch wasted no time in getting down to his task, and he spent a great deal of time at Holyhead that year, assessing the merits of two steam driven paddle steamers, the *Anglia* and the *Scotia*, which were based there. The two vessels, together with the *Hibernia*, had been bought by a subsidiary of the Chester & Holyhead Railway Company in 1847, in anticipation of winning a government contract to carry mail between Holyhead and the Irish port of Kingstown (Dun Laoghaire). In 1850 however, the mail contract was unexpectedly placed with the City of Dublin Steam Packet Company, much to the consternation of the railway company and its subsidiary and the two vessels became surplus to their requirements. As a result of Bulloch's covert negotiations, the *Anglia* and the *Scotia* were both sold to the Confederate States Navy, in which service they had somewhat lacklustre careers.

In view of Britain's neutrality however, it was not possible for Bulloch to purchase warships openly, and he had to resort to the subterfuge of ordering unarmed ships on the pretext that they were required for commercial purposes. The design of these vessels was based on those approved by the Admiralty for the Royal Navy, and it is highly unlikely that anyone with an intimate knowledge of warships would have been fooled for one moment by the pretence.

Across the Mersey from Bulloch's office in Liverpool was the shipbuilding yard of Laird Brothers, and it was with this firm that he placed an order for a specially designed barque rigged steamer, known initially as the 290, her yard number. It would appear that Bulloch associated himself quite openly with the vessel as she was being built, and it is not surprising therefore to learn that the United States Ambassador in London, advised of the situation in Liverpool by his Consul there, protested to the British Government about the evident violation of its declared neutrality. It is quite apparent that the British Government was most unwilling to interfere with the building of the vessel, presumably arguing that the US Government was unable to prove that the vessel was indeed intended for the Confederate Navy; and no doubt suggesting that if that proved to be the case, it would not prove difficult for the US Navy to arrest the unarmed vessel once she was outside British territorial waters.

Still known only by her yard number, the 290 was launched on 15 May, 1862, much to the consternation of the US Ambassador in London. Her fitting out was carried out with great haste, and by the 29 July, she was ready for her first sea trials. Bulloch was well aware of the moves to prevent the 290 from ever reaching her destination, and he devised a brilliantly simple ruse that was to allow the vessel to escape, albeit at enormous cost to the British Government.

Well aware of the pro-Confederate sentiments on Merseyside, Bulloch, with a great deal of prior publicity, invited local businessmen and their wives to join him on board the 290 for a cruise in Liverpool Bay, which was ostensibly to be a proving voyage for the new vessel. As a supposed precaution against engine failure however, Bulloch had arranged for the 290 to be accompanied by a steam tug, the *Hercules*, which was to tow the new ship back to Birkenhead in the event of her engines failing. During the late evening however the *Hercules* returned to Liverpool laden with the guests who had sailed on the 290 that very morning. As Bulloch had correctly anticipated, arrangements had been made to seize her when she returned.

Amongst the guests who sailed back on the *Hercules* was the Confederate Commissioner, who had been given a list of all the stores necessary to equip the 290 for her escape, together with the name and address of the person whose task it had been to recruit sufficient men to complete the ship's complement. These were to be taken to join their vessel at Moelfre on the following day.

The American Ambassador, who had been informed of the ruse by his Liverpool Consul, wasted no time in arranging for a warship, the USS *Tuscarora*, which had just put into Southampton, to sail westwards immediately in order to intercept and detain the 290. According to the captain of the *Hercules*, the 290, which had by then be named the *Enrica*, had undergone speedy but comprehensive sea trials off Amlwch. As soon as he was satisfied with the vessel's performance and seaworthiness, her British commander, Captain Butcher, anchored his new vessel in Moelfre Bay, where she underwent final checks.

In a later account of his part in the escape of the *Enrica*, Captain Butcher described how in the first instance he had been approached by a friend acting on behalf of a foreign government, with a view to taking temporary command of the new vessel. If he was agreeable to the proposal a suitable crew would be procured before sailing to an undisclosed destination. In return he was offered, in his own words, "very liberal remuneration" as well as a commission in that government's navy, which he refused.

Once the *Enrica* was safely anchored off Moelfre, all the remaining checks were carried out, and when they were complete the vessel slipped away northwards on 31 July. In anticipation of intercepting the *Enrica*, the *Tuscarora* had sailed immediately for Queenstown (Cobh), and having found nothing there proceeded northwards, still searching for her quarry, until she arrived off Amlwch on 1 August, bound for Moelfre. In the meantime Captain Butcher had taken his vessel around the north coast of Ireland, and was then sailing down its west coast towards the Azores, where it was to rendezvous with a supply ship, the CSS *Aggripa*. There it took on board coal, ammunition and clothing for its crew, and it was there also that the vessel took on its new identity as the CSS *Alabama*.

In a career that was to last only 666 days, the warship sank or captured no fewer than 64 ships, amongst which number was the vessel on which `Captain' Sam Roberts was serving when he was captured.

Her success made the *Alabama* the most feared, and without doubt, the most successful raider of the American Civil War; a fact that was reflected in the $15,500,000 compensation that had to be paid by Britain to the US Government, for failure to use diligence in the performance of its neutral obligations.

Might Captain Thomas have been the mysterious man who recruited the *Enrica's* crew, and was it perhaps nothing more than a coincidence that her crew embarked, and her sea trials arranged, off the coast of Anglesey? The answers may never be known, but if he had indeed played a part in the matter, it would have been prudent for him to have kept the fact a closely guarded secret, in the light of the resulting litigation and financial cost to the British Government.

In 1859, the same year that saw the launch of the *Clara Jane* and the *Grace Evans* from Treweek's new yard, William Cox Paynter his successor in the old yard, launched his first vessel, the *Charles Edwin*, a 94 ton wooden schooner. Cox Paynter was clearly more concerned with ship repairing than with shipbuilding for up until his death in 1884, the yard had built only four other vessels, all of which were schooners. The second and the third, the 92 ton *Mary Fanny* and the 123 ton *Jane Gray* were launched in 1862 and 1865 respectively; to be followed by the 48 ton *Charles,* and the 97 ton *Pary's Lodge*.[140]

Following William Cox Paynter's death, the yard continued to trade under its original name, but under the directorship of Captain Thomas Morgan, an Amlwch man. It would appear that he also was firmly committed to the ship repairing trade, for over a period of 14 years the yard went on to build only three other vessels, all of which were 3 masted schooners: the 118 ton *Camborne*, the 130 ton *Ailsie*, and the 142 ton *Donald & Doris*.

The *Camborne*, built in 1884, described as being "of graceful shape and good qualities", was owned and managed by the Cox Paynter Company up until the First World War. Crewed almost invariably by Amlwch men, she sailed mainly in the home trade, but made some voyages to Germany and North Africa. After the war she passed to Swansea owners, who in 1920 sold her to a colliery company whose intention was to use her to export anthracite products to northern France. She fared badly in that trade, mainly because of the unreliability of a diesel engine with which she had been fitted and, in 1920 she was laid up before being sold yet again. Under her new owner, Captain Shaw, she arrived at the port of Limerick at the time of the Irish troubles in 1922, and because she was the only powered vessel in the port she was pressed into service by the government for use as a troop carrier. The *Camborne's* seaworthiness was confirmed in 1936, when 52 years old, she weathered a particularly bad storm whilst on passage from Gloucester to Tralee. During the storm in which the *Nellie Fleming*, another three masted topsail schooner disappeared without trace, the wind was said to have gusted up to 108 miles an hour, and the *Camborne* was blown so far off course into the Atlantic, that it took her Master no fewer than four days to make landfall once the wind had abated.

The *Ailsie*, a typical coaster, was crewed by 5 men: her master, mate, two able bodied seamen and a cook. Her master, Captain John Hughes was from Llanfairfechan, and her crew members were for the most part drawn from the counties of Caernarfonshire and Anglesey. During her first year's operation she was in almost constant employment, and her varied cargoes included slates from Port Dinorwic to Germany, Portland stone to London, oilcake from the Elbe port of Harburg to Great Yarmouth, firebricks from Sunderland to London and herring from Lowestoft to Dublin.

The *Donald & Doris* was named after the children of W I Barratt, managing director of the Hodbarrow Mining Company of Millom in Cumberland. The relationship between the ports of Amlwch and Millom is discussed in a later chapter, but the significance as it relates to the *Donald & Doris*, is that Thomas Morgan her builder was the brother of Captain William Morgan, the harbourmaster at Millom.

The *Donald & Doris* was, over the years, to prove to be a most successful vessel, regularly paying good dividends to her owners, but her career almost came to an end in 1902 when having taken shelter in Belfast Lough she dragged her anchors, and was driven ashore. Her crew of 5 were rescued by the Carrickfergus lifeboat, and there were fears that the abandoned vessel would become a total wreck. She withstood the battering however, and the cargo of pitch she was carrying from Ayr to Swansea was taken off, allowing her to be refloated. Her recovery and subsequent repair in a Belfast dry dock cost her owners no less than £512, and her dividend that year amounted to no more than 5 shillings a share. Despite this, some doubt had been expressed regarding the strength of her hull, but in a letter to Basil Greenhill, Captain W J Slade had this to say of the schooner:

> I owned no part of the *Donald & Doris* but if my cousin who was Master and part owner of her could read about her alleged weakness I am sure he would rise from his grave. During the years my family owned her she never had a caulking iron put in her butts or seams. I was talking to a man who was Master of her during the War before she was taken over by the Admiralty. He said she was a very strong vessel and never made any water. To say the *Donald & Doris* was weak only proves to me that the man responsible for this knew nothing about the ship.

The war referred to was the Second World War, when the vessel was 42 years old.

Chapter 12
Captain William Thomas

Trevor Morgan, the Cumbrian maritime historian, has described the association between the ports of Amlwch and Millom, in what is now Cumbria, as the 'Cumberland Connection'.

This affiliation began when iron ore was discovered at a site on the Duddon estuary, close to Hodbarrow Point. The discovery was successfully exploited by Nathaniel Caine, a Liverpool metal merchant, and John Barratt, a Cornishman with extensive mining experience.[141] By a strange coincidence, Barratt came from the same Cornish parish of Gwennap, as did James Treweek, and it was he and his family who contributed the expertise, as well as much of the money to make a success of the venture. Up to that time, there had been little incentive for the railway companies to serve the area, and in the absence of a rail link, Nathaniel Caine had no option but to carry the ore to the smelters by sea. This made economic sense, for much of it was destined for the long established iron smelters located on the North and South Wales coalfields; and the remainder to stockpiles on Merseyside and Deeside, from where it was transported by rail to smelters in the Midlands.

Under normal circumstances, shipowners and captains alike, were more than happy to pick up freight wherever they could, if the price was right. Three factors made the Duddon trade an unattractive proposition however. The first was the dangerous nature of the Duddon estuary itself, which with its constantly shifting sand banks, made every passage along it a most risky undertaking. Having successfully negotiated the channel, the captain was then faced with harbour facilities which were woefully inadequate; leading inevitably to long delays. This meant that the vessels were less profitably employed than they might have been elsewhere. The third factor was the nature of the iron ore itself, which caused great damage to vessels not specifically designed to carry it.

In an effort to persuade owners to enter the Duddon iron trade, Nathaniel Caine travelled to Liverpool in 1867, and then to several of the small ports along the North Wales coast, where many of the shipowners in the Irish Sea trade lived. One such owner was Captain Thomas who, during their meeting, formally agreed to supply vessels to the trade. This was later confirmed when he wrote to Caine to tell him that he had already bought two vessels specifically for that purpose. There can be little doubt that the Captain agreed only on condition that he was guaranteed a certain annual tonnage of freight, at a rate which reflected the risk he was taking. In view of the delays then being suffered at Duddon he would also have negotiated demurrage, to compensate him for any delays outside his control.

By 1869, the congestion at the port had become such that Caine had to convince his fellow directors of the need to appoint a harbourmaster to direct its operation. The man appointed to the post in May of that year, was Captain William Morgan of Amlwch, and there is reason to believe that Caine had first sought Captain Thomas' advice before making the appointment.

Captain William Thomas.
[Thomas Family Archive]

William Thomas' shipping interests were in no way confined to the coastal trade, for in 1869, he and two others, who were also by coincidence both named William Thomas, bought shares in the 680 ton, fully rigged ship *William Melhuish*. The popular account that the vessel made her owners a profit on her first voyage equal to five times her original cost, may be apocryphal, but there can be little doubt that she yielded sufficient to enable at least two of her owners to expand their shipping interests quite considerably.

The second William Thomas, born in the Anglesey parish of Llanrhuddlad, distinguished himself by becoming a pupil-teacher in his village school at the age of 13, before sailing to Liverpool at the age of 19 to seek his fortune. There he found employment as a clerk in a shipping office, and by the age of 23 he had gained sufficient experience and confidence to set himself up as a ship insurance broker and manager. In his masterly work, *Ships & Seamen of Anglesey*, Aled Eames describes how the two men first met in a Welsh Calvinistic Methodist chapel in Liverpool where the broker was a deacon. It is evident that both had a great deal more in common than their name and the county of their birth however, for both went on to profit from extensive maritime interests, much of it in joint enterprises.

A Curious Place

The third namesake, yet another islander from the village of Newborough, took command of the *William Melhuish* and, however good the land-based management of the vessel may have been, it must be true to say that her great profitability was in no small measure directly attributable to him.

Captain William Thomas of Amlwch, further diversified his shipping interests in 1869, by building the 99 ton wooden schooner *Welsh Girl*. Where exactly the vessel was built at the port is a matter for conjecture, as available evidence suggests that he had no yard of his own at that time.

By 1870, a shortage of vessels was again creating a problem for the Hodbarrow mine, which Caine and some of his fellow directors endeavoured to solve by forming the Duddon Shipping Association. The Association appointed Captain William Morgan, the harbourmaster, and William Postlethwaite, an experienced ship manager - who was then Secretary to the Hodbarrow mine company, as managers. As with the Amlwch Shipping Company, the venture was financially independent of the mine itself, but there can be little doubt that both enterprises benefited by being given preferential treatment when it came to freight and loading.

The number of vessels using the port was quite considerable, and as they suffered a great deal of wear and tear due to the nature of the iron ore they carried, the need for ship repairing facilities became obvious. Captain Thomas, always with a keen eye for business, saw potential for profit in the situation, and with the help of the Hodbarrow mineowners, he was able to establish a shipbuilding and repair yard on the sandy shoreline adjacent to an area of land known as Crab Marsh. One of the first references to the new yard is contained in a letter written by Captain Thomas to Nathaniel Caine on 3 October, 1870, in which he says:

> When the gridiron will be completed and the smithy completed I shall be ready to build any size of vessel that I may get orders for. I shall be very happy to submit you a model for a schooner suitable for the Bristol Channel trade and to draw a light draft with a cargo of about 150 to 160 tons and to sail without ballast. Such vessel will answer for the Bristol Channel or Mersey or Dee as the wind blow and (I) can build her as cheap as any one and will if required take a share in her myself as this plan will establish Duddon. The terms on which I shall build you a schooner it depend on what class vessel you required. If I was to suggest to you it would be a suitable vessel it will be as follows. Length of keel 75ft, 20ft beam, by about 8 to 9ft hold. The frame to be English Oak with large dimensions for heavy trade. Planking, bottom A(merican) Elm, Bilge to Wales Pitch Pine and binding strakes Hardwood E(nglish) Oak or Teak, Ceiling Hackmatack or Red Pine. Fit out to be as customary and to class 8 years that the vessels they generally built in that neighbourhood. I could build a vessel to carry 150 tons, 8 year class with extra strong frame completed for sea for £1,700 as can agree for and will guarantee the vessel to be a first rate one entirely for the trade as Capt. Morgan can look after the building of her.

The success of Captain Thomas' venture depended almost entirely upon his selection of a yard foreman, who was not only skilful, but also completely reliable. For such a vitally important position one might have expected the Captain to have appointed a well proven man of many years standing, but having himself proved his abilities at an early age, he chose instead to select a comparatively young man for the job.

The man he appointed was Hugh Jones, a 30 year old, unmarried ship's carpenter from Amlwch. He had clearly impressed Captain Thomas with both his skill and his character, and it is very likely therefore that he had been previously employed by the Captain.

Three other young men, all from Amlwch, accompanied Hugh Jones to Duddon, the youngest being his 14 year old brother Miciah, an apprentice ship's carpenter. The two remaining members of the small party were 21 year old ship's carpenter, John Morris, and Hugh Owens, a 19 year old blacksmith. Their address at Millom, as Duddon later became known, was given simply as Crab Marsh, and it is believed that their first home was in an old hulk cast up on the sand dunes, which was known to have been occupied by several of the later yard workers.

Captain Thomas's coasting activities continued to expand, and according to the Amlwch Harbourmaster's log book for 1870, no fewer than 15 different vessels belonging to him made a total number of 32 visits to the port during that year. Of these, 14 brought in coal from the Lancashire and Welsh coalfields, one carried phosphate from Bristol, and another brought in rock-salt from Liverpool. The rock-salt may well have been intended for Hill's Chemical Works, but it could also have been used to pack between the timbers of vessels under construction to prevent the wood from rotting. Many of his other vessels came in carrying only ballast and it is very likely that these came to be repaired, for the Captain made it a point to oversee the repair of all damage sustained by his own ships. In those cases where there was no other option but to have the damaged vessel made seaworthy elsewhere, he insisted that only the bare minimum should be done to allow the master to bring his craft back to Amlwch safely, where permanent repairs could be carried out under his direct supervision.

Of the outward bound voyages, 40 were destined for Duddon, which gives a good indication of his commitment to, and involvement in the iron ore trade.

Despite having established a yard at Millom, the Captain was also keen to further expand his activities at Amlwch by building more ships there. The confined nature of the port was such that there was little or no private land available for expansion, but ever resourceful, he sought the assistance of the Harbour Trustees, for the minutes of their meeting held on the 25 July 1870 record:

> Mr William Thomas, Shipbuilder having made application to be allowed to lay and build a vessel at the upper end of the Harbour to the extent of 100 feet for her keel. - Ordered that permission be given him on payment of two Guineas to the Trust, for the use of such place, he agreeing to pay such sum and to take every risk upon himself, and not place any incumbrance (sic) or cause any obstruction to the Harbour, and not to occupy such room longer than 18 months from this date, otherwise a payment of 2 Guineas will be enforced for every month beyond that time.

The subject of the application turned out to be the 79 ton schooner *Lewis & Mary*, launched on 2 June 1870, which was named in honour of the eldest of the Captain's children. It would seem that the vessel was launched fully rigged, for within six days she sailed on her maiden voyage to Runcorn with a cargo of ochre from Dyffryn Adda. Two days before Christmas she returned to Amlwch with a full load of phosphate from Bristol for Hills Chemical Works, and left on 18 January 1871, in ballast for Duddon. During the first four years of her life the vessel returned to her home port eight times, more often than not with coal or culm from South Wales; on six of those occasions she returned to Duddon in ballast. On 5 September 1874 however, she returned in ballast from Dublin, and remained at Amlwch until 23 October, where she probably underwent repairs. On that date, her Master and part owner, Edward Pritchard sailed with a cargo of sulphur to Antwerp, but the schooner's return voyage to Greenock was to be her last, for she and her crew were never heard of again. The captain and at least two members of his crew of three were Amlwch men – one of whom it is thought, was the captain's son.

Within four months of making his offer to build Nathaniel Caine a vessel, Thomas received a letter from William Postlethwaite in which he wrote:

> I now beg to hand you specifications for a new schooner which we offer you to build at the rate of 12 5 0 (Twelve Pounds five shillings) per ton Builders Measurement. We would give you two to build at that price, one to be built at Amlwch in 6 months, and one at Duddon in 12 months from time of signing agreement. If you agree to it please make out agreement, sign and send it to me and we will send you ours as well.

In due course William Thomas received a further letter from Postlethwaite stating that, "We accept your offer for two vessels. I will attend to agreement in a day or two. This is just to say you may commence at once".

On the basis of this letter, William Thomas went ahead with the necessary arrangements at both Amlwch and Millom. There is nothing in the minutes of the Amlwch Harbour Trustees meetings to suggest that he repeated his request to be allowed to build another vessel at the upper end of the harbour, but in May 1871, the Trust denied him permission "to place a strong gate near the mouth of the cove at the upper end of the harbour for the purpose of constructing a Graving Dock".

Two things can be deduced from this. First, that Postlethwaite's Amlwch vessel was built somewhere other than at the upper end of the harbour, as was the *Lewis & Mary*, and secondly, that William Thomas had either begun to trade as a ship repairer or was particularly anxious to do so. In any case work went on apace with the building of the 119 ton schooner *Holy Wath* [142] at Amlwch, and the 113 ton, two masted, schooner *Nellie Bywater* at the Millom yard.

Under normal circumstances, shipbuilders required what are known as 'stage payments' as the vessel's construction progressed. These instalments, usually three or four in number, were paid when the vessel had reached certain stages in its construction programme, and Captain Thomas' utter dismay can be imagined when, having applied to Postlethwaite for payment, he was told that no formal agreement regarding either of the vessels existed. In desperation, Captain Thomas wrote to his friend Nathaniel Caine, reminding him of all that had transpired:

> You will no doubt remember that I made an agreement with Mr Postlethwaite, on behalf of the Company to build two vessels, one in Amlwch and the other in Duddon, the former having been completed, and I hope to the perfect satisfaction of yourself and the Co. Another one now being built at Duddon is ready for planking according to the specification. Had I thought for a moment that there would be any dispute about her or refusal - I would not have gone to such expense with her for I cannot make my money out of her in the market as she is built expressly for your trade with so much more strength than would be required for a vessel of ordinary dimensions. I beg to enclose for your inspection and return, 3 letters from Mr Postlethwaite to me on the subject, (on behalf of the Company), and I shall be glad to hear from you at your very earliest convenience, for if you will not take the vessel I shall indeed be greatly disappointed, and the loss to me will be very great. But I should hope you would kindly contribute toward it and not suffer me to be the loser. But I cannot understand the reason why you don't take her after agreeing to do so. However I hope this will be settled to our mutual satisfaction when you move in the matter for you will no doubt remember having spoken to me yourself about this identical vessel, cautioning me against putting any inferior timber in her &c &c

Some illuminating facets of William Thomas' character are revealed by his letter, the first being his self restraint in not threatening any form of legal action against the Hodbarrow company, which he would clearly have been fully justified in doing, choosing instead to appeal to his friend's code of honour. The fact that he sent Caine the three letters he had received from Postlethwaite, the only evidence he had of an agreement between them, might suggest that he was totally naive regarding such matters, but that was clearly not the case and his action must be seen as an act of faith in Caine's integrity.

His confidence was fully justified, and in due course the agreement was honoured. Instead of following what could have been a bitter course of litigation, the parties went on to enjoy a harmonious and mutually profitable association over many years.

The management of the new Millom shipyard was entrusted to Captain Thomas' son, John. Although Postlethwaite was not at first a partner in the business, he later acquired a one-third holding in the venture, which might account for the fact that the company was not taken to task for failing to complete its first vessel within the stipulated 12 months. The *Nellie Bywater* was eventually christened on 20 December 1873, by Mary Morgan, the Harbourmaster's wife. This was done to the sound of the town band and the clamour of the hundreds of townspeople who had turned out to witness the event. The customary dinner given to mark the occasion, was by all accounts a very happy, traditional Welsh evening, during which a poem written in honour of the vessel was recited.

For some reason, Captain Thomas was absent from the celebrations, and the company was represented by William Postlethwaite who replied to the criticism of the time taken to build the vessel by claiming that she was: "only a sideshow on which the men worked when they had little else to do". By that, it is evident that the yard had been concentrating on the more lucrative repair side of the business, to the exclusion of shipbuilding. What is significant however is that he challenged anyone to deny that the vessel was all that any demanding shipmaster could desire.

Another link with Amlwch was forged when Richard Morgan of Amlwch was appointed the *Nellie Bywater's* first Master, and who remained with her until April 1878, when yet another Amlwch man, Captain Solomon Ellis, took over command. The vessel traded mainly in home waters, carrying coal and iron ore to and from Duddon, and over the years she proved to be a most profitable vessel to her owners. She survived the First World War, and was subsequently bought by the McKibbin family of Northern Ireland. During the Second World War she was requisitioned by the Admiralty, under whose control she became a supply and refuelling vessel. When the schooner came off charter at the end of the war she was refitted and bought by Captain Richard England, whose apprenticeship had been served 'before the mast' in schooners. In his book *Schoonerman*, he describes how, before buying the 73 year old vessel, he examined her in a Belfast dry dock, where

> . . . I spent several hours down in the dry dock, thoroughly examining the bottom of the schooner, which was bone dry and scraped to the bare wood. Keel, garboards and skin planking were in excellent condition and all she needed was the renewal of a few trunnels and a bit of recaulking and hardening up of seams. I was amazed at the skill of her builders in constructing such a fine run to the schooner with scarcely any stealers [143] and it was obvious she was the work of superb craftsmen.

Hugh Jones and his colleagues could not have wished for a better epitaph.

Under Captain England's command the *Nellie Bywater* appeared in several films, the most famous being *The Elusive Pimpernel*, but when this and other work became scarce,

A Curious Place

Captain England decided to sail her to the West Indies where he hoped to find sufficient employment, trading between the islands, to maintain both his family and his vessel. On 28 December 1951, whilst bound for St Lucia with 14 people aboard, the vessel encountered a storm off the south Devon coast, which is probably best remembered for the loss of the 6,700 ton vessel *Flying Enterprise*, commanded by Captain Kurt Carlsen. Conditions were atrocious, with recorded wind speeds of 97 miles an hour, and one newspaper reported that the 78 year old vessel was blown off course several times before her fore topmast and topsail yard were carried away, and her sails torn to shreds by the wind.

Although at least one member of the crew had been on the pumps for over 30 hours, the vessel gradually sank lower in the water, and a tow line was put aboard her by the tanker *British Birch*. Captain England knew that, in her sinking condition, with 30 foot high waves breaking over her, she could not take the strain of a tow, and the line was reluctantly severed. The *Nellie Bywater* immediately heeled over, and the master of the tug *Careful*, which was standing by, reported seeing those on board walk over the side into the sea as she finally sank. The tragic incident cost the lives of two of those on board, the Captain's 17 year old daughter Josephine, and the ship's carpenter.

Chapter 13
Iard Newydd - The New Yard

As Captain Thomas' business affairs gathered momentum, Nicholas Treweek's interest in his new shipyard at Amlwch was ebbing and, following the launch of the *Perseverance* in 1866, he took no further interest in shipbuilding. This it is thought, was precipitated by his continuing ill health, but, for whatever, he finally decided to retire, and in May 1872, Captain William Thomas was pleased

> . . . to inform his Friends and the Public generally, that he has lately purchased Mr NICHOLAS TREWEEK'S Extensive and Commodious SHIP-BUILDING YARD and DRY DOCK, and that he is now in a position to execute any work entrusted to his care, with the greatest promptitude, and upon the most reasonable terms. He employs a most efficient staff of Workmen, including Carpenters, Joiners, Smiths, Sailmakers, Blockmakers and others. He also begs to intimate that he keeps all sorts of SHIP CHANDLERY STORES, &c, and has constantly on hand a Large Stock of BUILDING MATERIALS; such as Boards, Bricks, Chimney Tops, Laths, Nails (in great variety), Ridge and other Tiles, Slabs, Slates, Timber, &c, &c. W T begs to state that his Ship Building Yards are very conveniently situated, and are some of the most extensive in the Principality. He has also a large Grid Iron Yard at Duddon in Cumberland.

It should be noted that Captain Thomas refers to his ownership of more than one yard in the Principality. There is no evidence to suggest that he owned yards other than those at Amlwch and Duddon, and it must therefore be taken to mean that he owned more than one at Amlwch. In that case, he must already have owned a shipyard at the port when he bought Iard Newydd from Nicholas Treweek, and it is probably true to say that he was the owner of that yard in 1871, when he agreed to build the *Holy Wath* for the Duddon company. The remains of two slipways are evident on the western side of the harbour and, as the more northerly of the two is known to have belonged to William Cox Paynter, it must surely follow that the other was the one belonging to William Thomas.

The sight of two vessels nearing completion on the western side of the harbour must have gladdened the eye of all those taking an after dinner stroll along Pencei (Upper Quay Street) on Christmas Day 1871. From their vantage point on the opposite side of the harbour, overlooking the two shipyards, they would have seen the schooner *Charles*, rigging almost complete, resting on blocks, with her newly painted hull ringed about with supporting timber props. The slipway down which she would glide on her launching day a week later, would have been almost finished and the yard would have looked a great deal tidier than it had been for many a month.

A little further to the south, a much larger vessel was taking shape in Captain Thomas's yard. Half way to being completed, the hull's massive oak frames, made purposely large to suit the very demanding iron ore trade, conveyed a clear indication of her innate strength. Her planking would not have been started, but the several ribbands tying her frames together while she was being built, would have given an excellent idea of the *Holy Wath*'s attractive and purposeful lines.

The Watchhouse Pier at Amlwch with a vessel in the slipway of the Thomas Yard in the background. [National Library of Wales]

The town itself would have had little to celebrate however, for the mines were still in decline, and the ore they now produced was but a small fraction of that raised in former years. The copper and ochre ponds were still working however, but the limited employment they provided provided little comfort to the majority of the townspeople. Nevertheless the feeling at the port was one of optimism, with a steady stream of vessels coming and going, and the shipyards working to capacity. By this time William Thomas had largely transferred his shipbuilding activities to the new yard, but there is evidence to suggest that he continued to make use of the old premises as a builders' yard.

Well satisfied with the *Holy Wath*, Postlethwaite and his associates placed an order with the Captain for a 230 ton wooden barquentine, the largest vessel to be built at Amlwch up to that time. The *Cumberland Lassie*, as the vessel turned out to be, was an elegant three masted ship with a square stern and she remained under Postlethwaite's control for 16 years, during which time she paid occasional visits to the port. Following her sale she was, in common with many other barquentines at that time, re-rigged as a schooner, and for many years she served as a collier plying between the north east of England and Dover, where she became one of the best known of the Kent colliers. The vessel met her end at 7.14 on the morning of 16 January 1918, when on a voyage from Gravesend with a cargo of burnt ore, she ran aground 1 mile south of the Martello Tower, at Aldeborough, Suffolk. Her Master and one lad were drowned.

Pilot vessels belonging to the Liverpool Pilotage Service made regular use of Amlwch when they needed to be repaired or to have their bottoms cleaned, and this may have led William Thomas to tender for the building of a new vessel for them. The boat, whose detailed specification and half model have survived, was a schooner rigged vessel of 110 tons, with a keel length of 76 feet, main breadth of 19 feet, and depth of 10 feet. The whole of the vessel's frame was to be of copper fastened English oak, classed 12 years at Lloyds.

The half model, usually built by the shipwright personally, had a very important purpose, for once the design had been agreed with the owners, it was used to determine the actual dimensions of the full sized vessel. As the name implies, a half model represented one half of the ship's hull, cut along its centre line from stem to stern, and which was usually built of several layers of prime mahogany. The layers, each accurately planed to a predetermined thickness, were normally held together by dowels or screws in such a way that the whole model could be easily taken apart. At intervals corresponding to the spacing of the vessel's frames the shipwright drew fine pencil lines perpendicular to the keel, which he would use to calculate the final size of the frames. In the case of William Thomas's pilot boat, each of the model's laminations was made exactly $^1/_2$ inch thick, which correspond to a lift of 1 foot in the height of the full sized vessel. When the model was taken apart, the width of the hull at each frame position was measured and multiplied by 24, to determine the corresponding full size offset from the vessel's centre line. This was done for each lamination at every frame station, and from the resulting multiplications the shape of each full sized frame was determined, and passed on to the sawyers in the form of a template.

It is evident from the specification that Captain Thomas had previously inspected other vessels already in service, for he offered features similar to those they possessed. The patent water closet, for example, was to be on the deck, as it was on vessel No 2 (*Leader*); the dining cabin and its tables were to be similar to those in No 7 (*Lancashire Witch*); the store room cupboards and aft gratings were comparable to those provided for vessel No 8 (*Pride of Liverpool*). This is hardly surprising, for pilot vessels were designed with a single purpose in mind, and it is generally true to say that those serving any one particular port

One of the best known of the Kent colliers, *Cumberland Lassie* photographed at Folkestone.

were, because of the conditions under which they operated, very similar to each other both in construction and appearance.

The almost vertical stem, and sharp clean lines of William Thomas's vessel were designed for speed, and the shape of the hull permitted the pilot vessel to heave to at sea, with some degree of comfort for the pilots whilst they awaited the arrival of their charges.

The materials used to build the vessel were of the highest order, and all the fittings were of the finest quality. The schooner had seven sleeping rooms, each accommodating two men, and the cooking and messing facilities could cater for no fewer than 30 men in a high degree of comfort.

The agreed price of £2,600 for the vessel had to be paid in four equal instalments: the first when the keel was laid, the second when the vessel was in frame, and the third when the deck was laid. The final instalment was to be paid when the vessel was complete and ready for sea, which was to be no later than November: in default of which the builder forfeited £100.

For some reason the *Mersey* (officially known as Liverpool Pilot Vessel No 11) was not launched until 6 April 1875, and the Amlwch Harbourmaster's log records the fact that she did not come out of dry dock until 8 May. Another entry for the same day records that the Harbourmaster sent Captain Thomas a note, reprimanding him for allowing rubbish from the yard to accumulate at the mouth of the harbour.

In common with her Liverpool contemporaries, the *Mersey* was a particularly attractive vessel, and she had the added distinction of being the largest sailing vessel ever built for that service. The ever increasing numbers of steam vessels then coming into service added greatly to the natural hazards to which sailing vessels had always been subjected and, by the very nature of their work, pilot vessels were more at risk than others and the *Mersey's* working life was short but eventful, for on 12 October 1877 she was run down by the steamship *Menelaus*, and sunk. The *Mersey* was successfully raised shortly thereafter, and following complete refurbishment she returned to her duties as No 3 boat. On the night of 2 December 1885, whilst on duty some 2 miles south-west of the Bar Light Vessel, she was run down and sunk by the steamer *Landana*. Her Master losing his life in the accident.

On 11 April 1875, Captain Thomas submitted to the Queensland Government Agent, his tender for the building of a pilot vessel for the rapidly developing port of Brisbane. As might have been expected, the vessel he proposed was based on the very same model as the *Mersey*. It is evident that the tender was seriously considered, for 9 months later the Brisbane Port Office sent back a list of alterations which had to be incorporated into her specification. These were matters of general building detail, but the yard had overlooked the fact that the vessel was destined to work in a tropical climate and, for that reason, Captain Thomas was asked to provide better ventilation below deck and to do away with all dividing bulkheads between the sleeping berths. More to the point perhaps, was the request to delete the cabin stove from the specification! Sadly for the Captain, the order went to the Trethowan yard of Little Falmouth, whose vessel, the *Governor Cairns*, arrived in Brisbane on 8 May 1877 to take up her duties.

In 1876, the Amlwch yard turned out two further vessels: the 224 ton, 3 masted schooner *Baron Hill* and the smaller, 99 ton schooner *Lady Neave*. The first of these was built for William Roberts, who almost immediately sold her to William Postlethwaite, accepting the smaller schooner *Elizabeth* in part exchange. On a voyage from Flint to Newcastle with a cargo of salt cake, the *Baron Hill* grounded in the Dee estuary, and took in water. Two days later, on 28 March 1898 the local Lloyds agent reported that the vessel had by then become a total wreck and, was almost completely covered with sand.

The *Lady Neave*, crewed mainly by Amlwch men under the command of Captain Isaac Jones, had a somewhat longer life, and was the epitome of a coastal schooner. She paid her owners good dividends under Thomas management, and following a 35 year life spent in a most demanding trade, her end came when she collided with another vessel, and sank some 30 miles north of South Stack.

On 9 May 1877 the Liverpool & Great Western Steam Ship Company's 400 feet long, 4,332 ton iron vessel, the *Dakota*, sailed out of Liverpool, bound for New York. On board the liner there were only 218 passengers, despite the fact that she had accommodation for over five times that number, and in her holds were 2,000 tons of general cargo, including mail. She, and her sister ship the *Montana*, were built by Palmers of Jarrow, and it was intended that the vessels should uphold the company's boast of operating the fastest transatlantic liners. Launched in 1875, both ships incorporated the latest in boiler and engine technology, which, as it turned out, was a little too ambitious, for both vessels proved to be dismal failures. Within a short time of their launching, their boilers had to be replaced by others of more conventional design; and it was found that their coal consumption far exceeded expectations.

It was about 10 o'clock at night when the *Dakota* arrived off Amlwch, and the Officer of the Watch who was standing on the open bridge, realised that the vessel was sailing a bit too close to land. He immediately gave an order to the helmsman to turn her away to starboard, in order to take her further out to sea. To his great dismay the huge vessel turned the opposite way, towards the shore, and he was forced to repeat his order for port helm. The Captain who was on deck, realising that something was amiss, raced back to the bridge where he ordered the engines to be run full astern. His action was too late to save the vessel however, and her bow reared up as she struck the rocks of Trwyn Costog, some 700 yards to the west of the entrance to Amlwch Port. The vessel's distress rockets soon brought the Bull Bay lifeboat to the scene and it was able to ferry all of the passengers ashore. The fact that the *Dakota* was firmly aground made it possible to recover the mail, as well as the greater part of her cargo.

An entry in Captain Thomas's cash ledger for 17 May 1877 records a payment of £675 made to Messrs C W Kellock & Co, which relates to the *Dakota*. There are no additional details which would throw light on the matter, but there can be little doubt that W C Kellock, who still are shipbrokers in Liverpool, had been engaged to dispose of the wreck, and that Captain Thomas had bought part of it. How much he salvaged is not known, but it would appear that the greater part of the hull was intact when the vessel eventually slipped back off the rocks, and sank in 75 feet of water.

At the subsequent Court of Enquiry, three of the ship's Quartermasters claimed that the vessel, for some unexplained reason, simply refused to turn to starboard. The Court however chose to believe that the helmsman on duty had in fact turned the wheel in the opposite way to that intended by the Officer of the Watch. The Court also dismissed the evidence of the three remaining Quartermasters, in the belief that they were covering up the truth by way of helping their colleague, the duty helmsman.

One possible explanation for the bizarre accident, was the then custom of issuing opposite helm commands, a throwback to the days of tiller steering, which could, but should not, have confused the helmsman. The practice of issuing such commands was finally discontinued in 1934.

The irony of the story is that three years later, on 14 March 1880, the *Dakota's* sister ship, the *Montana*, was also lost off Anglesey, almost within sight of Trwyn Costog.

Steady as the income was from Captain Thomas' many coastal vessels, it is evident that the greatest return on his investments came from the larger foreign going vessels and his expertise in shipping matters enabled him to persuade others to join him in his investments. This was never more evident than when he proposed the purchase of a new iron built barque, to be built by Duxford's highly respected yard in Sunderland. There were a total of 14 investors, including prominent local businessmen such as James Treweek and C H Hills, owner of the Amlwch Chemical Works. The shares varied from as little as $1/64$, held by a Mary Clark of Mold, to Captain Thomas himself, who was the majority shareholder with a $24/64$ holding.

The Master appointed to the *Barbara* was Captain T H Roberts, an Amlwch man, who had previously been Master of the Canadian built *Toronto*, of which Captain Thomas was the managing owner. Although Captain Thomas is reputed to have assisted Captain Roberts in purchasing shares in the new vessel, the latter's name is not amongst those who subscribed, and it is thought that Captain Thomas may have sold part of his holding in the vessel to him, when he assumed command.

After only four years trading the *Barbara* was lost in Freshwater Bay on 22 November

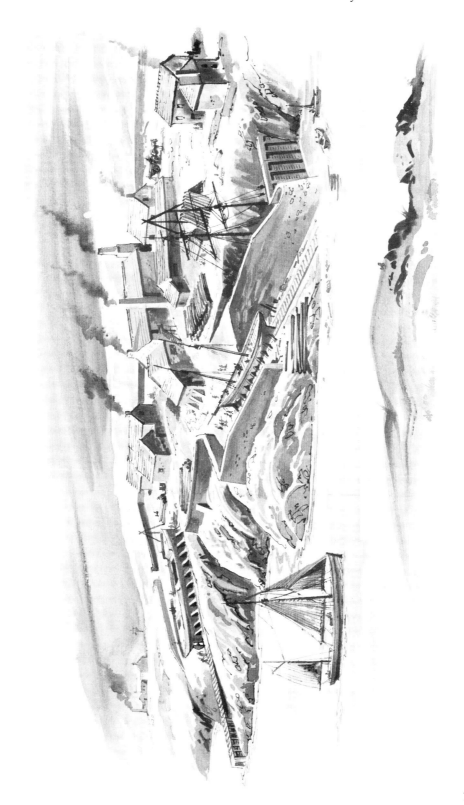

Artist's impression of Iard Newydd with two
vessels on the slips and a third in the dry dock.

1881, an event which led to the threat of litigation between Captain Thomas, her manager, and the Amlwch Mutual Marine Insurance Co Ltd, with whom the vessel was partly insured. It was then the usual practice to insure a vessel with several companies, or clubs as they were known, simultaneously; each company accepting only part of the total risk. The arrangement had obvious safeguards for both the clubs and shipowners alike, but unfortunately it was also open to abuse. Instances had come to light, of unscrupulous owners 'losing' vessels under mysterious circumstances, having first taken the precaution of insuring them in excess of their true value.

The litigation revolved around the refusal of the Amlwch Mutual to honour its cover of the *Barbara*, on the grounds that the total amount of insurance placed with the several clubs exceeded the vessel's worth. This, the directors claimed, was in contravention of their Byelaw 12, which by coincidence, Captain Thomas himself had approved of, as one of those Directors. There was apparently no suggestion of malpractice on the Captain's part, and the disagreement revolved around the annual percentage rate at which the vessel's value had depreciated from new.

The directors were of the opinion that the Captain's estimate of the vessel's worth exceeded their own, and for that reason refused to pay out, offering only to return the premium. To William Thomas' mind, this was grossly unjust, for he believed that his valuation of the *Barbara* was realistic and as a result was quite prepared to take the matter to court. A statement made by Thomas Fanning Evans, a director of the club, which was intended to be used as evidence, remains the only source of information regarding the matter. As the case does not appear to have been reported in the newspapers it would seem therefore that there was an out of court settlement and the disagreement between the parties did not permanently sour their relationship, for the Captain continued to patronize the club.

Three further schooners were to leave the Thomas yard in quick succession: the *Nantglyn* in 1877, followed by the *Nesta* and the *Eilian Hill* in 1878, the latter being commanded by William Thomas's eldest son Captain Lewis Thomas. As the registered tonnages of the three vessels were almost identical, it is probably true to say that they were all built to the same model as that used in the construction of the *Holy Wath*, some five years earlier. This would suggest that the design had proved to be so successful, that it induced others to have their vessels built along the same lines.

The small smack *Glyndwr* was the third vessel to leave the Thomas yard in 1878, and some time before 1883 she was re-rigged as a schooner. In order to do that, the smack would first have been lengthened, thereby giving her a greater carrying capacity. Her additional length and sail carrying capacity meant that she would also have been faster; which combined with her larger holds would have added quite considerably to her value.

On 7 April 1882 the following terse entry appeared in the Amlwch Harbourmaster's log:

> At about 11am the *Noah* was blon [sic] up in the bay by toing [sic] the *Victoria* out. Owen Pritchard, N Peters and E Jones of Holyhead were lost.

The *Noah*, a wooden, 35 ton, steam powered vessel had been jointly owned by Captain Thomas, William Cox Paynter and Thomas Fanning Evans until 1879, when she was sold to Owen Jones of Fagwyr, another local shipowner. She was mainly used to tow sailing vessels in and out of the port, but she was also used extensively in the recovery of cargoes from wrecked vessels.

On the afternoon preceding the accident she had been employed at nearby Cemlyn, on the wreck of the *Welsh Girl* which it will be recalled, was the first vessel to be built as a solo venture by Captain Thomas at Amlwch, some 13 years earlier.

On board the *Noah* was Edward Hughes, a young diver from Holyhead, who had been employed by Jones but a few days earlier to dive on the wreck of the *Welsh Girl*. The weather on the Thursday was such that salvage operations had to be cancelled, and the owner's son Evan, who was also the vessel's Master, had gone ashore at Cemlyn. Before doing so however, he gave Peters, himself a qualified captain, instructions to seek shelter at Cemaes until the weather improved. When he returned to Cemlyn on the following morning, Jones found that the *Noah* had left, and he set off for Cemaes on foot, only to find when he got there, that the *Noah* had sailed for Amlwch. No doubt cursing what he thought to be his bad luck, Jones decided to walk the remaining 5 miles to the port, and it was as he approached the town that he heard of the little vessel's dreadful fate.

In evidence at the subsequent inquest, the owner stated that no one was authorised to tow vessels without his express instructions: but despite that, Peters had agreed to tow the *Victoria*, a sloop which traded regularly between Amlwch and Liverpool, out of the harbour. When the two vessels were abreast of Llam Carw, some 3/4 of a mile out from the port, the tow was released and, while Owen Pritchard, described as being the engine driver, stoked the boiler, Peters turned the *Noah* back towards the harbour. Then,

The *W S Caine* (nearest the camera) and the *Trevor* alongside the pier at Dinmor Quarry, Penmon, Red Wharf Bay. [Gwynedd Archives Service]

Amlwch Port, c1905, clearly showing evidence of it's decline. The figures on the left are standing by the timber baulks which could be positioned across the harbour entrance.

according to witnesses, one of whom was Owen Pritchard's son, and who had himself been aboard the *Noah* some 30 minutes earlier, there was a loud, double explosion. He described how he then saw a cloud of steam, and fragments of wood and cinders flying through the air. Although the mate of the *Victoria* was hit by some of the flying debris, he was not seriously hurt. The bodies of Pritchard and Peters were recovered almost immediately by a rescue boat which put out from the port, but nothing was ever found of Edward Hughes, the young diver who had been married only a few days previously.

During the ensuing inquest held in the Dinorben Hotel, it was disclosed that the *Noah's* boiler was far from new, and had been bought second hand by the vessel's then owner, on the understanding that it had previously only been used in a private yacht. It was later discovered that it had in fact, been extensively used to power a donkey engine on board a large steamer.

The vessel's engine had a more curious history however, for it was revealed that it had begun life as a winch engine on board the *Dakota*, from which it had been salvaged when she ran aground at Amlwch, and there can be little doubt that it was one of the items recovered by Captain Thomas. Under the circumstances the Coroner had no option other than to conclude that there was insufficient evidence to enable him to determine the cause of the explosion.

Because of the fact that there could have been very few families in Amlwch whose lives had not been touched by disasters at sea, there was a profound sense of grief at the tragic loss of the *Noah*. Such was the extent of the sympathy felt towards the victims' families, that the members of the Coroner's jury formally requested that the old custom of allowing each juror the sum of one shilling for attending the court, should be revived in order that the money could be given to them.

In the same year as the *Glyndwr* was built at Amlwch, the 199 ton wooden, three masted, topsail schooner, the *Countess of Lonsdale* was launched from Captain Thomas' Millom yard. She was on the stocks for no less than 4 years, which suggests that she, like the *Nellie Bywater*, was built only when the yard had little else to do. The vessel was registered in the joint names of William Thomas and William Postlethwaite, who then respectively owned 2/3 and 1/3 shares in the yard. In April 1890, whilst outward bound from Runcorn with a cargo of coal for Bangor the schooner collided with the steamer *Sherbro*, and was sunk, fortunately without loss of life.

Between 1879 and 1881, Captain Thomas turned out three further schooners from Iard Newydd, the 83 ton *Margaret*, the 112 ton *Pearl*, which would appear to have been yet another built from the *Holy Wath* model; and the 54 ton *President Garfield* (the latter was launched in October 1881, and was named in honour of the 20th President of the United States, who was assassinated that same year).

On 12 May 1883, the following report appeared in the *North Wales Chronicle*::

> On Tuesday night last the 8th inst. the small schooner *Glyndwr* of Beaumaris, Owens (Master), of 26 tons register, from Liverpool bound to Amlwch with a cargo of iron to the owner, Mr Thomas, shipbuilder etc. of this place, when off Point Lynas, about l0pm the weather became very thick with rain and blowing a fresh gale from the east, with heavy sea. Some of the sails were blown away and the vessel became unmanageable. About ll pm by the force of wind and tide, she was driven ashore at Llaneilian, near Point Lynas, and is likely to be a total wreck. A portion of the cargo may be saved. The Mate took to the rigging and was saved, but the Master was washed overboard and drowned.

A Curious Place

At least part of the vessel's cargo was saved however, and eventually brought to Iard Newydd where it was used in the construction of the 155 ton steamer *W S Caine*, named after Nathaniel Caine's brother, William Sproston Caine. The report of the vessel's launching, and that of her subsequent maiden voyage, which appeared in the *Holyhead Weekly Mail & Anglesey Herald* are worth repeating in full, for not only do they give a good eye witness account of the occasion, they also impart a flavour of the times:

A very successful launch of the SS *W S Caine* was effected at 10 o'clock last Saturday morning from the shipbuilding yard of Captain Wm Thomas at this port. The launch was performed under exceedingly favourable conditions in respect of weather and tide, the christening having been entrusted to Mrs Fanning Evans of Mona Lodge (wife of the Sheriff of the County), who executed her onerous duties in a graceful and efficient manner, and amidst the hearty cheers of the vast assemblage present.

The *W S Caine* took to the water as naturally as the honourable gentleman whose good name she bears, and who, through teetotalism enables him to vie with the gallant vessel in the love of the limpid element. The W S Caine is built of iron, being the first iron steamer ever built in Amlwch, is of about 200 tons deadweight capacity, classed A1 for 100 years at Lloyds, and it is designed for the coasting trade. She will immediately be fitted with splendid boilers and engines by Messrs De Winton & Co, engineers, Caernarvon.

Great credit is due to Captain Thomas for his successful efforts to establish such an excellent shipbuilding yard in Amlwch. The vessel is only the first in a line of steamers which our enterprising fellow countryman contemplates building. Another vessel twice as large has just been started, and with his splendid machinery and efficient staff and appliances will very quickly be modelled into shape. The recent addition to his premises is an acquisition of incalculable benefit to facilitate the turning out of heavy tonnage.

Five weeks after the vessel's launching the same newspaper contained the following report:

On Thursday last week this new vessel, under the command of Captain L Thomas, left the Port of Caernarvon for a trial trip round the island of Anglesey, and to Llandudno, and back to Amlwch. This ship was launched five weeks ago from the extensive shipbuilding yard of our enterprising fellow countryman - Captain William Thomas; being the first iron steamer to be built in North Wales, but is to be quickly succeeded by several others of much heavier tonnage.

The *W S Caine* is 122 feet long between perpendiculars, beam 21 feet, depth of hold 8 feet, and capable of carrying about 200 tons on 8 feet of water, being thus practically of the most suitable dimensions for the coasting trade.

Shortly after the launch she was towed to Caernarvon to have her new boiler and engines fitted at the foundry of Messrs De Winton and Co. Her engines are of the compound surface condensing type of fifty nominal horse power, and upon the most recently improved pattern, the cylinders being 14 inches and 27 inches respectively by twenty one inches stroke, and her trial runs were most satisfactory.

A start was made from Caernarvon between nine and ten a.m. reaching Holyhead by twelve, where the vessel was inspected by several gentlemen, and a cruise of about two hours was made. At three pm a course for Amlwch was steered, and the distance of twenty miles covered in one hour and twenty minutes.

At Amlwch a numerous and distinguished party of ladies and gentlemen joined those who had previously embarked, and a prompt start for Llandudno was made . . . At five o'clock tea was served all round, and the weather being very fine, and the rich sea coast scenery, a most enjoyable trip was had. The party landed for two hours at Llandudno, and having viewed that fashionable watering place, re-embarked for the homeward trip at nine p.m.

The *W S Caine* behaved admirably, and will prove a very fast cargo boat. Her pretty model, fine lines, and other appurtenances are all worked by steam, and the steam winch is sufficiently strong to discharge a full cargo in five hours.

The vessel, worth £5,000, was eventually put up for sale by William Thomas & Co of Liverpool, in share lots of £20 each.

Facing into the outer basin as it did, the original slipway at Iard Newydd had severe limitations, and it was quite unsuitable for the larger iron vessels envisaged by Captain Thomas and he had no option but to construct another. The site chosen was to the north of the existing yard and which may have been the addition to the Captain's premises referred to in the report of the launching of the *W S Caine*. It was decided that because of the steepness of the rocks, the new slip would run obliquely across them, in a northerly direction. The slope of the rocks was still greater than might be wished for however, and in order to reduce this, brick piers were built to raise its lower end.

There can be little doubt that the steepness of the new slipway, combined with the fact that the first vessel to use it, the *Eilian*, was by far the largest yet built by the yard, worried the builders greatly for, unlike previous occasions, they refused, almost to a man, to remain on board as she was being launched. Neither was there a 'volunteer' crew of young people, as was the custom:

> . . . only Captain Lewis Thomas (Lloyds Agent) [145] and a youth in the employ of the firm ventured on board. However, gaily and gracefully this new born daughter of the ocean glided into her precarious future. The ceremony of christening was performed by Miss Lallie Evans of Mona Lodge, and hundreds assembled to witness the interesting spectacle.
>
> An exciting incident occurred. Like a self willed steed the *Eilian* broke loose from the little steamer which was engaged to bring her into port, and went off at full speed with the tide in the direction of Cemaes when a tug sighted her and towed her into desired waters.
>
> Amlwch is likely to be a great shipbuilding station. We understand that Captain Thomas has a new Manager who has had great experience in the construction of iron vessels.[146]

On 23 March 1884, three weeks after her launching, the *Eilian* was towed by the tug *Temple* to Caernarfon where she was to have her boiler and machinery fitted by De Winton. Seven weeks later however, the Harbourmaster's log recorded the fact that the steamer *Express*, having a captain of the same name as that of the *Eilian*, came into Amlwch on her trial trip from Caernarfon, carrying a cargo of slates and timber. Quite clearly, the vessel's name had been changed while she was away, and it can only be assumed that it already belonged to another ship. The same may have been true of the second choice also, for that too was changed, and the vessel was somewhat appropriately, renamed the *Exchange*.

Captain Thomas' youngest son William, was sent to Liverpool immediately he completed his public school education in November 1879. In the light of his subsequent career as a naval architect, it had been thought that he went there to receive professional training in that field. This may not have been the case, for there is evidence to show that he had returned home to Amlwch by May 1880, where he was assisting his elder brother Lewis in the family business. It can only be assumed therefore that he received his training at Amlwch, possibly as a pupil to his father's new yard manager. By the beginning of 1884, however, he was sufficiently confident in his abilities as a designer to write to W H Owen of Plas Penrhyn enclosing a tracing of a yacht he had drawn to the latter's specifications. In the event of the yard being favoured with an order to build the vessel, young Thomas strongly urged the prospective owner, ". . . to add greatly to her beam, as 13 feet appears very small in proportion to the length."

It is now thought very likely that it was the unnamed manager, and not young Thomas with his limited expertise, who designed the steamer *Sydney*, the next iron vessel to leave the yard. Once again, for some unexplained reason, the new ship's name was changed, and she became the *Anglesea*. [147] The half model of the *Anglesea*, the third of the yard's iron steamers, has fortunately survived. Unlike the earlier laminated half models belonging to the yard, the model is made from a single block of pine. This strongly suggests that it was not used in the vessel's construction; but was instead, intended to give three dimensional form to her lines, which had first been determined on the drawing board.

The little steamer was built as an addition to the Thomas family fleet, and her ownership was shared between the Captain and his two sons Lewis and William, the former having earlier that year been appointed Lloyds' agent at Amlwch, following the death of William Cox Paynter.

The second schooner to leave the Millom yard, the *Countess of Lonsdale*, was on the stocks for over four and a half years, which is a good indication of the volume of repair business then being undertaken. Initially owned jointly by the Captain and William Postlethwaite, the former acquired full ownership of her in 1880, when she was 2 years old. She remained in the Thomas family's ownership until April 1890, when on a voyage from Runcorn with a cargo of coal for Bangor, she was run down and sunk by a steamer homeward bound from Africa. The Captain, Lewis Hughes of Amlwch and his crew fortunately survived the ordeal.[148]

Unlike the yard at Amlwch, Millom did not have the facilities to build iron vessels. This however did not prevent Hugh Jones from turning out wooden steamers such as the *Lady Kate*, the *Lady Louisa* and the *Lady Bessie*, all named after the daughters of Thomas Massicks, who had recently built the Hodbarrow Ironworks. Captain Thomas was clearly very satisfied with the boilers and engines he had purchased previously from De Winton; for he arranged for both the *Kate* and the *Bessie* to be similarly fitted out at Caernarfon. Neither vessel had to be towed there as had the iron steamers built at Amlwch; for both had the added advantage of sail power.

The *Lady Kate* was already under construction when the Lady Kate Steamship Company was formed to purchase her. Amongst the shareholders were: Captain Thomas, his second son John, William Postlethwaite, William Thomas of Liverpool and two Amlwch men who described themselves as shipbuilders. The dinner given to celebrate the launching was attended by the Captain accompanied by two of his three sons. By all accounts the function was an occasion for a great deal of Welsh 'hwyl',[149] where the opportunity was taken to praise Hugh Jones' undoubted skills as a shipwright.

The celebration may have been one of the last at which the Captain and his son John were seen together, for the latter shortly afterwards left his wife, the daughter of an official of the Hodbarrow mine, and their two children. Such was the Captain's shame and displeasure with his son, that he practically disowned him, but being an honourable and caring man, he personally saw to it that the young man's family was taken care of thereafter.

Facing:
Top – *Eilian*, the first vessel to be built in Iard Newydd. [Late Miss Gertrude Thomas]
Bottom – *Camborne*, leaving Cardiff Docks under power, indicating that she had an auxilliary engine fitted. [Welsh Industrial & Maritime Museum]

William Thomas (right), son of Captain William Thomas. [Thomas Family Archive]

The last vessel to leave the Millom yard under Captain Thomas' name was the *Greyhound*, launched in 1886. Originally laid down as a steamer for the Lady Kate Steamship Company, she was refashioned as a three masted schooner when the steamship company became insolvent. She subsequently joined Captain Thomas' own fleet. Under his management she sailed regularly in the Spanish, African and Brazilian trades, and following her sale to a South African owner in 1891 she spent the next 20 years trading mainly in African waters, with occasional voyages to Mauritius and Saint Helena.[150]

For some reason, the relationship between the Captain and the directors of the Hodbarrow mine deteriorated, perhaps as a result of his son John's behaviour, but for whatever reason, he decided to abandon his control of the Millom yard in order to concentrate his business interests at Amlwch. A letter written on the Millom yard's headed notepaper by William Thomas Junior in April 1887, suggests either that he temporarily replaced his brother as the yard's manager, or that he was sent there to wind up the business.

The yard was sold to Hugh Jones and his brother Miciah, who went on to trade as the Duddon Shipbuilding Company. The ship repairing side of their business flourished, and Hugh went on to design and build four new vessels, all of which were a testimony to his undeniable skill as a Master Shipwright. He had by then married, and in common with several other fellow countrymen, many of whom hailed from Amlwch, he made his home in Millom. There, he and his friends formed part of a strong Welsh community with its own chapel which, although built of corrugated iron, is still standing, and is now used as a social centre.

Hugh Jones' gravestone describing him simply as a shipbuilder can be seen in St George's churchyard in Millom, but perhaps the greatest tribute to his skill lies in the fact that the last vessel he built, the *Emily Barratt* launched in 1913, is still afloat. She now lies in Barrow in Furness where she was due to be restored, but it is understood that the considerable amount of money needed to carry out the work has not been forthcoming, and her now rapidly deteriorating condition is giving rise to much concern.

After his first flush of enthusiasm for iron steamers, the Captain, for some reason, reverted to building sailing vessels, which he now built exclusively of iron, and two schooners, the *Elizabeth Peers* and the *Gelert* were launched from the Amlwch yard in 1885 and 1887 respectively.

According to the Harbourmaster's log, the weather at mid-day on 20 March 1889, was misty and raining, and the wind was freshening from the north-east. By 3.30 in the afternoon however, the weather was worsening, and he felt duty bound to send "Edward Griffith and Wm Hughes (Hobblers) to warn the masters of the vessels in the Harbour to have them well moored as the weather is threatening".

By 5pm, his log records that the wind was

. . . blowing right into the harbour. Strong gale and misty at 6 pm, had the baulks well secured, heavy sea and furious run coming in to the outer basin which continued to increase. At about 10.45 pm it was found that some of the lower baulks had been broken by the force of the heavy sea and run which broke over the pier heads. The tide being the highest spring of the year, between this (time) and midnight the vessels in the harbour parted from their moorings causing a great deal of damage to themselves and the harbour. Everything that could be done by the harbour officials to secure the safety of the vessels inside had been done, further service could not be rendered owing to the seas breaking over the pier head.

March 21.

NE whole gale and heavy sea, misty. At about 1.30 am the schooner *Emperor of Beaumaris* broke adrift from Captain's graving dock and came in contact with the watch house pier and caused damage to the lighthouse and buildings attached. The vessel became a total wreck. At about 2.45 am the remaining baulk got loose from the groove owing to the fall of the tide. Wind NE strong gale about 4 am Got carpenters to make new baulks. At 6 am employed the steam crane to raise the baulks out of the harbour and employed about two dozen men to have the baulks replaced.

Noon wind NE moderate gale, new baulks secured, and had the vessels put into their proper berths and got men employed putting chains across the entrance to the harbour to keep the wreck of the schooner *Emperor* from coming into contact with the baulks.

March 22.

Sun rise wind WSW strong breeze, misty and rain, 2 men employed in clearing wreckage inside the harbour. Vessels working, *Martha* discharging and repairing, also *British Queen* repairing. Baulks down, the wreck still laying across the entrance of the harbour. At noon wind WNW moderate breeze. At about 5 pm the *Pleadias* [Pleiades] came into the bay but could not come in as the wreck lay across the mouth of the harbour and too much ebb for her to float over her. At 6pm wind WNW moderate breeze and continued. Employed John Hughes and G Williams to clear wreckage in harbour.

Over the next three days, life at the port returned to some degree of normality, but the wreck continued to block the harbour entrance, and the Harbourmaster was forced to employ no fewer than 17 men to haul it to the back of the Watch House pier where it was chained to the rocks.

In order to warn vessels of the fact that they could not enter the port before the entrance was cleared, the Harbourmaster arranged to have the appropriate signal hoisted on the post at Llam Carw. How effective this method was in preventing vessels from entering port is open to debate, for there are numerous references in the Harbourmaster's log to vessels entering the outer basin 'contrary to the rules of the harbour', and in so doing, damaging or even breaking the baulks. Their Masters were made to pay for all the damage they caused, to which was added a nominal fine for breaking the rules. It is evident however that the fine was no great deterrent, for local captains, who were all too familiar with the regulations, were amongst the most frequent offenders.

Thomas Fanning Evans, himself a shipowner and businessman, owned the land on which the signal post stood, and for which he was paid a rent of one shilling per annum. The Harbourmaster's log for 24 January 1889 records that about 3 o'clock in the morning the signal pole was ". . . shot down with Dynamite by some person unknown". On the following day the Trust erected a replacement, and no sooner had it been put up, that it was cut down by Fanning Evans.

Four days later the weather made it necessary to lower the baulks, a fact which could not be communicated to a vessel wishing to enter. This angered the maritime fraternity to such an extent that in the afternoon of the 30th, a second pole was erected by the Trust's foreman, only this time he was assisted by no fewer than 30 sailors. Fanning Evans had no stomach for a fight against such odds, and there was no further trouble.

Facing:
Top – Amlwch Port, c1903. The vessel are – *Alice & Eliza* (rear centre), *Kate* (rear right) and *Thomas Pearson* (foreground). [Trevor Morgan]
Bottom – The *Prince Ja Ja* after she had been re-named the *Matje*, beached at Porthdinllaen. [Gwynedd Archives Service]

What brought about such extraordinary behaviour on Fanning Evans' part will probably never be known as nothing in the records gives an indication of the root cause of the problem, and despite its newsworthiness, no mention was ever made of the incident in the local newspaper.

Captain Thomas' ambition to have a vessel named in honour of his own parish saint was at last realised when the 116 ton, 3 masted iron schooner *Eilian* was launched on 27 September 1889. The Thomas family owned three quarters of the vessel, and her Master, R Griffiths owned the remainder. In 1899, she collided with another vessel in the English Channel, and was sunk.

On Saturday 8 March 1890, the only paddle steamer ever to leave the Thomas yard, was launched for Messrs P & H Lewis of Conwy. The *Prince George*, "a beautifully modelled boat in all respects," [151] was designed to cater for the rapidly expanding tourist trade of nearby Llandudno, by carrying passengers along the scenic river Conwy, as far as Trefriw. The channel up to the once busy slate quay at Trefriw had by then silted up to such an extent, that it could only be negotiated by shallow draughted vessels. The late Johnny Roberts of Amlwch, a former apprentice at the Grayson shipyard in Holyhead, was at one time the *Prince George's* engineer, and it was with great amusement that he recalled how the unsuspecting passengers were smudged with soot when he lowered her funnel in order to clear the Conwy bridges.

The next vessel to leave the yard, the 271 ton iron screw steamer *Prince Ja Ja*, was in its time, one of the best known vessels along the whole of the North Wales coast. Built to the order of the Liverpool, Caernarvon & Menai Straits Steamship Co, she regularly conveyed slates to, and general merchandise from Liverpool, to both Bangor and Caernarfon, and the quay close to the pier at Bangor where she berthed is still known as the Ja Ja Jetty. Renamed the *Matje* in 1902, she continued life as a tramp steamer, and was eventually broken up in October 1935, having served Monroe Brothers Ltd of Liverpool for the last four years of her life.

The two week period which separated the launching of the *Prince George* and the *Prince Ja Ja* must have meant that the latter, because of her size, was built on the yard's new, northern slipway which, for the same reason, must also have been the slip used to build and launch the 23rd and largest vessel ever to leave the yard, the 355 ton iron steamship *Cygnus*. The fact that she was launched a mere 11 months after the *Prince Ja Ja* suggests that some part of her structure at least, had been prefabricated before the latter was completed.

The 264 ton iron barquentine *Detlef Wagner* (yard No 24) was launched 7 months later from the old slipway. The name may seem unusual, but there were close links between the company and the Elbe port of Harburg, and it was often the custom to name vessels in honour of esteemed associates.[152] A photograph of the vessel on the stocks as she was nearing completion, shows quite clearly that at least part of the dry dock alongside the old slipway where she was being built, was planked over when not in use.

Chapter 14
The Thomas Brothers

It is evident that, as Captain Thomas' health deteriorated, his two sons Lewis and William, who had earlier been taken into partnership, were assuming greater resposibility for the running of the business. Lewis appears to have accepted responsibility for the management of the yard, and his younger brother, who had by then become a highly proficient naval architect, undertook the design work. The additional responsibilities involved in managing their own, as well as other peoples' vessels was a joint undertaking.

William Thomas (the younger) was an accomplished artist, as fine examples of his draughtsmanship in the family's possession testify, and it is evident that his eye for form contributed greatly to the widely acclaimed beauty of the vessels he designed. It is also evident that, despite being highly aware of the progression of steam power, his first love was for sail, and it is for these vessels that he will be best remembered. Basil Greenhill, the noted maritime historian and one time Director of the National Maritime Museum, paid William Thomas & Sons the following glowing tribute:

> . . . it was the iron and steel ships produced by this firm that were best remembered, for most of the few iron and steel schooners built seem to have been of very high standard of design and construction, William Thomas' vessels were considered in their time to be among the finest.[153]

Based on the same model as the *Gelert*, the iron, 3 masted schooner *Maggie Williams* was built to the order of William Postlethwaite. Although her specification was to the highest class for Lloyd's Rules of 100:A1, her new owner preferred to suit her with his own sails, which suggests that Postlethwaite preferred those from his own sail loft at Millom. When she was seven years old, the vessel was sold to Captain Alfred Tyrrell of Arklow, who in 1902, left Dublin bound for Great Yarmouth, with a cargo of timber. His faith, both in himself and his vessel, must have been considerable, for he was sailing her uninsured. The weather had deteriorated by the time he arrived off the Yare estuary, and rather than wait for a pilot, Captain Tyrrell decided to take his vessel in unaided. As the vessel passed Gorleston the wind was such that she became unmanageable, and she was driven against the pier with such force that that her plates were crushed.

Her plight had not gone unnoticed, and willing hands soon had lifelines aboard her, by which means all of the crew with the exception of her master, who had ostensibly gone below to recover the ship's papers, were saved. When he failed to reappear, a rescuer followed him below, and to his amazement found the Captain sitting on his bunk placidly awaiting his end: the loss of his vessel meant that he had nothing further to live for. He was eventually taken off the stricken vessel unharmed, but in a state of total shock.[154, 155]

The next three vessels built at the yard, the *Cymric*, *Celtic* and *Gaelic* were built to the same design as the *Maggie Williams*, and they exemplified clearly what would now be referred to as, state of the art technology.

The first of the vessels was launched in March 1893, 6 days before the death of Captain

William Thomas, who was then 70 years of age. He had attended to the yard's business almost up to the time of his death, and it is thought that he was then well enough to be present at the launch. The company had built the *Cymric* as a speculation, but the brothers, having failed to come to terms with potential buyers, absorbed her into the family fleet. The vessel was put to work immediately under the command of Captain Robert Jones of Amlwch, and she arrived at the Brazilian port of Porto Alegre on 24 June 1893.

Following in the wake of the *Maggie Williams*, the *Cymric* also ended up at Arklow where she remained, with the exception of a period during the First World War, when she was converted into a Q-ship. This was at a time when German submarines were inflicting great losses on the British merchant fleet, and many of those ships which were sunk were unarmed and unescorted sailing vessels, which could offer no resistance.

To counter this threat, the Admiralty converted several steam and sail driven vessels into armed decoys or 'Q-ships', which would have the outward appearance of being unarmed merchant ships going about their lawful business, but which in reality were more than able to deal effectively with their underwater adversaries. In this way many submarines were sunk, not all of which, unfortunately, belonged to the enemy for, on 15 October 1918, the *Cymric* , alias the Q-ship *Olive*, armed with one 4-inch gun, two 12-pounders, and one 7.5 inch howitzer, mistakenly sank the British submarine *J6*.

The *Cymric* survived until the Second World War, during which she disappeared without trace whilst on passage from Ardrossan to Lisbon with a cargo of coal. The circumstances under which she was lost may never be known, but it is probably true to say that she herself had become a casualty of war.

The *Cymric's* sister ship the *Celtic* was launched on 27 October 1894. Attempts had been made to sell her whilst she was still on the stocks, but although there were many enquiries from prospective buyers she remained unsold, and in the company tradition, joined the family fleet.

William Thomas was justifiably disappointed when his vessels failed to sell readily, particularly as he knew that by any standard, they were outstanding ships. In his letters to brokers he repeatedly stressed the importance of getting potential buyers to come and see the vessels for themselves, in which case: ". . . they could not fail to be impressed'. It is evident that Captain William Thomas was somewhat of a perfectionist, and that he had instilled into his sons the maxim that, 'good enough, is not good enough'. For this reason the yard's vessels were invariably built to Lloyds' highest specifications, and in its latter years under the brothers' control, even those high standards were regularly exceeded.

The vessels' structural excellence was matched by their speed, and it was with some pride that William Thomas was able to inform one potential buyer that their latest vessels were of

> . . . Class 100 A1 [non-wood], and built in excess of Lloyds' requirements for this grade, intended for any shallow trade such as Rio Grande and Porto Alegre, they are smart sailors, the *Cymric* went out to Rio Grande last passage in 34 days, and the *Celtic* arrived in Falmouth last round from Rio Grande with 15 months foul bottom, in under 60 days, beating vessels that had left the same time by 18 and 22 days. We are building them to sell, and failing this we sail them ourselves and they have paid us 12.5%.

In later correspondence, William Thomas stated that he believed the *Cymric's* fast passage to Rio Grande, under the command of Captain Robert Jones of Amlwch, to be a record.

Above: The completed *Elizabeth Roberts* on the slipway. She was launched on 3 May 1904. [Thomas Family Archive]

Below: Hospital ship *Morfudd*. [Thomas Family Archive]

The following translation of a report in *Y Clorianydd*, dated 17 March 1898 gives a good impression of the pride that was felt locally, whenever a vessel left the Thomas yard:

> On Wednesday the 8th of this month one of the most beautiful and valuable sailing vessels ever built at Amlwch was launched into her element from the extensive shipbuilding yard of Messrs W Thomas & Sons. One of several ships built by them to the same design, this latest vessel incorporates several constructional improvements. According to calculations she is expected to carry a load of 380 tons, and she has been designed to sail without ballast.
>
> The naming ceremony was performed by Mrs Thomas of Ponc Taldrwst, wife of the firm's senior member, who named the vessel *Gaelic*. It is certain that never before was there seen a more beautiful and perfectly executed launch; and both Captain Lewis Thomas and Mr William Thomas together with their foremen Richard Edwards and Richard Williams deserve high praise for the excellent manner in which it was done. The 3 masted vessel is rigged as a barquentine and is built of steel.
>
> The firm has secured the services of one of the most able men to command the vessel, namely Captain Ishmael Williams junior, of Chapel Street, Amlwch; and he is wished every success in employing her to the best advantage of all who are associated with her.
>
> The vessel sails next Saturday for Liverpool where she will take on a general cargo for Rio Grande do Sul.

The *Gaelic* did not to return to the Mersey until the beginning of November, when Captain Williams wrote to the company with his assessment of her performance. In his reply William Thomas wrote:

> We were very pleased to learn of your safe arrival and to receive such a favourable report of the vessel. This is most satisfactory for all concerned and naturally so to us, in particular being in the dual position of Builders and Owners. We hope that we shall be fortunate in securing good employment for her.

A month after the launch of the *Gaelic* a start was made on Yard No 29, the *Meyric*. Whilst she was still on the stocks, two iron lighters, the *Belfast* and the *Walton*, Yard Nos 30 and 31 respectively, were completed for The United Grain Elevator Company of Liverpool.

The schooner *Meyric*, the largest sailing vessel ever to leave the yard, was launched on 4 January 1904, and amongst her crew members on the maiden voyage to South America was William Williams, an Amlwch born seaman who, some ten yers later, at the beginning of the First World War, enlisted in the Royal Naval Reserve, in which he served with distinction as a seaman aboard several Q-ships [see Appendix 5]. This particular aspect of the war was of great concern to the Admiralty, for by April 1917, the German submarine service had sunk well in excess of 500,000 tons of British merchant shipping.

The smaller *Elizabeth Roberts* was launched some three months after the *Meyric*, and the two vessels also departed from the usual, inasmuch that they were both built of steel. The former was built on the southern slipway, and one photograph of her dressed overall on the day she was launched is thought to be the only remaining one showing a Thomas vessel actually entering the water for the first time.

Similarly, a recently discovered photograph in the National Library of Wales, is believed to be the only one known, which shows a vessel under construction on Thomas' northern slipway. The appearance of the vessel itself and that of the yard, looking strangely empty

Facing:
The *Donald & Doris* , built at Cox Paynter's Iard Ochr Draw. Photographed c1930. [Trevor Morgan]

Above: *Eilian II* at Amlwch Port prior to sailing on her maiden voyage in 1908.
[Thomas Family Archive]

Left: *Eilian II* at Barnstaple, Devon c.1935. Note the square wheelhouse which replaced the whaleback wheelhouse seen in the above photograph.
[Trevor Morgan]

and devoid of any activity, suggests that she was the schooner *Cenric*, which was launched on 2 August 1905, at a time when the fortunes of the yard were at a very low ebb.

The death of Captain Lewis Thomas at the age of 55 came when the yard was still far from busy, although one vessel was well advanced on the stocks. The new ship, which turned out to be the last sailing vessel, and the third to bear the name *Eilian*, to leave the Thomas yard. Launched on 14 August 1908, she is reputed to have been the first schooner launched as an auxiliary, her power being provided by a 52-horsepower paraffin engine made by Goedkoop of Amsterdam. The pole masted vessel was built for Captain David Richardson of Rock Ferry, a retired Master Mariner, who owned $^{40}/_{64}$ shares in her, whilst the remainder was held by the Thomas family.

Much of the *Eilian's* commercial history is already well documented,[156] and like her yard sisters *Meyric* and *Gaelic*, she also saw service as a Q-ship during the first World War, when she was known as the *Chromium*.

Renamed the *Fjordbo* in 1976, the vessel spent her last years in the West Indies where on the 9 January 1984, at the ripe old age of 76, she sank; her last reported position being LAT.12 21 N: LONG. 66 43W.

In 1911, during Herbert Asquith's tenure of office as Prime Minister, the House of Lords was forced, under threat of the creation of a large number of Liberal peers, to pass a parliamentary bill, which amongst other things, deprived it of the power of veto over finance bills. Amongst the names put forward for elevation to the peerage was that of William Thomas. In a private letter dated 17 July 1911, to an unnamed friend, which was recently discovered amongst the yard's business correspondence, he wrote:

My Dear Friend,
   I am much obliged for your letter of the 15th inst; but as I am one of the selected 500 New Members of the House of Lords your sympathy is misplaced, but strange enough you have correctly guessed my Title and as it has not yet been officially Gazetted I must ask you to keep it private for the present. Hoping to receive your congratulations when the announcement is made.
      I am,
      Yours Very Truly,
      Wm Thomas (For a few days only) [157]

The announcement was never made, for the House of Lords, fearful of Asquith's threat, eventually agreed to the passage of the controversial bill. The blow must have been a particularly bitter one for William Thomas, for there was no later mention made of the matter within the family and the contents of the letter came as a complete surprise to his daughter Gertrude.

After the launch of the *Eilian* the yard undertook no further building until June 1911, when the keel of a new hospital ship was laid down for the Beaumaris Port Sanitary Authority. Having a length of just over 81 feet, a breadth of 23 feet, and a side depth of 11 feet, her functional shape, not unlike that of a smoothing iron, could have given William Thomas no pleasure at all as he viewed her construction from the Counting House window.

The *Morfudd*, as she was to be known, was launched on Monday 4 March 1912, and within four days was towed to a mooring at Bangor by Bangor Corporation's own vessels *Lady Magdalen* and *Torbay*. [158] In a letter addressed to the Clerk of Anglesey County Council, the Local Government Board stated that its attention had been drawn by the

Amlwch Port, c1910. The vessel *Gaelic* is moored nearest to the camera. In the foreground is 'Iard Ochr Draw'. Centre right is the probable location of Captain Thomas' first shipyard. Left centre are the storage bins and, top right, the site of Hills' Chemical Works, formerly the site of the smelter.

Medical Officers of Health for the various districts within the county, to the fact that apart from the hospital ship belonging to the Beaumaris Port Sanitary Authority, no accommodation had been provided by sanitary authorities in the County for the isolation, in hospital, of cases of infectious diseases occurring in their districts. Despite the Board's concern, it is believed that the *Morfudd* was never called into use as a hospital ship, and that she was later converted into a houseboat.

As the yard was near enough idle, more of William Thomas' time was taken up with the problems arising from the management of the many vessels under his control, but the needs of the Government, during the First World War brought some relief to the hard pressed yard. Two ammunition barges, referred to only as *B384* and *B499*, were built some time before May 1918, when the keels of what it is thought were two others, were also laid down. Work on Yard Nos 40 and 41, referred to only as Admiralty Duffers, appears to have been started, but was never completed and it must be assumed that they were both cancelled when they were no longer needed at the end of the war.

William Thomas & Sons were always in the market for cheap second-hand vessels which were basically of sound construction, for the purpose of modifying them to their own requirements and standards. Not only were the working lives of such ships extended, the refits also added greatly to their market value. Until such time as they could be profitably sold, it was usual for the vessels to serve in the Thomas' own fleet. Notable amongst the steamers purchased in this way were the Scottish built vessels: *Nar, Ardgowan, Black Rock, Dunleith* and *Ardri*. [159]

Of the above, perhaps the best known locally was the *Black Rock*. She was acquired by the family after she had been raised, following her sinking by the steamer *Balniel* close to the Liverpool Bar lightship. Brought to Amlwch, the vessel's superstructure was stripped down and extensive modifications carried out to her structure. A violent storm arose whilst she was in the dry dock however, and in a recurrence of the way in which the *Emperor* had broken free from the same dock in 1889, the steamer crashed through the gates, destroying them completely. Driven by fierce northerly winds, the hapless vessel demolished the lighthouse at the end of the watch-house pier before capsizing, and totally blocking the harbour entrance. The repaired section of the pier on the opposite side of the harbour, where her bow dug into the masonry, is still evident.

Following an extensive refit the vessel was renamed *Eleth*, in honour of the patron saint of Amlwch, but despite being a sound ship structurally, she turned out to be highly unpopular with her crews. Legend somewhat cynically relates how during the Second World War she was renamed *Empire Lethe* in order to disguise her true identity from crews who might otherwise have been reluctant to sail on her. The *Eleth* eventually foundered on 1 February 1951, with the loss of 9 members of her crew.

Chapter 15
Epilogue

The devastating effect wrought by the run-down and closure of an industry on which a whole community depends for its livelihood, is a phenomenon that is familiar to most. In today's economic climate, such closures can happen almost overnight, making their effect appear more calamitous still. Fate was a little kinder to Amlwch however, for the decline in the town's fortunes, from a time when the mines' output controlled the world price of copper, to relative obscurity, was more gradual.

Despite the generally low quality of ore found at Parys Mountain, the relative ease with which vast quantities could be raised made the whole concern a phenomenal success. There can be little doubt that Roe & Company's fortunes, and to a lesser degree, those of Nicholas Bayly, were greatly enhanced by their early association with the mountain, but it was not until Thomas Williams' active participation in the concern, that its true wealth was fully realised. His commercial genius, to which can be added no small measure of compassion, courage and ruthlessness in business, made him both rich and powerful. He undoubtedly made equally powerful enemies along the way, and it may have been for that reason that his achievements went unrecognised by the Establishment, but there can be little doubt however that the wealth he generated for the Hughes family of Llys Dulas was instrumental in the elevation to the peerage in 1831, of Edward Hughes' son, William Lewis Hughes, as Lord Dinorben.

Of greater relevance to Thomas Williams perhaps, would have been the claim that he should have had the recognition due to him as a pioneer of a revolutionary commercial strategy which made use of heavy capital in an organisation of wide dispersion and great complexity, [160] a strategy that has since become a norm.

His death was soon followed by the piecemeal disintegration of the empire he had so assiduously built, and with the exhaustion of the more easily worked beds of ore, the mines at Parys Mountain went into steep decline. The resurgence in their fortunes, which began with the arrival of the Vivians, revitalised the economy of the town - a fact that was in no small measure due to the expertise of the oft maligned James Treweek. Whilst the output of ore was, by comparison with the mines' heyday, on a much reduced scale, they continued to provide well-paid employment over a period of some 40 years to many who would otherwise have been destitute.

The greater importance placed on the local smelting industry, which was claimed by its managers to be more efficient than that at Swansea, also had the effect of ameliorating the decline in the mines' fortunes. Indeed, such was its efficiency that it continued to compete successfully with its southern rivals, despite having to import both coal and foreign ores. Ores from the Caernarfonshire mines of Sygyn and Llandudno were also brought in, and their importation reached a peak in 1850, the year of James Treweek's death. After that there was a sharp decline in the output of refined copper and other products from the smelters.

Attracted to the town in 1840 by the availability of cheap sulphur, Charles Henry Hills' chemical works added to the diversity of local industry, and contributed greatly to its economy. When the supply of locally produced sulphur ended with the closure of the smelter, Hills moved his chemical works from Llam Carw to the vacant smelter buildings, where he continued operations using sulphur imported directly into Amlwch from Spain. Under the able managership of Lewis Hughes, a local man, the firm went on to manufacture great quantities of high quality fertilizers, for which it became renowned. The site of the chemical works continued to be known as Gwaith Hills (Hills' Works) until the building of the present housing estate, despite the fact that all that remained of them were numerous heaps of firebricks and slag.

Following the Second World War, the Associated Octel Company relocated its bromide extraction plant, previously sited at Hayle in Cornwall, to Amlwch. The company established the new works on the headland to the west of the harbour entrance, much as Hills had established his on the headland on the eastern side some one hundred years previously. As Hills manufactured sulphuric acid from locally produced sulphur for use in his own chemical processes, so the Octel company now produces it in vast quantities at its plant, as part of the bromide extraction process. The similarities between the two concerns are manifold, but perhaps the most significant of which is that they have both in their time added significantly to the economy of the town, when there was very little other employment to be had.

Although further shafts were sunk at Morfa Du, in the north western corner of Parys Mountain, the escalating cost of extracting an ever diminishing reserve of minerals, eventually brought mining at Parys Mountain to an end. All that remained of the once flourishing industries were the precipitation ponds, and these continued working until the end of the Second World War.

There is renewed hope for Parys Mountain however, for the recently established Anglesey Mining Company firmly believes that by using modern mining methods, it can profitably extract what still remains of the mountain's hidden wealth.

The shipbuilding industry represented by the Treweek and Paynter yards, were rightly renowned for the excellent vessels they turned out, and the building in 1859 of the *Mary Catherine*, the first iron vessel to be constructed in North Wales, is fitting testimony to the progressive spirit of the locality. Of all the firms however, the honours must surely go to that founded by Captain William Thomas, the quality of whose vessels was legendary. The yard's reputation was further enhanced by the later sailing vessels designed by his son William, of which the record breaking *Cymric* was a fine example. The launching of the *Eilian* in 1908, heralded the end of a proud tradition of shipbuilding at the port, and the vessel's survival in commercial service until 1984 is adequate confirmation, if that were needed, of the quality of her construction.

The additional work occasioned by the needs of the First World War brought some measure of relief to what was rapidly becoming a hard pressed yard, and in a last effort to keep it going, the Thomas's bought two redundant naval vessels, believed to have been the largest ever to enter the port, for breaking. No doubt much of the scrap produced in this way found its way to the ponds at Dyffryn Adda.

With the port very much in decline, an attempt was made by the Harbour Trustees in 1913, to interest the Mersey Docks and Harbour Board in taking over its management as a pilot station. This met with no success however, and following the end of the war, all responsibilities relating to the port were transferred to the Amlwch Urban District Council. Thereafter, apart from a few Thomas owned vessels brought there for repair and refitting, or the visit of an occasional collier, there was little other commerce at the port worth mentioning, and warehouses and yard buildings, by then boarded up, fell into total decay.

Later developments have, surprisingly, left many of the industrial sites untouched, although the ravages of time are all too evident. The building of the Craig y Don estate on the Smelter/Gwaith Hills site has left nothing that would be of interest to the industrial archaeologist, and apart from the sail loft, the dry dock, and two tall chimneys, little now remains of Iard Newydd, following the building of the Shell Marine Terminal on the site. The Harbourmaster's office, in which were housed valuable records of ship movements in and out of the port, was vandalised and later demolished, the records being lost in the process.

The Ynys Môn Borough Council however, has recently and very commendably, carried out some restoration work at the harbour, amongst which have been the refurbishment of the interior of the old Watch House with its little lighthouse, as well as the original two seater toilet in Treweek's old yard. What little now remains of the Newhaven public house has been partly cleared and the walls stabilised. The square based limekiln with its stone flagged charging floor has been partly restored, but some more work needs to be done to ensure its survival.

The attractive little harbour, once described as being one of the most important ports in Wales, continues to attract hundreds of visitors each year, and there can be little doubt that, were the sites of the various early local industries (the diversity of which is unique in British industrial history) to be taken as a whole, they could prove to be the foundation of an industrial heritage centre of national importance.

Appendix 1
Amlwch Built Vessels, 1788-1918

Year	Vessel	Built	Notes*		
1788	*Lovely Nancy*		15	W	Sloop
1791	*Swallow*		7	W	Sloop
1825	*Unity*	TR	68	W	Sloop
1826	*Marquis of Anglesey*	TR	65	W	Sloop
1827	*Margaret*	TR	43	W	Sloop
1829	*Eleanor*	TR	17	W	Smack
1830	*James & Jane*	TR	130	W	Brigantine
1832	*Amlwch Packet*	TR	37	W	Smack
1834	*Sarah*	TR	17	W	Smack
1836	*Cymraes*	TR	21	W	Sloop
1836	*Sarah*	TR	21	W	Sloop
1837	*Jane & Margaret*	TR	57	W	Smack
1839	*Marianne*	TR	53	W	Sloop
1840	*Economy*	TR	46	W	Schooner
1842	*Catherine*	TR	62	W	Schooner
1844	*Cymro*	TR	20	W	Smack
1858	*Alliance*	TR	93	W	Schooner
1858	*Mary Catherine*	TR/HT	77	I	Schooner
1859	*Charles Edwin*	CP	94	W	Schooner
1859	*Grace Evans*	TR	89	I	Schooner
1860	*Sea Queen*	TR	82		Schooner
1862	*Mary Fanny*	CP	92	W	Schooner
1864	*Princess of Wales*	TR	99	I	Schooner
1865	*Jane Gray*	CP	123	W	Schooner
1866	*Perseverance*	TR	110	W	Schooner
1869	*Welsh Girl*	WT	99	W	Schooner
1870	*Lewis & Mary*	WT	79	W	Schooner
1871	*Charles*	CP	48	W	Schooner
1872	*Holy Wath*	WT	119	W	Schooner
1874	*Cumberland Lassie*	WT	230	W	Brigantine
1875	*Mersey*	WT	79	W	Schooner
1876	*Baron Hill*	WT	224	W	3M Schooner
1876	*Lady Neave*	WT	99	W	Schooner
1877	*Nantglyn*	WT	115	W	Schooner
1878	*Parys Lodge*	CP	97	W	Schooner
1878	*Nesta*	Wt	117	W	Schooner
1878	*Eilian Hill*	WT	113	W	Schooner
1878	*Glyndwr*	Wt	26	W	Smack
1879	*Margaret*	Wt	83	W	Schooner
1880	*Pearl*	Wt	112	W	Schooner

Appendices

1881	*President Garfield*	WT	54	W	Schooner
1883	*W S Caine*	Wt	155	I	Steamship
1884	*Camborne*	CP	118	W	3M Schooner
1884	*Exchange*	WT	274	I	Steamship
1884	*Anglesea*	WT	149	I	Steamship
1885	*Elizabeth Peers*	WT	183	I	3M Schooner
1887	*Gelert*	WT	223	I	Schooner
1889	*Eilian*	WT	116	W	3M Schooner
1890	*Cygnus*	WT	355	I	Schooner
1890	*Prince Ja Ja*	WT	294	Stl	Steamship
1890	*Prince George*	WT	24	Stl	Paddleboat
1891	*Detlef Wagner*	WT	264	I	Barquentine
1892	*Ailsie*	CP	130	W	3M Schooner
1892	*Maggie Williams*	WT	226	I	3M Schooner
1893	*Cymric*	WT	226	I	Barquentine
1894	*Celtic*	WT	226	I	Barquentine
1897	*Donald & Doris*	CP	142	W	3M Schooner
1898	*Gaelic*	WT	224	I	Barquentine
1900	*Belfast*	WT	60		Flat
1902	*Walton*	WT	82		Steam Flat
1904	*Meyric*	WT	132	Stl	3M Schooner
1904	*Elizabeth Roberts*	WT	132	Stl	3M Schooner
1905	*Cenric*	WT	98		3M Schooner
1908	*Eilian*	WT	140	Stl	Sch/Aux Scr
1912	*Morfudd*	WT		Stl	Hosp Ship
1914	Barge B 384	WT			
WW1	Barge B 499	WT			
WW1	A C Barge 1308	WT			
WW1	A C Barge 1309	WT			
WW1	*Blush*	WT			Admiralty Duffer
WW1	*Bluster*	WT			Admiralty Duffer

*The three columns indicate the tonnage, construction material and the class of each vessel.

Abbreviations:
W - wood; I - iron; M - mast; St - steel; Sch - schooner; Aux - Auxiliary engine; Hosp - Hospital ship.

Builders:
TR - Treweek; HT - Hughes/Thomas; CP Cox Paynter; WT - William Thomas.

Sources:
Gwynedd Archives, doc WM/1131
Private papers of William Thomas & Sons

Appendix 2
Vessels in the Amlwch Copper Trade, 1763-1852

See National Library of Wales note re Amlwch Shipping, dated 1793: "30 years ago [1763] there were but one small sloop of 20 [tons?] called the *Gracy* and another of 15 [tons?]".

1769-70 (see *Copper Mountain* pp 153-4, John Rowlands).

Speedwell	*Providence*
Molly	*True Lion*
Morning Star	*Royal Briton*
Peggy	*Jonney*
Anne	*George*
Sea Horse	*Darling*
Grey	

In 1771 the following vessels were added to the trade (see Mona Mines Mss 3540, 3541, 3543, UCNW, Bangor) –

Nancy	*William & James*
Catherine	*Charming Peggy*
Betty	*Caernarvon*
Diligence	*Richard & Robert*
John	*Eagle*
Sampson	*Wikker*
Dove	*Elizabeth*
Success	*Hopewell*
Heart of Oak	*Mary*
Torbay	*Happy Return*
Unity	*William & Mary*
Hawk	

1771 (see M M Mss, 3750) –

Warrington	57 tons	*Richard & Robert*	16 tons
Betty	26 tons	*William & James*	8 tons
Gray	12 tons	*Jenny*	16 tons
Caesar	7 tons	*Peggy*	29 tons
Providence	20 tons	*Betty*	34 tons
Diligence	23 tons	*Sea Horse*	17 tons
Speedwell	20 tons	*Hopewell*	16 tons
Catherine	31 tons	*Speedwell*	21 tons
Mary	21 tons	*Sampson*	12 tons

Appendices

1771 (see M M Mss 2242) –

Peggy	30 tons	*Catherine*	48 tons
Nancy	24 tons	*Success*	24 tons
Providence	28 tons	*Trulove (True Love?)*	46 tons
Caesar	6 tons	*Richard Roberts*	35 tons
Betty	33 tons	*William & James*	70 tons
Diligence	23 tons	*Heart of Oak*	33 tons
Speedwell	20 tons	*Fourboy (?)*	27 tons
Molly	35 tons	*Charming Peggy*	26 tons
James ?	46 tons	*Happy Return*	38 tons
Speedwell	42 tons	*Unity*	40 tons
Sampson	40 tons	*Jenny*	30 tons
Sea Horse	16 tons	*John*	24 tons
Dove	25 tons	*Hawk*	52 tons

27 vessels averaging 34 tons

1775 (see Mona Mines Mss 3543) –

William & James	William Ward	Master
Peggy	Lewis Thomas	
Providence	David Edwards	
Happy Return	David Griffiths	
William & Mary	Edward Owens	

1786 (see *Mynydd Parys*, Owen Griffith) –

Ann	*Mary*
Amlwch	*Mayflower*
Benjamin	*Nancy*
Blessing	*Nelly*
Betty	*New Loyalty*
Eagle	*Portland*
Edward & Mary	*Providence*
Elinor	*Prince of Orange*
Fame	*Phoenix*
Happy Hopewell (?)	*Speedwell*
Jamaica	*Susannah*
Jane	*Sally*
Jenny & Peggy	*Sandwich*
Morning Star	*Swan*
Molly	*True Britain (True Briton?)*
Mona	*Uxbridge*
Maria	

In 1787, the following vessels were added to their number (see *Mynydd Parys*, Owen Griffith) –

Amity	*Barmouth*
Ann & Betty	*Beginning*
Britannia	*Constant Trader*

Catherine	*Resolution*
Endeavour	*Royal Escape*
Elizabeth	*Squirrel*
Greenfield	*Swallow*
Green Linet	*Stanley*
Harmony	*Tom*
Happy Return	*Two Brothers*
Industry	*Upper Bank* (Captain Th^os Landeg)
Magdalen	*Venus*
Mersey	*William & Betty*
Parys	

A great deal of ore was carried to Swansea during this year. In the following year (1788), the following vessels were added to the list –

Berkin	*Lord Bulkeley*
Concord	*Lark*
Favoured	*Unity*
Nightingale	

The following were added in 1789 –

Druid	*Lady Caroline*
Earl of Uxbridge	*Miner*
Friendship	*Union*

1793 (see documents in the National Library of Wales) –

Maria	170 tons	10 men
Greenfield	150 tons	8 men
Jane	150 tons	8 men
Parys	130 tons	7 men
Earl of Uxbridge	150 tons	8 men
Mona	140 tons	7 men
Kitty	115 tons	6 men
Amlwch	115 tons	6 men
Eleanor	100 tons	6 men
Mary	96 tons	6 men
Portland	100 tons	6 men
Sandwich	86 tons	5 men
Mersey	85 tons	4 men
Union	85 tons	4 men
Stanley	85 tons	4 men
Peggy	90 tons	5 men
Diana	150 tons	10 men
Fanny	18 tons	2 men
Hopewell	20 tons	2 men
Shark	16 tons	2 men
Pennant	30 tons	8 men

Appendices

William	85 tons	5 men
True Love	20 tons	2 men

Average 95 tons

1822 (see M M Mss, 448, 449, 488, 531) –

Wellington	*Jane & Ellen*
Dublin	*Voryd*
Vigour	*Favourite*
Hero	*Menai*

1830 (see M M Mss 3684 – Petition for advance in freight) –

Maria	Evan Griffith Master
Marchioness of Anglesey	William Hughes
Unity	John Griffith
Marquis of Anglesey	Hugh Thomas
Elizabeth	Owen Roberts
Amlwch	John Thomas
Earl of Uxbridge	Solomon Ellis
Agnes	John Hughes
Portland	
Neptune	John Thomas
Diana	Richard Morgan
Juno	John Jones
Margaret	Hugh Hughes
Tower	Griffith Rowlands
Vigour	John Griffiths
Hero	
Happy Return	William Jones
Samson (Sampson ?)	Owen Pritchard

1845 (see M M Mss – Petition for an advance in freight) –

Agnes	John Hughes – Master
Hero	Evan Griffith
George	Griffith Rowlands
Thomas	William Owens
Earl of Uxbridge	John Thomas
Unity	David Owen
Mary	Owen Parry
Concord	John Williams
Diana	John Price
Juno	Richard Evans
Marchioness of Anglesey	John Hughes
Providence	William Hughes
Anne	Ellis Jones

Webster Family in Anglesey (private document)

Sampson	*Diana*
Centurion	*London*
Marquis	*Elizabeth*
Margaret	*Glynrhonwy*
Union	*Betsy*
Neptune	*Dove*
Jane	*Irons*
Tower	*Unity*
Hope	

Appendix 3
Amlwch Inns, Taverns & Public Houses, 1828 -1911

Adelphi Vaults
Amlwch Harbour
Belmont Vaults
Blue Bell
Britannia Bridge
Buck
Bull
Bull Inn
Bull's Head
Castle
Clock
Clock Inn
Coach & Horses
Crown
Crown Inn
Crown & Anchor
Dinorben Arms
Druid
Druid Arms
Duke of Wellington
Eagle
Eagles
Eleth
Farmers' Arms
Freemasons' Arms
Gardeners' Arms
George & Dragon
George the Fourth
Harp
Hope & Anchor
Jolly Sailor
King William IV
King's Arms
King's Head
Liverpool Arms
Marquess of Anglesey
Marquis of Anglesey
Menai Bridge

Mona Tavern
New Haven
New Mill
Oddfellows' Arms
Old Post
Old England
Packet House
Pilot
Plough
Prince of Wales
Queen's Head
Raglan Castle
Railway
Railway Inn
Red Bull
Red Lion
Rifleman's Arms
Royal Oak
Sailors' Home
Ship
Ship & Castle
Ship Inn
Skerries
Stag
Stars
Sun
Swan
Two Frigates
Ty Mawr Inn
Union
Uxbridge Arms
Vaults
Vigour Arms
Waterman's Arms
Wheatsheaf
White Lion
Windmill

The names of some of these would appear to be variations of the same name and probably refer to the same establishment.

Appendix 4
Brand Names of Amlwch Made Tobaccos

E Morgan & Co

Pride of Wales Light Shag   *Old Watchmen*
Workmen's Friend   *Baco'r Aelwyd*
Yr Hen Wlad   *Baco'r Byd*
Taffy Twist   *Sunkist Virginia Cigarette Tobacco*

E Morgan Hughes & Co

Best Bright Birds-Eye   *Gelert Shag*
Baco Amlwch   *Four in Hand*
The Old Favourite   *Cambrian Smoking Mixture*
Baco'r Cymro   *Welsh Terriers Cigarettes*

Hugh Owen & Sons / Amlwch Tobacco Co

Young Wales   *Baco'r Werin*
Blended Virginia Smoking Shag   *Amlwch Twist*

Appendix 5
William Williams, VC, DSM and Bar, Medaille Militaire

At the beginning of the First World War, some ten years after his trip to South America on the *Cymric's* maiden voyage, William Williams enlisted in the Royal Naval Reserve, in which he subsequently served with exceptional gallantry as a seaman engaged in anti-submarine duties. This particular aspect of the war was of great concern to the Admiralty for, by April 1917, the German submarine service had sunk well in excess of half a million tons of British merchant shipping.

Enemy submarine commanders at that time were known to favour three means by which to sink their victims: torpedo, gunfire, and time bombs. The use of torpedoes had its drawbacks inasmuch that they were both expensive and notoriously unreliable; and in those cases where the victim sank rapidly following a direct hit, the commander was left with no proof of a 'kill'. Both of the remaining methods overcame this problem by facilitating the capture of crew members or documents, and they became the preferred means of attack whenever conditions were favourable. As a result, the Admiralty decided that one way to combat the submarine menace was through the use of armed decoys: the basic concept of which was brilliantly simple.

By employing what appeared to be unarmed sailing vessels and small steamers which would not normally warrant the expense of a torpedo, as decoys, it was thought that most submarine commanders would choose to make a surface attack. The advantages gained by doing this were to a great extent outweighed by the fact that whilst the submarine was on the surface, she was herself very vulnerable to a counter attack.

In order to give the appearance of being unarmed, many of the Q-ships had their guns hidden in false deckhouses, the sides of which were designed to drop down to give a clear field of fire. Others had their guns concealed in what appeared to be conventional rowing boats resting in their cradles on deck; but which in reality were two separate halves, hinged in such a way as to allow them to drop down to expose the gun. Further realism was given to the deception by having what was known as a 'panic party', composed of what would have been the ship's normal complement, to take to the boats whenever there was an attack; thus giving the impression that the vessel was being abandoned.

On 7 June, 1917, William Williams was serving aboard the Q-ship, HMS *Pargust*, when she was torpedoed off the south west coast of Ireland. He was no stranger to mystery ships (as the decoys were often referred to) for earlier that year he had been awarded the Distinguished Service Medal whilst serving aboard HMS *Farnborough*, otherwise known as *Q-5*.

At 8 o'clock that morning, a torpedo struck the *Pargust's* water line close to her engine room, blowing a 40 foot long hole in her side and bursting her aft bulkhead. Her remaining bulkheads held however and she remained afloat and stable. The 'panic party', which included an officer dressed in captain's uniform and carrying a stuffed parrot, took to the boats. As they were pulling away a periscope appeared some 400 yards off the stricken vessel's port side, watched all the time by Captain Gordon Campbell VC, the *Pargust's* commanding officer who has remained on board. Some 30 minutes after her torpedo struck the decoy, during which time he had satisfied himself that his victim was not a 'Q-ship', the commander of *UC-29* surfaced his vessel in order to finish the job by gunfire. During the whole of this time the *Pargust's* gun crews were safely hidden to all but Campbell in his hidden vantage point. What Campbell saw however must have appalled him, for the releasing weight of the starboard gun port had been freed by the torpedo's explosion, threatening to reveal the gun prematurely. With what Campbell described as great presence of mind, Williams took the whole weight of the port upon himself, and although injured and in great pain as a result of the explosion, he supported the plate for well over half an hour.

Leading Seaman William Williams, VC, DSM, 1917.
[Mrs Conwy Evans]

During this time, the submarine commander brought his vessel around to the *Pargust's* starboard side in order to be better positioned to deliver the *coup de grace*, but where he also presented his vessel as an ideal target to the decoy's gunners, at what was almost point-blank range. Presented with what was an ideal target, Campbell ordered his gun crews to open fire. Hit several times, the submarine heeled over to port, and many of her crew managed to escape on to her deck with their hands up. In the belief that the vesssel was surrendering, Campbell gave the order to cease fire; but the submarine commander made an attempt to escape, sweeping many of those on deck into the sea. Under the circumstances, Campbell had no option but to re-engage the enemy, and after several more shots the *UC-29* exploded and sank.*

In recognition of the bravery of the *Pargust's* crew, the King approved the award of the Victoria Cross to one officer and one crew member, each to be selected by the officers and men respectively by secret ballot. The officer's award went to Lieutenant Stuart and the other to Seaman Williams, who was later that year to be awarded a bar to his DSM following service aboard HMS *Dunraven*, another Q-ship. The French government also was pleased to recognise William Williams' courage on board the *Pargust* by awarding him the Medaille Militaire.

* Rear Admiral Gordon Campbell, *My Mystery Ships*, London, 1929, p229.

Notes

Chapter 1 - Introduction
1. *The Observer*, Sunday 16 October, 1988.
2. Owen Jones, *Amlwch & the Celebrated Mona & Parys Copper Mines*, 1848, 2nd edition, p6.
3. Oliver Davies, *Excavations on Parys Mountain*, TAAS.
4. The author was fortunate to discover one such stone, which despite weighing over 4 lbs, is surprisingly comfortable to hold. It is evident that it had once been used as a hammer, for several flakes had spalled off at one end, in much the same way as had those discovered by Davies.
5. John Pickin, 'Stone Tools and Early Metal Working in England & Wales', *Early Mining Workshop Occasional Paper*, No1, p39.
6. Andrew Lewis, 'Firesetting Experiments on the Great Orme, 1989', *Early Mining Workshop Occasional Paper*, No 1, p56.
7. Peter Crew, 'Fire Setting Experiments at Rhiw Goch, 1989', *Early Mining Workshop Occasional Paper*, No 1, p57.
8. Janet Ambers, 'Radiocarbon Calibration and Early Mining', *Early Mining Workshop Occasional Paper*, No 1, p61.
9. Paul T Craddock, 'Copper Smelting in Bronze Age Britain', *Early Mining Workshop Occasional Paper*, No 1.
10. In his paper, 'The Parys Mountain Copper Mines in the Island of Anglesey', *Archaeologica Cambrensis*, pp87-111, Edwin Cockshutt refers to a long flue climbing the hillside in what he describes as the roasting kiln area of the mine. This however does not accord with his description of the smelter.
11. Owen Griffith, *Mynydd Parys*, Caernarfon, c1897, pp29, 32.
12. Paul T Craddock, 'Copper Smelting in Bronze Age Britain', *Early Mining Workshop Occasional Paper*, No 1, p71.
13. Richard West, *River of Tears*, p 13.
14. Catherall, *The History of North Wales*.
15. Public Records Office, ref MPF11 (SP46/36).
16. It is known that the land on the western side of the harbour was in the ownership of the Bishopric of Bangor in the 19th century, on which a farmhouse known as *Plas* (palace or mansion) stood, before it was demolished in 1972. An outhouse belonging to the farm had survived however, and although it bears no resemblance to the building shown on the map, it also is divided into four sections. What is remarkable is the fact that the outhouse contains the remains of fireplaces, which clearly do not accord with its' later use.
17. M B Donald, *Elizabethan Copper*, pp243, 300.
18. Bangor Mss 484, UCNW.
19. H Owen, *History of the Island of Anglesey* , 1775, p25.
20. Lewis Morris, *Plans of Harbours, Bars, Bays and Roads in St George's Channel, 1748*, Shrewsbury, 1801.
21. H Owen, *History of the Island of Anglesey,* J Dodsley, p51, London, 1775.
22. Llwydiarth Esgob Mss FS638. UCNW.

Chapter 2 - Changes and Early Industries
23. T S Ashton, *The Industrial Revolution 1760-1830*, p2.
24. See*Windmills of Anglesey*, Barry Guise & George Lees, Attic Books, 1992.
25. trans - the fulling mill field.

Chapter 3 - Bayly and Hughes
26. trans - the wolves' stones.

27. Loose sheet accompanying Mona Mines Mss 2242.
28. Thomas Pennant, *Tours in Wales*, p276.
29. p57.
30. Mona Mine Mss 3544.
31. Mona Mine Mss 2242.
32. Thomas Pennant, *Tours in Wales*, p281.
33. Mona Minc Mss 2242.
34. Mona Mine Mss 1276.
35. Mona Mine Mss 2242.
36. J R Harris, *Copper King*, Liverpool University Press, 1964.
37. *ibid*, ppxvi, xviii.
38. Edwin Cockshutt, 'The Parys & Mona Copper Mines', *Transactions of the Anglesey Antiquarian Society*, 1960, pp1-25.
39. W Bingley, *A Tour round North Wales performed during the Summer of 1798*, London, 1801.

Chapter 4 - Sulphur
40. February would have had two fewer days at least!
41. Owen Jones, *Amlwch the Celebrated Copper Mines*, p7.
42. Thomas Pennant, *Tours in Wales*, 1784, p279.
43. Thomas Pennant, *Tours in Wales*, 1784, p275.
44. Richard West, *River of Tears*, p14.
45. J R Harris, *Copper King*, p163.
46. *ibid*.
47. Augustin Gottfried Ludwig Lentin, *Briefe uber die Insel Anglesea, vortzuglich uber das dasige Kupfer-Bergwerk und die dazu gehorigen Schmelzwerke und Fabriken*, Leipzig, 1800.
48. A G L Lentin, *Briefe uber die Insel Anglesea*.
49. A G L Lentin, *Briefe uber die Insel Anglesea*. Schester brief.

Chapter 5 - Early Smelting
50. J R Harris, *Copper King*, p36.
51. Dafydd Thomas, *Old Ships & Sailors of Wales*, p57.
52. UCNW Misc 3/113.
53. Arthur Aikin, *Journal of a tour through North Wales*, p139.
54. Arthur Aikin, *Journal of a tour through North Wales*, p138.
55. J R Harris, *Copper King*, p145.
56. J R Harris, *Copper King*, p ix.
57. *ibid*.
58. National Library of Wales Mss 10885c.
59. R R Toomey, *Vivian & Sons 1809-1924*, p81.
60. Toomey thesis, p84.
61. J R Harris, *Copper King*, p183.
62. R R Toomey, *Vivian & Sons 1809-1924*, p85.
63. John Rowlands, *Copper Mountain*, p60.
64. Mona Mine Mss 172 and 173.
65. Mona Mine Mss 175.
66. Later known as the Dinorben Arms Hotel.
67. D J V Jones, 'The Amlwch Riots of 1817', *Transactions of the Anglesey Antiquarian Society*, 1966, p95.
68. *ibid*.
69. Mona Mine Mss 179.
70. Mona Mine Mss 181.
71. Lieut C G Robinson, RN, *Sailing Directions for the north and north east coast of Anglesey*, p20.
72. Mona Mine Mss 184.
73. D J V Jones, 'The Amlwch Riots of 1817', *Transactions of the Anglesey Antiquarian Society*, 1966, p99.
74. Mona Mine Mss 187.
75. Mona Mine Mss 220, 221, 226, and 227.
76. Mona Mine Mss 233.
77. Reverberatory furnaces were those possessing curved roofs which reflected heat on to the charge without bringing it into direct contact with the fuel.

78. Dafydd Tomos, *Michael Faraday in Wales*, p77.
79. *ibid*, p33.
80. Owen Jones, *Amlwch & the Celebrated Mona & Parys Copper Mines*, p11.
81. Mona Mine Mss 434.
82. Owen Jones, *Amlwch & the Celebrated Mona & Parys Copper Mines*, p12.
83. Probably the place now known as Llam Carw, to the north of the eastern quay, where Henry Hills subsequently had his vitriol works.
84. Faraday's travelling companion.
85. Captain Lemin.
86. The quoted description of Faraday's visit to Amlwch is contained in a letter addressed to Margaret, whose identity is not known. Faraday was later to marry Sarah Barnard on the 12 June 1821.
87. Copper Ladies.
88. Owen Griffith, *Mynydd Parys*, p38.
89. Owen Griffith, *Mynydd Parys*, p39.
90. D B Barton, *The Cornish Beam Engine*, p92.
91. This was probably the one known as the Engine Shaft, which is recorded as having been 360 feet deep.
92. Cockshutt estimates this to be no more than 75 gallons per minute, all told. *The Parys and Mona Copper Mines*, p11.
93. Pennant, *Tours in Wales*, p279.
94. Mona Mine Mss, 3201 and 3202.

CHAPTER 6 - The Francis Map
95. Llwydiarth Esgob Mss FS 639/640/641, UCNW. Several versions of this map exist, each varying slightly from the other.
96. Colonel Sir Charles Close, *The Early Years of the Ordance Survey*, p38.
97. Mona Mine Mss 2242.
98. Hugh Hughes, *Hanes Amlwch a'r Cymydogaethau*.
99. Samuel Child, 'Every Man His Own Brewer', quoated in the Brewer's Society publication, *How Beer is Brewed*.
100. The creek of the King's ship.

Chapter 7 - Vitriol & Precipitation Works
101. J R Harris, *Copper King*, p20.
102. A Aitkin, *Journal of a Tour through North Wales*, p140.
103. Cartwright's disbursements incurred in the early working of the Parys mine included a sum paid for "freight of old iron from Chester to Port Amlwch". The extent to which the precipitation process was exploited by Bayly is not known, but one of the charges levelled against him by Hughes, during one of their frequent legal wrangles, was that he was not doing so to the fullest extent possible, thereby wasting their joint resources.
104. The ruins of the engine house compound, and what remains of the boiler house chimney, are still evident.
105. Dafydd Tomos, *Michael Faraday in Wales*, p137: quoting from the 'Parys Mona Ore Deposit Report', 1956, Gilbert McPherson.
106. *The Railway Supplies Journal*, 23 November 1889, p14.
107. *The Railway Supplies Journal*, 23 November 1889.

Chapter 8 - Later Smelting
108. Admiral W H Smith, *The Sailor's Word Book of 1867*.
109. Mona Mine Mss 554.
110. Mona Mine Mss 675.
111. Mona Mine Mss 564.
112. Mona Mine Mss 566.
113. John Rowlands, *Copper Mountain*, p66.
114. Mona Mine Mss 752.
115. Mona Mine Mss 906.
116. John Rowlands, *Copper Mountain*, p73.

Chapter 9 - Chemicals

117.   T I Williams, *The Chemical Industry*, p36.
118.   *Y Clorianydd*, 20 April 1893.
119.   Mona Mine Mss 2160.
120.   Mona Mine Mss 2164.
121.   The Harbourmaster's log for 25 November 1889 records that the vessel *Jane* was put into her berth to load salt cake, indicating a relaxation of the agreement. Gwynedd Archives, WM 427/149.
122.   Mona Mine Mss 2166.
123.   Gwynedd Archives WM 427/149.
124.   An advertisement in *Y Clorianydd*, 20 April 1893, gave the year of establishment as 1840.
125.   *Y Clorianydd*, 1 June 1893.
126.   *Y Clorianydd*, 19 July 1900.

Chapter 10 - Tobacco

127.   The firm was in fact first established in 1822.
128.   The outbuilding at Madyn Droliau which housed the original tobacco works is extant, but there is no evidence left of its former use.
129.   *The Life and Opinions of Robert Roberts, a Wandering Scholar*, p315.

Chapter 11 - The Port

130.   Mona Mine Mss 3750.
131.   J R Harris, *Copper King,* p167.
132.   Although many of the vessels employed in the Amlwch copper trade are known by name, it has not been possible to identify those owned by the Amlwch Shipping Company.
133.   The viaduct appears quite clearly in a photograph of the harbour taken in 1913. It is evident however that it has since been reconstructed, which suggests that it either became unsafe and had to be filled in, or that it had collapsed.
134.   *North Wales Gazette*, 16 April 1818.
135.   The reference to the "traffic in articles" appears to relate to the then common practice of paying wages in tokens which were redeemable only in the employer's own truck shops, where prices were usually higher than elsewhere. This iniquitous practice was resorted to by many and renunciation of it by the Mona mineowners may well have stemmed from the time when Thomas Williams was actively involved in the management of the mine.
136.   Over the period of his employment as the principal mine agent many charges of corruption were levelled against James Treweek, many of which were born of spite and petty jealousy. It is note-worthy, however, that despite them all he retained his employers' complete confidence.
137.   Mona Mine Mss 467, 3609.
138.   Legend has it that at least one wooden vessel was lengthened at Amlwch, a process which involved the unfastening of the ship's structure where its' beam was greatest, and then drawing the two ends sufficiently far apart to enable a whole new centre section to be married into the hull structure. Despite its' complexity, this was a technique that was often employed, and was clearly more economical than having a new vessel built.
139.   *Enwogion Môn 1850-1912*, p124 (An anthology of the notables of Anglesey), North Wales Chronicle, 1913.
140.   The registered name would appear to have been a spelling mistake, for the vessel sailed as the *Parys Lodge*.

Chapter 12 - Captain William Thomas

141.   A Harris, *Cumberland Iron*, p19.
142.   *Holy Wath*, pronounced as in 'lath', was also the home of John Barratt, the Hodbarrow Mine's Director, at Coniston.
143.   Sections of timber used for infilling.

Chapter 13 - Iard Newydd (The New Yard)

144.   William Thomas, Llanrhuddlad.
145.   Son of Captain William Thomas.
146.   *Holyhead Weekly Mail*, 3 March 1884.

147.   *Holyhead Mail*, 15 November 1884.
148.   Trevor Morgan, 'The Cumberland Connection', *Maritime Wales*, No 7.
149.   Trans - enthusiasm.
150.   Trevor Morgan, 'The Cumberland Connection', *Maritime Wales*, No 7.
151.   *North Wales Chronicle*, 8 March 1890.
152.   Aled Eames, *Ships and Seamen of Anglesey*, p395.

CHAPTER 14 - Thomas Brothers
153.   Basil Greenhill, *The Merchant Schooners*, p182.
154.   *Arklow, Last Stronghold of Sail*, Jim Rees and Liam Charlton, p77.
155.   Whilst walking along the Yare estuary some 90 years later, Miss Emma Potter of Dereham found the builder's plate from the *Maggie Williams*, which had lain hidden in the sand following the destruction of the vessel.
156.   R E Williams, *Sea Breezes*, Volume 53, No 405, p512, September 1979.
       Robyn Williams, *Sea Breezes*, Volume 54, No 412, p245, April 1980.
157.   William Thomas & Sons, Private Document.
158.   *Holyhead Chronicle*, 8 March 1912.
159.   R S Fenton, *Cambrian Coasters*, pp176-9.

CHAPTER 15 - Epilogue
160.   J R Harris, *Copper King*, pxiv.

Bibliography

Aikin, A	*A Journal of a Tour through North Wales*, Johnson, 1797.
Ambers, J	'Radiocarbon Calibration and Early Mining', *Early Mining Workshop Occasional Paper*, No 1. Snowdonia National Park Study Centre.
Ashton, T S	*The Industrial Revolution, 1760-1830.* Oxford, 1972.
Barton, D B	*The Cornish Beam Engine*, Truro, 1969.
Bingley, W	*A Tour Round North Wales performed during the Summer of 1798*, London, 1801.
Butcher, M J	'The Delivery Voyage of the *Alabama*', *Sea Breezes*, Vol LXII, No 515, November, 1988.
Campbell, Rear Admiral G	*My Mystery Ships*, London, 1929.
Catherall, W	*History of North Wales*, Manchester, 1828.
Close, Col Sir Charles	*The Early Years of the Ordnance Survey*, Chatham, 1926.
Cockshutt, E	'The Parys Mountain Copper Mines in the Island of Anglesey', *Archaeologica Cambrensis*, 1965. 'The Parys and Mona Copper Mines', *Transactions Anglesey Antiquarian Society*, 1960.
Craddock, P T	'Copper Smelting in Bronze Age Britain', *Early Mining Workshop Occasional Paper*, No 1.
Crew, P	'Fire Setting Experiments at Rhiw Goch, 1989', *Early Mining Workshop Occasional Paper*, No. 1. Snowdonia National Park Study Centre.
Davies, J H (Ed)	*The Life and Opinions of Robert Roberts, a Wandering Scholar.* Cardiff, 1923.
Dodd, A H	*The Industrial Revolution in North Wales*, Wrexham, 1990.
Donald, M B	*Elizabethan Copper*, London, 1955.
Eames, A	*Ships and Seamen of Anglesey*, Llangefni, 1973.
Fenton, R	*Cambrian Coasters*, World Ship Society, 1989.
Greenhill, B	*The Merchant Schooners*, London, 1988.
Griffith, O	*Mynydd Parys*, Caernarfon, 1897.
Guise & Lees	*Windmills of Anglesey*, Builth Wells, 1992.
Harris, A	*Cumberland Iron*, Truro, 1970.
Harris, J R	*Copper King*, Liverpool, 1964.
Jenkins, J G	*Maritime Heritage*, Llandysul, 1982.
Jones, O	*Amlwch and the Celebrated Mona and Parys Copper Mines*, Beaumaris, 1848.
Lentin, G L L	*Briefe über die Insel Anglesea, vorzüglich über das dasige*

	Kupfer-Bergwerk und die dazu Gehörigen Schmelzwerke und Fabriken, Leipzig, 1800.
Lewis, A	'Fire Setting Experiments on the Great Orme', *Early Mining Workshop Occasional Paper*, No 1. Snowdonia National Park Sudy Centre.
Morgan, T	'The Cumberland Connection', *Maritime Wales*, Vol VII, Caernarfon, 1983.
Morris, L	*Plans of Harbours, Bars, Bays and Roads in St George's Channel*, Shrewsbury, 1801.
Owen, H	*History of the Island of Anglesea*, London,1775.
Pennant, T	*Tours in Wales*, reprinted Wrexham, 1991.
Pickin, J	'Stone Tools and Early Metal Working in England & Wales', *Early Mining Workshop Occasional Paper*, No 1. Snowdonia National Park Study Centre.
Rees & Charlton	*Arklow, Last Stronghold of Sail*, Arklow, 1986.
Ritchie, C	*'Q' Ships*, Lavenham, 1985.
Robinson, C G	*Sailing Directions for the North and North East Coast of Anglesey*, 1837.
Rowlands, J	*Copper Mountain*, Llangefni, 1966.
Smyth, W H	*The Sailor's Word Book of 1867*, London, 1991.
Thomas, D	*Old Ships and Sailors of Wales*, Cardiff, 1949.
Tomos, D	*Michael Farraday in Wales*, Denbigh, nd.
Toomey, R R	'Vivian and Sons, a Study of the Firm in the Copper Related Industries', Phd Thesis, UW, 1979.
West, R	*River of Tears*, Earth Island, 1972.
Williams, T I	*The Chemical Industry*, Wakefield, 1972.

Index

People

Aiken, Arthur 47-48, 76
Ashton, T S 23
Asquith, Herbert (Prime Minister) 147
Barratt, John (mine owner) 114
Barratt, W I 113
Bayly, Henry, 1st Earl of Uxbridge
45-49, 98, 102
Bayly, Sir Nicholas
28-33, 38, 44, 45,98 , 150
Bingley, Rev Edward 33, 80
Boulton, Matthew 31, 38, 39, 40
Brunel, Isambard Kingdom 109
Bulloch, Cpt James D, CSN 110-111
Butcher, Cpt 112
Caine, Nathaniel (metal merchant)
114, 116, 118, 132
Caine, William Sproston 132
Carlsen, Cpt Kurt 120
Cartwright, John 28, 29
Champion, John 38, 39
Clark, Mary (of Mold) 126
Cockshutt, Edwin 14, 35
Darby, Abraham 47
Davey, Cpt William 49
Davies, Oliver 11
Davy, Sir Humphrey 54
Dawes, John 32, 48
Elias, John 100
Elizabeth I, Queen 15, 17, 22
Ellis, Cpt Solomon 119
England, Josephine 120
England, Cpt Richard 119, 120
Eure, Lord 15-16
Evans, Evan (mine agent) 89
Evans, Cpt John 101, 102
Evans, Thomas Fanning 128, 138
Faraday, Michael
54, 56, 57-58, 59, 61-62
Francis, Ann 65
Francis, Cpt William
65-67, 68, 69, 70, 72, 73, 74
Frazier, Alexander 28
Garfield, President 131
Gaunt, Mr 84

German, Cpt John 107
Greenhill, Basil 141
Griffith, Owen (miner) 14-15, 34, 62
Griffiths, Cpt R 140
Harris, Professor J R 31
Henry, John 49
Hills, Charles Henry (see also Chemicals)
88, 89, 90, 91, 99, 126, 151
Hughes, Edward (diver) 129
Hughes, Rev Edward 29, 30, 31, 32, 44, 48
Hughes, Edward Morgan 92, 96, 97
Hughes, Evan 100
Hughes, Hugh 69
Hughes, John (ship owner) 103
Hughes, Cpt John (of Llanfairfechan) 113
Hughes, Lewis 151
Hughes, Mary 29
Hughes, Michael 49
Hughes, Cpt Richard 98
Hughes, Cpt Thomas 103
Hughes, William (of Madyn Dysw) 86
Hussey, Richard 49
Jones, Prof Bedwyr Lewis 79
Jones, E 128
Jones, Hugh 116, 117, 119, 137
Jones, Cpt Isaac 125
Jones, John (wheelwright) 68
Jones, Miciah 117
Jones, Owen (of Fagwyr) 128
Jones, Richard (shoemaker) 68
Jones, Cpt Robert 101, 142
Jones, Thomas (ship owner) 103
Jones, William (weaver) 68
Jones, Wynne 53
Legg, Mr 89
Lemin, Cpt 57
Lentin, Dr Augustin 38, 39, 40, 42, 48, 99
Lewis, William 28, 29
Lincoln, President Abraham 110
Llwyfo, Llew 59-61
Mackay, John 44
Martin, Major Alexander 53
Mary I, Queen 15
Medley, Mr 75

A Curious Place

Morgan, Mrs Mary   119
Morgan, Cpt Richard   119
Morgan, Cpt Thomas   112, 113
Morgan, Trevor   114
Morgan, William   49, 55, 82, 84, 86,114,116
Morgans, Edward   92, 96, 97
Morris, John   117
Morris, Lewis   19-20
Mostyn, William   92
Owen, Hugh   92, 97
Owen, Rev Richard   30
Owen, Richard   20-1, 65, 69
Owen, W H (of Plas Penrhyn)   133
Owens, Hugh   117
Paget Henry William, Marquess of Anglesey
                             49, 51, 52, 69
Parr, Dr Joshua   75, 76
Pavnter. William Cox
             108, 109, 112, 113, 121, 128, 135
Pennant, Thomas
             28-29, 32-3, 36, 37, 79
Peters, Cpt N   128, 129, 131
Postlethwaite, William   118, 119, 125, 131
Price, Hugh   31
Price, Thomas   28
Pritchard, Cpt Edward   117
Pritchard, Owen   128, 129, 131
Rees, William   86
Richardson, Cpt David   147
Roberts, 'Johnny'   140
Roberts, Owen (ship's carpenter) 101
Roberts, Robert   96
Roberts, Cpt Sam (of Groeslon) 110, 112
Roberts, Cpt T H   126
Roberts, Cpt William (Portland)   68
Roberts, Cpt William (Thomas)   68
Roe, Charles   29, 38
Roe, William   38, 45, 67
Roose, Jonathan   28-29
Rutty, Dr   75
Sanderson, John   52, 53, 64, 82, 84, 100, 102
Shaw, Cpt   113
Slade, Cpt W J   113
Thomas, Miss Gertrude   147
Thomas, John (brother of Cpt W Thomas)
                                 109
Thomas, John (son of Cpt W Thomas)
                             119, 135
Thomas, John (author)   20
Thomas, Lewis (ship owner)   106
Thomas, Cpt Lewis

             108, 128, 132, 133, 135, 141-49, 147
Thomas, Cpt William
             106, 109, 110, 112, 114-20
             121-40, 141, 142, 151
Thomas, William   108, 133, 135, 137, 141-49
Thomas, William (of Llanrhuddlad) 115
Thomas, William (of Newborough) 115, 116
Treweek, Francis   101, 103
Treweek, James
    49, 50, 51, 52, 53, 54, 55, 56, 64, 82-6, 87, 100
       101, 102, 103, 104, 107, 109, 114, 150
Treweek, Nicholas   101, 104, 106, 121
Tyrrell, Cpt Alfred (of Arklow) 141
Vignoles, Charles   86, 87
Vivian, John   49-50, 54, 84, 150
Watt, James   31, 49
Webster, James   86
Webster brothers   76
Webster, Robert   101
Wedgewood, Josiah   31
Wilkinson brothers   31
Wilkinson, John   36
William IV, King   64
Williams, Cpt Ishmael   145
Williams, John   48
Williams, Owen   48
Williams. Thomas
             31-2, 44, 45, 46, 48, 76, 98, 150
Williams, Thomas   23
Williams, William VC, DSM   145, 155-6
Wynn, Sir John (of Gwydir)   15-6

Places & Industries

Aberdyfi   19
Afon Amlwch (see Afon Goch)
Afon Goch (Red River)   27, 46, 78, 81
Amlwch
    Bank Street   92
    Brewery   70, 71, 72, 73, 74
    Chapel Street   21, 69, 72.
    Dinorben Hotel   131
    Haven (see also Amlwch Port)
                              16-21
    Machine Street   87
    Madyn Works   92
    Market Place   92

Methusalem Street (Mona St) 92
New Haven Public House *85*
Parys Lodge Square 65
Petters Street 92
Ponc yr Odyn (Lime Kiln Bank) 68
Quay Street
20, 30, 43, 67, 68, 69, 74, 121
Royal Oak 68
Smelter 49, 50, 53, 82-7, 85
Well Street 68, 69, 99
Amlwch Port (see also Amlwch Haven)
36, 39, 44, 48, 49, 52, 53, 67, 73, *85*
105, 98-113, 126, *130*, *146*, *148*
Act of Parliament, 1793 98
Baulks Pier 74
Harbour Board 90, 98-99, 102, 117
118, 138, 151
Harbourmaster 90, 102, 109, 138, 152
Iard Newydd 121-40, *122*, *127*,
141-149, *143*
Turkey Shore 47, 67
Porth Cwch y Brenin 74, 106
Watch House Pier 74, *122*, 152
Anglesey 9
Ardrossan 142
Arklow, Ireland 142
Bangor 38, 47, 48, 147
Beaudesert, Staffordshire 45
Beaumaris 19, 52, 100, 107, 147, 149
Belfast 113, 118
Bersham Ironworks, Wrexham 36, 38
Birmingham 48
Bishop's House, Amlwch 17
Bod Ednyfed Estate 20, 65, 104
British Museum 12, 15
Brosely 38
Buckley Brickworks, Flintshire 74
Caernarfon 48, 54, 65, 76, 98, 110, 132, 140
Cae Pant 106
Cae'r Pandy Vitriol Works 76
Cemlyn 129
Cerrig-y-Bleiddiau (see also Mona Mine)
28, 32, 44, 45, 64
Chelmsford 101
Chemical Industry 88, 89, 90, 91
Henry Hills & Son 90
Charles Henry Hills 88-9, 90, 91, 99
Hills Chemical Works
(Gwaith Hills) 91, 117, 151, 152
Chester 30, 38, 48, 101
Coalbrookdale 47

Conwy 19, 38, 140
Cox Paynter's Yard 109, 112, 113
Craig y Don Estate 46
Cwmystwyth 11
Dinmor Quarry, Red Wharf Bay *129*
Dublin 19, 82, 113, 117, 141
Duddon 117, 118, 121,137
Dulas 17, 18, 19, 78, 81
Dyffryn Adda 79,151
Fagwyr 128
Fleet Prison, London 31
Flintshire 19, 29, 48
Garston Vitriol Works, Liverpool 48, 76
Glanllyn Estate 20
Great Orme 11, 12
Great Yarmouth 141
Greenfield 49
Grogan Goch 86
Gwydir Estate 15
Harburg, Germany 140
Hern Grundt Mines, Hungary 77
Hodbarrow 116, 137
Holyhead 19, 53, 76, 109, 110
Holywell 38
House of Lords 147
Iard Ochr Draw 42
Jarrow 125
Kilns 39, 40, 41, 42, 43, 80, 89
Kingstown, Ireland (Dun Laoghaire) 111
Lancashire 19
Lead Mining, Parys Mountain 29
Leipzig University 38
Lisbon 142
Liverpool 20, 48, 67, 76, 91, 92, 100, 101, 104
107, 108, 110, 111, 114, 115, 125
129, 131, 133, 135, 145, 149
Liverpool Pilot Vessel 123, 124
Llaethdy Bach 79
Llam Carw 88-89, 99, 102, 129, 151
Llaneilian 131
Llandudno 132, 150
Llanelli 84
Llanerchymedd 52
Llanfairfechan 113
Llanwenllwyfo 51
Llanrhuddlad 115
Llys Dulas 28, 29, 100, 150
London 31, 32, 48, 56, 82, 88, 92
98, 111, 113
Malaga, Spain 19
Millom 113, 114, 117, 118, 119

131, 135, 137
Mills 24, 60
    Amlwch Fulling Mill 79
    Cae'r Pandy 27
    Melin Adda 79
    Pentrefelin Adda 27
    Rholdy 27, 79
    St Eilian Colour Works Mill 81
Moelfre 111, 112
Mona Lodge 54, 133.
Mona Mine (see also Cerrig-y-Bleiddiau)
    38, 44, 45, 48, 50, 55, 67
    74, 88-89, 104, 108
Nantyreira 11
National Library of Wales 145
National Maritime Museum 141
National Museum of Wales 12
Neath, Vale of 17
Newborough 116
Oxen Quarry 64
Parys Farm 28, 30, 46
Parys Mountain (Mynydd Parys)
    11, 12, 13, 14, 15, 18, 28-9, 30, 31, 32,
    33, 35, 36, 37, 45, 48, 49, 55,
    57, 58-61, 67, 74, 78, 150, 151
Parys Smelter 49, 50
Pembrey 84, 86
Pembrokeshire 19
Penrhoslligwy 103
Penrhyn Du Mine, Caernarfonshire 28, 29
Pentre Eirianell Farm 19
Plas Farm 27
Plas Newydd 28, 32
Plas Penrhyn 133
Ponc Taldrwst 145
Port Dinorwic (Y Felinheli) 113
Porthaethwy 54
Porth Llam Carw 88
Pumping Engines 60, 61, 62, 63, 64
Pwll Fanogl 30
Queen's University, Belfast 11
Queenstown, Ireland (Cobh) 112
Ravenhead 44, 49, 50
Rhos Mynach Mine 28
Rhyl 106
Rio Grande 142
Rio Tinto, Spain 15
River Mersey 44
Rock Ferry 147
St Eilian's Church (see St Hillary's Church)
St Eilian Colour Works 81

St Elaeth 17, 69
St Hillary's Church 17
Shrewsbury 38
Stanley Smelter 49
Sulphur 34-43, 117
Swansea 44, 49, 54, 55, 56, 84, 101, 113, 150
Tharsis Copper Mine, Spain 38
Tobacco Industry 92-7
    Morgans & Jones 92
    Edward Morgan 92, 93, 94
    96, 97, 161
    William Mostyn & Co 92
    Hugh Owen & Sons 92, 97, 161
    Edward Morgan Hughes 92, 96
    97, 161
Treweek's Yard 42, 43, 101, 103, 104
    105, 106, 107
Trysglwyn Isaf 76, 78, 101
Ty Mawr (Dinorben Hotel) 51, 54
Upper Bank Works 44
Vitriol Works (Y Fudrol) 75-7, 78
    Mona Vitriol Company 76, 86, 101
Warrington 30
Wicklow Mines, Ireland 77
Woollen Industry 24-7

Ships

Aggripa, CSS 112
Agnes 109
Ailsie 112, 113
Alabama, CSS 110, 112
Alice and Eliza 139
Alliance 107
Amlwch Packet 103
Anglesea 104
Anglesea Lass 106
Anglia 110, 111
Ardgowan 149
Ardri 149
Arethusa 104
Balniel 149
Barbara 126, 128
Baron Hill 125
Belfast 145
Black Rock 149
British Birch 120
Camborne 112, 113, *135*

Careful	120
Catherine	104
Celtic	141,142
Cenric	147
Charles	105, 112
Charles Edwin	108, 112
Charlotte Maule	90
Chromium (see Eilian II)	
Clyde	106
Cotton	19
Countess of Lonsdale	131, 135
County of Lancaster	90
Cumberland Lassie	123, 124
Cygnus	140
Cymraes	103
Cymric	141, 142, 151
Cymro	104
Dakota	125, 126, 131
Deveron	82
Donald and Doris	112, 113, *144*
Dunleith	149
Economy	104
Edmond	90
Eilian	133, *134,*
Eilian	140
Eilian	*146, 147,* 151
Eilian Hill	90
Eleanor	*101*
Eleth (see Black Rock)	149
Elizabeth	125
Elizabeth Peers	137
Elizabeth Roberts	*143,* 145
Emily Barratt	137
Emperor of Beaumaris	138
Empire Lethe (see Black Rock)	149
Enrica	112
Exchange	133
Express	133
Fjordbo (see Eilian)	
Florence Vivian	108
Flying Enterprise	120
Gaelic	141, 145, 147, *148*
Gelert	137, 141
Glyndwr	128, 131
Governor Cairns	125
Grace Evans	109
Great Britain	107
Great Eastern	107, 109
Greyhound	137
Helen	104
Hercules	111, 112
Hero	101, 102
Hibernia	110
Holy Wath	105, 121, 123, 128, 131
Hopewell	19
James and Jane	103
Jane Gray	112
Jane and Margaret	103
Kendal Castle	106, 109
John Morgan	107
Kate	139
Lady Bessie	135
Lady Kate	135
Lady Louisa	135
Lady Magdalen	147
Lady Neave	125
Lovely Nancy	100
Leader	123
Lancashire Witch	123
Landana	125
Lewis and Mary	117, 118
Maggie Williams	141, 142
Marchioness of Anglesea	99
Margaret	101, 131
Marianne	103
Marquis of Anglesea	101
Martha	138
Mary	104
Mary Catherine	90, 107, 108, 151
Mary Fanny	112
Matje (see Prince Ja Ja)	
Menelaus	125
Mersey	124, 125
Meyric	145, 147
Montana	125, 126
Morfudd	*143,* 147
Nantglyn	128
Nar	149
Nellie Bywater	118, 119, 120, 131
Nellie Fleming	113
Noah	128, 129, 131
Olive (see Cymric)	
Pary's Lodge (known as Parry's Lodge)	112
Pembroke	19
Perseverance	108, 121
Pleiades	138
Portland	68
President Garfield	131
Pride of Liverpool	123
Prince George	140
Prince Ja Ja	139, 140
Princess of Wales	108

A Curious Place

Red	106	*Torbay*	147
Royal Charter	108	*Trevor*	*129*
Sampson	67, 98	*Tuscarora*, USS	112
Scotia	110	*Victoria*	128, 129, 131
Sherbro	131	*Unity*	101
Sarah	103	*WS Caine*	*129*, 132-3
Speedwell	19	*Walton*	145
Swallow	19, 100	*Wellington*	51
Temple	133	*Welsh Girl*	116, 129
Thomas	68	*William Melhuish*	115,116
Thomas Pearson	*138*		